PREACHING THE
Sermon ON THE Mount
The World It Imagines

David Fleer & Dave Bland, EDITORS

D1304912

CHALICE
PRESS
ST. LOUIS, MISSOURI

Cover art: *St. Matthew and the Angel* by Josh Lackowski
Cover and interior design: Elizabeth Wright

Visit Chalice Press on the World Wide Web at
www.chalicepress.com

10 9 8 7 6 5 4 3 2 1   07 08 09 10 11 12

Library of Congress Cataloging–in–Publication Data

(pending)

To
Mae Fleer
for her affirming love
and unfailing encouragement
and
Nancy Bland
for her untiring gift of ministry
to her family and others

PREACHING THE
Sermon ON THE Mount

About the Cover Image

In the seventeenth century the Vatican commissioned Italian artist Guido Reni to create *St. Matthew and the Angel*. More than three centuries later, family and friends commissioned Rochester artist Josh Lackowski to paint an ectype of Reni's work, the painting featured on this volume's cover.

Lackowski's twenty-first–century ectype refers back to Reni's work and modifies it, creating a new expression of the original. Lackowski uses slightly different style, lighting, and structure than Reni, with which the current artist "speaks" through the painting.

It is altogether fitting that Lackowski's *St. Matthew and the Angel* adorns this volume's cover. With respect for the rich and diverse history of interpretation and preaching from Matthew's sermon, revealing fresh scholarship and in light of the events of our times, this volume promises to dare us to imagine living in and preaching from the world depicted in the Sermon on the Mount.

Contents

Contributors

RONALD J. ALLEN—An ordained minister in the Christian Church (Disciples of Christ), Ron Allen has taught preaching and Second Testament at Christian Theological Seminary in Indianapolis since 1982. Author or coauthor of thirty books on the relationship of biblical studies and preaching, his most recent publications are (with Clark M. Williamson) *Preaching the Letters Without Dismissing the Law* and (with Mary Alice Mulligan) *Make the Word Come Alive: Lessons from Laity.* Allen is married to an ordained minister of the Disciples, and they are the parents of five children, ages fifteen to twenty-five.

CHRIS ALTROCK has served as preaching minister for the Highland Street Church of Christ in Memphis, Tennessee, for the past nine years. Prior to that, he preached in Las Cruces, New Mexico. He is the author of *The Cross: Saved by the Shame of It All; Mark: A Call to Service;* and *Preaching to Pluralists.* Chris is also an adjunct professor for Harding University Graduate School of Religion (where he earned his M.Div. and D.Min.) and Oklahoma Christian University. He and his wife of seventeen years have a five-year-old son and ten-year-old daughter.

DAVE BLAND—For more than two decades, Dave Bland has devoted his life to preaching tenures with the Eastside Church of Christ in Portland, Oregon, and, currently, with the White Station congregation in Memphis. Dave complements his life's activity in preaching with a background in rhetoric and has long cultivated an interest in wisdom literature. In addition to preaching, for the past fourteen years Dave has served as fulltime professor of homiletics at Harding University Graduate School of Religion in Memphis. He and his wife, Nancy, have three sons.

LEE C. CAMP is in his eighth year of teaching at his undergrad alma mater Lipscomb University. He received his Ph.D. in moral theology at the University of Notre Dame and has served in churches preaching and ministering in Kentucky, Indiana, and Tennessee. He and his wife, Laura, have three sons.

CHARLES CAMPBELL is the Peter Marshall Professor of Homiletics at Columbia Theological Seminary in Decatur, Georgia. An ordained minister in the Presbyterian Church (U.S.A.), Campbell has degrees from Hendrix College, Union Theological Seminary in Virginia, Yale Divinity School, and Duke University (Ph.D.). Campbell was born and raised in Little Rock, Arkansas. From 1982 to 1988 he served as pastor of First Presbyterian Church in Stuttgart, Arkansas, and then joined the faculty of Columbia Seminary in 1991. He currently serves as the first vice president of the Academy of Homiletics. He and his wife, Dana, have two children.

WARREN CARTER is originally from New Zealand. After five years of pastoral ministry there, he came to the United States for doctoral study at Princeton Theological Seminary before moving to Kansas City to teach New Testament in 1990. He is professor of New Testament at Saint Paul School of Theology in Kansas City, Missouri. He has written a number of books on Matthew's gospel, John's gospel, and about the way New Testament writers negotiate the Roman imperial world. He regularly teaches in conferences and church adult Christian education programs.

JEFF CHRISTIAN has ministered to churches in Texas for the past fifteen years. He began preaching part-time in a small West Texas church outside of Abilene when he was a sophomore at Abilene Christian University. He has preached almost every Sunday since with churches in Munday, Paris, and—since 2002—Tyler, Texas, at the Glenwood Church of Christ. He received his M.Div. from ACU in 1999 and is scheduled to finish the D.Min. program in 2007 there, where he has written on the role preaching plays in the formation of a person's character. The ministry of preaching is especially important to Jeff in its asking listeners to welcome the world of the Bible into daily lives.

DENNIS DEWEY has engaged in a ministry of biblical storytelling for fourteen years, a vocation he describes as helping people hear the biblical stories again for the first time. An ordained minister in the Presbyterian Church (U.S.A.), he has also served as executive director of the Network of Biblical Storytellers, an international organization whose mission is to encourage everyone to learn and tell biblical stories. His performing and teaching work has taken him all over the United States and to every continent except Antarctica. He helped establish the Academy for Biblical Storytelling and the NOBS Seminar, an ongoing gathering of scholars and practitioners committed to exploring the performance of biblical texts in antiquity and in contemporary settings.

DAVID FLEER'S devotion to preaching first found expression through a long-tenured pulpit ministry with the Vancouver, Washington, Church of Christ. His Ph.D. in speech Communication at the University of Washington moved him into teaching at Rochester College, and now he is professor of religion and communication and special assistant to the president at Lipscomb University in Nashville. For the last decade he has directed the Rochester Sermon Seminar. David's work is characterized as a thoughtful and passionate attempt to walk afresh in the world of scripture that readers and listeners may experience the reality of the Gospel of God.

KENNETH R. GREENE received his A.A. in theology at Southwestern Christian College in 1976, his B.S. in religious education from Abilene Christian University in 1978, a M.Div. degree from the same school in 1981, and a D.Min. from Fuller Theological Seminary in 1991. He served as a colonel in the Texas Army National Guard from 1989 to 2006. He was selected as the Distinguished Alumni of ACU in 2002 and Southwestern in 2003. He is the minister at Metro Church of Christ in Dallas, Texas. He and his wife, Mary, have been together for twenty-eight years and have two children.

STANLEY HAUERWAS is the Gilbert T. Rowe Professor of Theological Ethics at the Divinity School of Duke University. Though he is often identified as an ethicist, his work is more properly described as theology. The primary intent of his work has been to show in what way theological convictions make no sense unless they are actually embodied in our lives. He delivered the prestigious Gifford Lectures at St. Andrews and has authored many books, including *The Cross-shattered Christ.* A graduate of Yale Divinity School (B.D., 1965) and Yale University Graduate School (M.A., M.Phil., Ph.D., 1968), Hauerwas did his undergraduate work at Southwestern University, Georgetown, Texas. He taught for two years at Augustana College in Rock Island, Illinois, before joining the faculty of the University of Notre Dame, where he taught from 1970–1984. He joined the faculty of Duke University in 1984, where he served as director of graduate studies from 1985 to 1991. He is married to the Reverend Doctor Paula Gilbert and has one son.

LUCY LIND HOGAN has devoted her ministry to helping guide and shape the preaching of those who have been called by God to share the good news. She has been ordained in the Episcopal Church for twenty-five years. With a D.Min. in preaching and a Ph.D. in rhetoric and speech communication from the University of Maryland, Lucy has taught preaching and worship at Wesley Theological Seminary in Washington, D.C. for twenty years. She preaches all over the country and all over the world, and is the author of *Graceful Speech: An Invitation to Preaching.*

RICHARD HUGHES has explored the intersection of Christianity and culture with college students for thirty-five years, ever since earning his Ph.D. from the University of Iowa in 1971. His longest tenure was at Pepperdine University, where he taught for twenty-four years. He teaches at Messiah College in Grantham, Pennsylvania. Hughes has authored or coauthored sixteen books and scores of articles on Christian history and related themes. His books include a history of the Churches of Christ entitled *Reviving the Ancient Faith: The Story of Churches of Christ in America, Myths America Lives By,* and *The Vocation of a Christian Scholar: How Christian Faith Can Sustain the Life of the Mind.*

CHARME ROBARTS is the involvement minister at Skillman Church of Christ in Dallas, Texas. She received a master's degree in biblical studies at Abilene Christian University. She has written numerous articles on biblical topics and speaks and teaches in a variety of settings, including recent instruction for church leaders in Uganda.

RUBEL SHELLY–For twenty-seven years Rubel Shelly preached for the Woodmont Hills Church of Christ (Nashville) and taught at Lipscomb University, Vanderbilt School of Medicine, and Tennessee State. He became professor of religion and philosophy at Rochester College in 2005. The author of more than thirty books, Shelly is a community leader, working with Habitat for Humanity, American Red Cross, and Metro Public Schools. Congregational missionary work has taken Shelly to Africa, Central America, and Eastern Europe.

JOHN SIBURT, a third-generation preacher, has served as the preaching minister at the Richardson, Texas, East Church of Christ since October 2002. John earned B.A., M.Div., and D.Min. degrees from Abilene Christian University, as well as a graduate certificate in conflict resolution. He is devoted to the craft of preaching and to the high calling of congregational leadership. John loves reading, sports, music, and most of all, spending time with his wife, Sarah, and their two children.

DEAN SMITH has preached for more than thirty years, half of that time in the Midwest and half in Texas. He has been a leader in community development and social justice activities and organizations ranging from the Human Rights Commission in Chicago to a nationally recognized ministry for the homeless in San Antonio. He currently preaches for the University Avenue Church of Christ in Austin, Texas.

JERRY TAYLOR earned the D.Min. from Perkins School of Theology at Southern Methodist University and was recently presented the Outstanding Leadership Award at the NAACP National Convention. A frequent speaker at college and church conferences around the country, Taylor is known for his engaging and challenging oratory. A remarkable preacher in the spirit of the Sermon on the Mount, Taylor presently serves as assistant professor of Bible and ministry at Abilene Christian University and associate pulpit minister at the Highland Church of Christ in Abilene, Texas.

Preaching the Sermon on the Mount

The World It Imagines

DAVID FLEER AND DAVE BLAND

We live in troubled times. During one eventful and characteristic week—in the very season that we write this introduction—acts of violence terrorize the world. Israeli soldiers and tanks amass on the Lebanon border and make another expansive war appear imminent. North Korea tests nuclear weapons. Violence increases in Iraq, with Baghdad reporting an average of five bombings or shootings each day. Meanwhile, Iranian President Mahmoud Ahmadinejad sends a letter to the German chancellor labeling the holocaust a "myth" and calling for Israel's annihilation. In the midst of this turmoil the *Detroit Free Press* op-ed section features a quarter-page cartoon, backdropped with a huge human skull. An Israeli soldier stands in one eye socket, and a Hezbollah combatant in the other. A voice coming from the skull asks, "All in favor of retaliating in retaliation of the retaliation for the retaliation..." Both soldiers raise their hands, and the caption reads, "An aye for an aye..."[1] The world is exploding, and half the nations seem to be involved in war.

During this same eventful week the popular American novelist Cormac McCarthy celebrated a birthday. *The New York Times* labeled his early prose, *Blood Meridian,* "the bloodiest book since the *Iliad.*" McCarthy claims, "There's no such thing as life without bloodshed. I think the notion that the species can be improved in some way, that everyone could live in harmony, is a really dangerous idea. Those who are afflicted with this notion are the first ones to give up their souls, their freedom. Your desire that it be that way will enslave you and make your life vacuous."[2] Evidently, McCarthy attempts to creatively mimic the violent reality of our existence. But must we live in an imagined world that is now, and always shall be enslaving, and violent? We think not.

Of course, principalities and powers are on the move today. *That is* dangerous and horrific. Weapons testing, preemptive strikes, and ceaseless bombings all signal the terrible threat the principalities and powers pose, a threat that endangers our existence and challenges Jesus' vision for his disciples.

Principalities and powers advance by force and violence, with bombs and bullets. But, Jesus imagines disciples who turn the other cheek, walk the second mile, and volunteer undergarments as they relinquish their outer garments. Principalities and powers claim that war cures war and violence ends violence. But Jesus implies, "An eye for an eye…leaves a lot of people blind."

This volume proposes that Matthew's Sermon on the Mount was written with our particular situation in mind. We hope to recapture the Sermon's themes and images that our Western churches seem to have forgotten. We hope to bring fresh eyes to Jesus' Sermon and suggest new ways of preaching its message. We intend to break from the romantic notion of an easy primitivism and a distorted "Christianity" that compromises with the world's empires.

The Sermon on the Mount usually comes to us preachers handicapped by a convoluted eschatology or shut down by common sense ("that can't mean what it appears to say") or reduced to an interior world. What would happen, however, if we did not flatten Jesus' Sermon, did not inoculate the congregation, preaching a little dose here and there to ward off its full impact? What if we preachers approached this Sermon as a serious proposal for an alternative society?

This volume works with the assumption that Matthew's audience belongs to a "minority community" situated in the emergence of the early Christian movement, amidst the stress and difficulties of life in the Roman Empire.[3] Matthew's gospel challenges the Roman Empire and all secular powers by requesting social change through a different vision and experience of the human community. Thus, the Sermon on the Mount is a counter-narrative, a work of resistance providing a plausible and persuasive worldview that creates an alternative community, one that is identified as inclusive, egalitarian, and merciful.[4]

The church's relationship to the secular government is always tenuous. For instance, one church is currently being threatened because of its minister's antiwar sermon.[5] Under federal tax law, church officials can legally discuss politics, but to retain tax-exempt status, churches may not endorse candidates or parties. The dispute is located in a particular church where the minister, two days prior to the 2004 presidential election, imagined Jesus in a debate with John Kerry and George W. Bush. The preacher concluded that Jesus would condemn Bush's doctrine of preemptive war. This was cause for the IRS to intervene and sound the warning that before the next term's congressional races, it would be "scrutinizing churches and charities for unlawful activity."

This case raises pertinent questions such as, Who draws the lines we must not cross? What's at stake? Whom do we follow? Why should a nation's threat prevent us from following Jesus and examining every nuance of discipleship? By deeply engaging these questions, this volume hopes to better enable preachers to grapple with the issues for themselves.

As resources to this end we present the following essays (part 1) and sermons (part 2). Warren Carter opens the volume with two chapters, setting the context for understanding and living in the world Matthew's Sermon on the Mount imagines. Carter suggests that to put the Sermon in context we must understand it as *Matthew's* Sermon, which comes to us as three chapters embedded in his larger gospel story. In his first chapter, Carter vividly describes two important contexts: the Sermon's narrative and imperial-historical setting. The narrative context includes Matthew's first four chapters, which identify Jesus' character and ministry and therefore shape our reading and preaching. The imperial context depicts Rome's domination as utterly contrary to God's purposes. The Roman Empire benefited society's elite while exploiting and tyrannizing common citizens. Jesus' Sermon calls disciples to embody God's life-giving ways through an alternative community, offering different experiences than the falsities of Rome's empire. The chapter concludes by examining the beatitudes as embodiment of this vision.

The second chapter maintains that we must read the Sermon through the lens of the imperial contexts of militarism, consumerism, and poverty that plague the twenty-first century. Carter contends that we engage Matthew's Sermon, not by moving away from the pain in our societal mess, but by moving into God's transforming work as community. These demands are woven into renewal as Carter finds hopeful rhythms in three acts of justice in Matthew 6:1–18.

Stanley Hauerwas extends this focus with an interpretive framework for the last third of Matthew's Sermon, finding the Sermon's ecclesial implications in its climactic ending. Contending that the church is unintelligible when not shaped by the Sermon, Hauerwas claims the difference between church and world is not of realms or levels, but of response. The church's only advantage is that it acknowledges its sinfulness and therefore is able to embody a life of forgiveness. Yet Hauerwas reveals that Matthew 7 expects Jesus' disciples to permeate boundaries with the world through dialogue—not through judgmental words or actions—but by treating others, regardless of background or lifestyle, the way we want to be treated.

Richard Hughes offers three historical examples of persons and communities who have embodied the Sermon on the Mount. Striving to incarnate the world imagined in Matthew's Sermon and live counter to society's values, William Stringfellow, David Lipscomb, and the sixteenth century Anabaptists practiced nonviolence, loved their neighbors, resisted materialism, and embodied concern for the poor. They lived by the politics of the kingdom of God, encouraging us to preach its message of concern for the marginalized and its prohibition against violence.

Charles Campbell sees the Sermon on the Mount inverting the language of foolishness and making it something positive. The lifestyle imagined in the Sermon looks completely foolish in the eyes of the world. But we are fools…for Christ's sake. Jesus turns the world's notion of power upside down, taking on the role of a jester and engaging in irony. Similarly, gospel foolishness subverts the world's presuppositions and myths that prevent us from imagining alternatives. Foolishness, he argues, characterizes a gospel that shatters commonsense presuppositions in order to help us glimpse the odd new creation imagined in the Sermon on the Mount.

Dennis Dewey provides a pragmatic bridge from the essays to this volume's sermons with keen observations as a biblical storyteller. Dewey urges us to internalize the text before we retell and perform it. The first step is to embody the text in our own hearts, acting out the Sermon's words in our lives, not paying lip service to the text but giving life service. Dewey records his four-month preparation for his oral performance of Sermon on the Mount, an experience that elicited the response, "I felt as if Jesus was talking to me."

These heuristic essays from biblical scholar, theologian, historian, homiletician, and storyteller provide the guiding work for the sermons that make up the second part of this volume. Fourteen sermons cover the textual landscape of Matthew 5–7, with compositional comments identifying some dependence on the volume's essays and others more subtly blending insights. All the sermons were preached prior to their inclusion in this volume, which means they've been tested and tried in the trenches of church life. These sermons offer rich perspectives from a variety of Christian traditions including Disciples of Christ, Churches of

Christ, Presbyterian, and Episcopalian churches. These sermons approach the Sermon as an act of imagination, challenging us to follow Christ, calling followers to embrace his alternative lifestyle, encouraging the church to become salt and light in messy relationships even with those who are our enemies, and exhorting disciples to resist the powers that run counter to the ethics of God's kingdom.

These sermons challenge us to live in God's new world and stand against the contemporary empires. These preachers do so by standing with us in the challenge, confessing their own struggles along the way. One senses the years of pastoral care coming through the sermons, offering a word of grace while at the same time holding us accountable to the demands of discipleship. They demonstrate that the Sermon on the Mount is a Sermon that puts before us, not an impossible ideal, but a vision of what God's people can be when they choose by God's grace to live in God's kingdom.

These troublesome times demand that we construct an alphabet of discipleship, an alphabet that will give us the vocabulary to create the sentences, to form the paragraphs, to possess the language, to frame the conversation so we might begin to speak with and listen to one another about matters central to our faith.

To create such a reality takes a grammar of honesty and love; truth telling and repentance; forgiveness and reconciliation. This volume intends to help build that grammar by starting with the building blocks of research, essay, and sermon all for the larger task of equipping the church for the ministry of Christian living. Given the violent realities of our existences, it is altogether appropriate that we begin with the Sermon on the Mount.

PART ONE

Essays on the
Sermon on the Mount

1

Power and Identities

The Contexts of Matthew's Sermon on the Mount

WARREN CARTER

It is my pleasure to join with you in this task of thinking about and wrestling with preaching and Matthew's Sermon on the Mount.[1] In this essay, I take up one of the primary issues that I think preachers must engage in preaching from Matthew's Sermon, namely how one understands the Sermon as a whole. What sort of text is it? What are we reading? Answering that question involves at least three further related questions: What content are we preaching? To whom are we preaching? And to what end, purpose, goal, are we preaching from Matthew's Sermon on the Mount?

These are complicated questions and have been answered in various ways in the Christian tradition.[2] One approach has seen Matthew's Sermon as articulating an impossible and unfulfillable ideal. To regard the Sermon as impracticable and full of impossible demands means preaching from it to convict hearers of their sin, to have them cry out for God's mercy, and to beg for God's forgiveness.

A second approach has regarded the Sermon as extra-special instruction for extra-special Christians, a text for ecclesial professionals (leaders, clergy) and serious Christians. To regard the Sermon as specially demanding in its instruction is to preach to a select audience of serious or professional Christians, and to mark out divisions between them and the not-so-serious.

A third approach has regarded Matthew's Sermon as laying out God's eternal will for individual Christians. This approach focuses on explicating God's eternal will for human lives to apply God's eternal will to the circumstances of individual lives. Such preaching focuses on the "be-happy attitudes," "how to improve your prayer life," or, as I saw recently, "you are the salt of the earth—a sodium-free diet is not for you."

For various reasons (which space prevents me from arguing in any detail), I do not think any of these options is a satisfactory one for framing preaching from Matthew's Sermon. Much, though, is at stake in determining what sort of text we are reading, the audience, purpose or goal, and content of one's preaching. How do we decide what sort of text we're reading?

My approach is reflected in part in the title of a little book I wrote some time ago, *What Are They Saying about Matthew's Sermon on the Mount?*[3] As part of the WATSA series, it reviews scholarly discussions of a particular topic, identifying important issues and different ways of thinking about them. While I was writing the book, a scholar friend asked me at a conference what I was working on and I told him about the book. He nodded approvingly and asked, "But why include 'Matthew' in the title? Isn't that redundant?"

Why insert *Matthew* in front of Sermon on the Mount? Because the Sermon on the Mount does not come to us as a free-floating document, though it has often been treated as such. It does not exist as a separate or separated entity. It comes to us as three chapters embedded in a larger story, three chapters embedded in a gospel story, three chapters embedded in Matthew's gospel. It comes to us in context as a contextualized text, and that context is, I am suggesting, crucial for meaning. It creates meaning and it limits meaning. And that matters for preaching.

In fact, and I say this hesitantly and with all due respect, I would like to make a small but significant editorial change to this volume's proposed title. "Dare We Live in the World Imagined by the Sermon on the Mount?" is the key question before us.[4] I would like to reword it just a little, "Dare We Live in the World Imagined by *Matthew's* Sermon on the Mount?"

In this essay I attend to two contexts of Matthew's Sermon on the Mount that I think are crucial for determining what we're reading and therefore crucial for what we preach, to whom, and for what end. These two contexts are not the only ones that are important for preaching Matthew's Sermon; I will name a third in my second essay.[5] I first address the narrative or literary context of Matthew's Sermon and then, second, its imperial-historical context. Then I will elaborate some of the consequences of attending to these two contexts in interpreting and preaching Matthew's Sermon.

Narrative Context

First, let's begin with the narrative or literary context. It is important to recall that chapters 5–7, Matthew's Sermon, follow chapters 1–4 of the gospel. The beginning of Matthew's Sermon points out this connection.[6] Chapter 5 begins–and I translate rather literally–"and seeing the crowds, he went up the mountain and after/when he had sat down,[7] his disciples came to him." Notice the numerous occurences of "he," "his," and "him." Four times in the Greek text of this verse we have an unspecified referent. Three times it's explicitly articulated in personal pronouns with two genitives, and a dative, and in the fourth instance it's in a verb ("he went up") with an unspecified subject. Who is this "he," "his," and "him"?

The answer of course seems obvious: Jesus. But the implications of the text *not* naming Jesus are huge. The unspecified subject in the verb in 5:1 requires us to contextualize the verse if we are going to put any content to it. The unspecified subject and unspecified pronouns require us as readers of the gospel to link Matthew's Sermon with what has preceded 5:1 to identify the "he." And when we do that, we do not just get a one-word answer "Jesus," but rather "Jesus as defined by the first four chapters of the gospel." The first four chapters have given an enormous amount of attention to defining who Jesus is and what he is commissioned to do. The speaker of Matthew's Sermon is the Jesus defined by chapters 1–4 of the gospel. Those pronouns bring forward from chapters 1–4 all that we have learned about Jesus and his commission up to this point and put the Sermon in that context. What do we know about Jesus by the time we get to Matthew's Sermon in chapter 5?

In 1:1–17, the genealogy, Jesus is introduced in relation to God's good, just, and life-giving purposes demonstrated through Israel's experiences.[8] Jesus is son of Abraham through whom God promised that all the nations of the earth would be blessed (Gen. 12:1–3). Jesus is son of David to whom God promised a life-giving reign forever, a king who–according to the job description of a royal psalm like Psalm 72–would represent God's care for the poor and needy, God's justice and protection for those threatened by oppressive powers. Jesus is the Christ–anointed or set apart for divine service in the line of priests (Lev. 4:3, 5, 16), prophets (1 Kings 19:16) and kings (Ps. 2:2), but anointed for what?[9] Jesus is introduced in the context of God's life-giving and just purposes for all people, especially the poor and needy.

In 1:18–25, the conception, Jesus is commissioned to manifest God's saving presence. The angel says to Joseph in 1:21–23, "You are to name him Jesus, for he will save his people from their sins…and they shall name him Emmanuel, which means 'God is with us.'"[10] In line with other biblical stories, such as those involving Isaac, Jacob, and Jeremiah, this commission and job description are given in the womb before Jesus is born. In the womb Jesus is commissioned to manifest God's saving presence, and that commission stands over the whole of the gospel story, including Matthew's Sermon on the Mount.

In 2:1–23 Jesus is opposed by the imperial status quo, that is, by the Judean power group allied with and dependent on Rome. In verse 3, Herod, puppet king of Rome, representative of Roman interests, defender of the imperial hierarchical status quo, king of the Jews because Rome says so, murderer of sons and wives, is terrified because some not-so-bright "wise men" ask a politically unwise question, "Where is the one born king of the Jews–and we don't mean Herod?" Of course King Herod is terrified; there can only be one king by definition, and he has so much to lose and so much to defend. When the empire feels threatened, it always strikes back. So Herod resorts to the usual repertoire of imperial weapons: allies, spies, and lies. He summons his allies–the rest of the Jerusalem leadership, the elite, the chief priests and scribes–to find out where the Christ was to be born (2:4). He turns the wise men/magi into spies: "Go and search diligently for the child" (2:8a). And he lies to them: "that I also go and pay him homage" (2:8b). But allies, spies, and lies are only the starters. Inevitably in killing the baby boys around Bethlehem he turns to murderous violence to thwart God's purposes, eliminate God's anointed, and defend the status quo in which the elite 2–3 percent of the population rule for their own benefit and at the expense of the rest.

In 3:1-12 Jesus is witnessed to by John: this Elijah lookalike prepares the way, confronts the elite Pharisees and Sadducees, and announces Jesus' task to baptize with the Spirit and fire–a phrase that identifies Jesus' saving and judging impact.

In 3:13–17 Jesus is sanctioned by God in baptism: the heavens open, the Spirit descends, and for the first of only two times in Matthew's gospel, God speaks directly, "This is my beloved Son, in whom I am well pleased" (KJV). God confirms Jesus' identity as agent of God's saving presence.

In 4:1–11, Jesus is tested in temptation by the devil. The devil holds out good things for Jesus to do: feed the hungry, trust God, take charge of all the empires of the world (4:8). Jesus eventually does all these things (14:13–21; 26:36–46; 28:16–20). But the issue is not what he is to do, but *who* is doing the bidding. As *God's* son or agent he carries out *God's* will and purposes, God's saving presence, at God's bidding, not Satan's bidding.

In 4:12–16, Jesus is located in imperial Galilee and in scripture. Quoting Isaiah 9, he is in Galilee under the Gentiles, under Rome, land of darkness and death in which light, an image of God's saving presence, has now dawned in the person of Jesus commissioned to manifest God's saving presence.

In 4:17, Jesus begins his public ministry. Jesus as defined by these first three and a half chapters announces that God's kingdom, reign, empire–the *basileia ton ouranon*–has come near. In the context of God's commissioning of Jesus in 1:21–23, this phrase "re-languages" Jesus' commission. God's rule, God's empire, is established when God's saving presence–Jesus' commission from 1:21–23–is asserted. The two are synonyms. What does it look like when God's reign/empire/saving presence breaks into human experience?

In 4:18–22, we get a first answer as Jesus calls disciples. He calls two sets of brothers in sequence, disrupting life as they know it–its priorities, commitments, and tasks. He gives them a new identity ("follow me"), a new task ("I will make you fish for people"), and a new community focused on himself. He is a caller of disciples. When God's empire, God's saving empire, comes among people, it claims their lives, disturbs the status quo, creates new priorities and identities, gives new purpose, commissions people to new tasks, and creates a new and alternative community that is going to need formational instruction as in the Sermon on the Mount.

In 4:23, what does it look like when God's empire, God's saving presence comes among humans? Jesus teaches and preaches. God's empire comes among people with demand, invitation, possibilities, challenge, and gift. Explanation accompanies action. Action requires interpretation.

In 4:24–25, what does it look like when God's empire, God's saving presence comes among humans? Jesus engages the imperial world by healing the sick. He enacts God's life-giving purposes for all people as son of Abraham. There is an epidemic of wholeness, of transformation. Jesus rolls back imperial damage caused by consigning 97 percent of the population to poverty and inadequate nutrition.[11] Diseases of contagion and deficiency abound in imperial contexts because taxes, tribute, rents, and tolls literally transfer goods from nonelite producers (most of the population) to elite consumers (a very small percentage) to sustain the elite's extravagant lifestyle.

What does it look like when God's empire, God's saving presence comes among humans? It's the beginning of the end. In 5:1, "he went up the mountain." The phrase "he went up the mountain" is a quotation from earlier in scripture. Nine times in the Pentateuch it refers to Moses going up Mount Sinai to receive the Decalogue, the revelation of God's will.[12] Six times the clause is used in reference to Mount Zion, to the coming of God's new age of justice and life in which the nations go up to Zion and learn God's ways.[13] By quoting this phrase Matthew presents Jesus as the revealer of God's ultimate or eschatological purposes for the world underway now in his ministry, even in his words.

So in verses 1:1 to 5:1 Matthew introduces Jesus, who is:

- Contextualized in God's life-giving purposes (1:1–17)
- Commissioned from conception to manifest God's saving presence (1:18–25)
- Opposed by Herod (2:1–23)
- Witnessed to by John (3:1–12)
- Sanctioned by God in baptism (3:13–17)
- Tested by the devil (4:1–11)
- Located in Galilee and in the scriptures (4:12–16)
  and who:
- Announces God's empire (4:17)
- Calls disciples and creates an alternative community (4:18–22)
- Preaches the good news of the empire (4:23)
- Heals the sick (4:24–25)
- Reveals God's eschatological purposes (5:1).

Why bother to rehearse all of this material from the opening chapters? Because it answers the question: What type of sermon are we engaging? This is the narrative context of Matthew's Sermon. All of this frames, locates, contextualizes Matthew's Sermon, and thereby it shapes our reading of and preaching from chapters 5–7. It is this Jesus who is referred to by those pronouns in 5:1. It is this Jesus, commissioned to manifest God's saving presence as God's son or agent who enacts that commission in preaching Matthew's Sermon on the Mount.

What kind of writing is it? Matthew's Sermon addresses disciples in 5:1–2, people who have encountered in Jesus' call and commission the kingdom or empire of the heavens. The phrase "the kingdom or the empire of the heavens"[14] provides the opening words, the theme, the thesis, the focus, the headline of Jesus' public activity in 4:17; it is enacted in calling disciples and healing the sick; it is the content of his preaching in 4:23, and it occurs seven times in Matthew's Sermon.[15] In the Sermon Jesus carries out his commission from chapter 1 to manifest God's saving presence, the commission that is re-languaged as "the kingdom/empire of the heavens" in 4:17. Jesus carries out that commission in the Sermon by envisioning God's saving presence at work, by painting pictures of the kingdom or empire at work. Matthew's Sermon, like the scene depicting the call of disciples in 4:18–22, like the scene depicting the healing of the sick and desperate in 4:23–25, provides examples, visions, vignettes of the sort of life, the sort of community, God's empire and saving presence creates among human beings.

In envisioning for disciples and for the crowds that comprise the secondary audience (7:28–29) life shaped by God's empire, Matthew's Sermon is a work of imagination.[16] By that I do not mean it is a fantasy or escape that has nothing to do with how people live. Rather, I mean that it sets about enabling disciples to envision life shaped by God's reign/empire. Its purpose is to enable disciples to imagine life created by God's saving presence. Why? So that disciples can live accordingly, so that we can embody God's empire in practices and social structures, so that we can articulate what it does among humans. It is an identity-shaping, community-forming sermon. It shapes the identity of a community of disciples who enact, who live out this way of life. It trains us in the ways of God's saving purposes, God's reign. Good preaching will concern itself with the same task.

Why is such imagining necessary? Why is such identity-forming work needed? Why do these newly called and commissioned disciples who have just encountered God's empire in their lives need such formative, envisioning, training work? The short answer is that their everyday world, their cultural context, just like ours, trains them in very different practices, shapes a very different identity.

Imperial-Historical Context

That brings us to the second context for Matthew's Sermon that I mentioned earlier. I've written so far about the importance of seeing Matthew's Sermon in relation to chapters 1–4, its narrative context, and in that context it emerges as a visionary, imaging text. Now I take up the second context for Matthew's Sermon, the imperial-historical context.[17] The Roman Empire was a very hierarchical, vertical society with a small group possessing all the power. The elite were some 2 to 3 percent of the population, marked by power, wealth, and status, with the remaining 97 or so percent consigned to varying degrees of powerlessness and to varying degrees of poverty, hunger, and poor health. The society featured great disparities of wealth and power with essentially no middle class, though it did have varying levels of wealth and degrees of poverty. The people knew no "Roman dream" in which folks pulled themselves up by their sandal straps. The system was set up by the elite, for the elite.

Matthew's gospel was probably written in the 80s of the first century, perhaps in the city of Antioch in Syria.[18] The key date here is the burning and destruction of Jerusalem and the temple in the year 70 C.E., some ten to fifteen years previously. Antioch had been the staging area for Roman troops before they moved south to siege and destroy, to shock and awe Jerusalem.[19] Special levies of corn and other supplies had been made on Syrian peasant farmers—on top of normal taxes—to provision the troops.[20]

Violence had broken out against Jewish folks in Antioch.[21] The city's debt recording office had been attacked and burned.[22] After the war in Judaea the victorious general Titus, son of Emperor Vespasian and himself the future emperor from 79–81 C.E. visited Antioch, addressed the assembled citizens, and paraded booty and captives from Jerusalem on his way to a triumphal entry into Rome.[23] After the fall of the temple in 70 C.E., the Emperor Vespasian co-opted the temple tax and made Jews pay it to himself as a reminder of their subjugation. To add insult to injury, he used it to rebuild the temple of Jupiter Capitolinus in Rome.[24] Jupiter was one of the deities on whose behalf and at whose will Rome ruled, the deity that had blessed Rome's efforts in being victorious over the Jewish God.[25] Rome issued Judea Capta coins to proclaim the Roman victory and intimidate anyone else out of any thoughts to rebel.[26] This is the empire at work. Military power, political control, economic exploitation, religious sanction, spin or propaganda, rhetoric, and xenophobia linked up together to preserve the interests of the ruling 2 to 3 percent at the expense of the rest.

This post-70 C.E. situation required Jewish folks and groups to negotiate this fresh assertion of Roman power, to reformulate distinctive identity and practices without the temple, to make sense of this past, and to find a way ahead. It is out of this context of various options and much debate that the rabbinic movement would eventually come to dominate.[27] One of the players in the debates, as a group, are the Jesus followers. Matthew's gospel attests plenty of conflict with a local synagogue community over the way ahead.[28]

A key part of what Matthew's gospel is doing is providing ways for followers of Jesus, crucified by the empire, to negotiate Roman power in the light of this fresh assertion of Rome's military power. It offers a whole spectrum of views of the empire.

The gospel does not hesitate, for example, to name the empire as utterly contrary to God's purposes. God would have no need to commission Jesus to manifest God's saving presence, God's reign or empire, if the Roman Empire enacted God's purposes. The Herod story in chapter 2 reveals standard ways in which imperial powers operate—lies, spies, allies, and murder—contrary to God's purposes. Herod seeks the death of God's anointed agent, but ironically Herod's death is mentioned three times in the chapter.[29] God thwarts him. I mentioned that in the temptation scene in 4:8 the devil offers Jesus "all the [empires] of the world" if Jesus will pay him homage. But we must not overlook the content of that claim. The empires of the world—including Rome—are thus said to be in the devil's control. This means the Roman Empire is demonic. It is diabolical. It is fundamentally opposed to God's life-giving and just purposes. The Roman Empire is not a blessing for all the nations of the earth, God's promise to Abraham. It benefits the elite and exploits and tyrannizes the rest. This is not God's vision of a just society.

Yet Matthew also sees Rome's empire as an agent of God's purposes. Jesus tells the parable of the king who invites his elite allies to his son's wedding banquet (22:1–14). They refuse. The king burns their city and then invites others, the nonelites. The reference to the burning in verse 7 is Matthew's addition to the Q parable in Luke 14:15–24, and disrupts the sequence and creates an unlikely scenario of a wedding feast held in the ruins of the burned city. It recalls and interprets Rome's burning of Jerusalem in 70 C.E., thus presenting it as an act of punishment on the city's elite for rejecting God's son Jesus. Rome is the instrument of God's punishment on the city. This is Matthew's theological interpretation of 70 C.E.

But in turn Rome will be judged by God. Twice in these opening chapters Matthew includes citations from Isaiah 7–9.[30] First in 1:23 in naming Jesus Immanuel–God with us–and again in 4:14–16 right before Jesus' public ministry begins, a citation from Isaiah announces light in darkness and life in death. Isaiah 7–9 addresses the situation in the eighth century when Syria and Israel to the north threaten King Ahaz of Judah in an effort to fend off Assyrian imperial aggression. God gives Ahaz a sign of Immanuel, a child to be born who represents the future, the next generation; they will survive if they trust God. But fear dominates, and judgment falls. Samaria is wiped out in 722 B.C.E., and Jerusalem is occupied by 701 B.C.E. But that is not the end of the story–after judgment comes redemption. Isaiah 9:2 is restated in Matthew 4:16, which reads, "The people who sat in darkness / have seen a great light, / and for those who sat in the region and shadow of death / light has dawned," perhaps a reference to Hezekiah–and the nation continues in the seventh century B.C.E. There is life after death. Imperial power does not have the final word. Matthew cites this very text, Isaiah 9:1–2, in Matthew 4:14–16 at the end of his introduction to Jesus, and before Jesus' public activity begins with the announcement, "The kingdom, the empire of the heavens, has come near" (4:17). The end of Rome's world is under way.

The eschatological discourse of Matthew 24 pictures that end.[31] At Jesus' parousia, a term used to identify the coming or arrival of imperial figures at cities, a battle occurs and the eagles, the standards of the Roman legions, will be gathered amid the corpses (24:28). This is God's judgment on Rome, God's victory over Rome.

Matthew's gospel, then, exhibits various attitudes attributed to the Roman Empire: the empire is devilish (4:8); it is totally contrary to God's will for just and life-giving human community, yet it carries out God's purposes of judgment in the destruction of Jerusalem (22:7)–which is not the final word; it is under God's judgment (4:15–16, evoking Isaiah 7–9) to be enacted finally at Jesus' return (24:27–31).

But in the meantime, until this judgment takes place, in the light of this fresh assertion of Roman power in the destruction of Jerusalem in 70 C.E., how are disciples of Jesus, one crucified by the empire, yet the revealer of God's saving purposes and reign, to live in its midst?

Matthew's Sermon on the Mount addresses precisely this question. It sets about training disciples by having them imagine a different identity, that of being followers of Jesus, not imitators of Rome. It has them imagine a different way of life, a life that differs from imperial values and practices. It has them envision different ways of being, different social structures, different practices, different community.

Why? To bring down the empire? No–that is God's work, in God's time, by God's means, according to Matthew. No democratic processes are available to these followers, no letter-writing campaigns, no petitions, no elections, no PACs. And no violence. Rather, they are to engage the empire by enacting in the midst of it, by embodying in the midst of the empire God's just and life-giving purposes in an alternative community that offers a different experience of being human, that bears witness to the falsity of Rome's empire, and offers an alternative to it: the empire or saving presence of God.

Matthew's Beatitudes (5:3–12)

How does Matthew's Sermon do this? Consider the beatitudes, the opening section of Matthew's Sermon in 5:3–12.[32] As a way of talking, beatitudes express God's blessing, God's favor on situations and actions. That word translated "blessed" has the sense–"God is pleased with, God is pleased when, God's favor rests on...Esteemed are...Honored are..." Beatitudes focus on present situations, declare God's blessing, and promise and anticipate a future eschatological transformation connected to how followers live in the present. That first word meaning "blessed" or "honored"–*makarioi* in Greek–is a plural term, not a singular term. These beatitudes are directed to groups, to communities, not to individuals. They concern communal practices much more than they do individual qualities.

Immediately in the first beatitude the focus falls on a most unlikely group of people in this Roman world, "Blessed are the poor in spirit" (5:3). In an empire the important folks, of course, are the elite. The whole world is organized to bless them, to honor them, and to exhibit their blessing; but this first beatitude asks disciples to imagine something very different—that God's favor falls not on the elite but on the nonelite. They are the honored ones.

The phrase "the poor in spirit" is not to be spiritualized. They aren't the humble or the voluntary poor or the deserving poor or the lazy poor or those with soft spiritual dispositions or the patient or any other spiritualization. They are the literal poor, the destitute, those without options and with few resources who are part of the 97 percent or so of the empire's population.[33] They are folks like the fishermen of 4:18–22 who fish only because they are licensed to do so by Rome's representatives in Galilee. They especially include the sick and damaged in 4:23–25, those who bear in their bodies the cost and damage of taxing imperial ways that deprive them of land, adequate food and nutrition, of health and strength, and consign them to desperate daily circumstances. They are the powerless, the exploited. To be "poor *in spirit*," though, is to recognize that poverty is very physical and material, but also so much more. Poverty not only physically damages people but also crushes people's spirits. It eats away at the very core of a person. Poverty deprives people of material resources as well "spiritual" ones such as hope, dignity, and value. These are the poor in spirit, those crushed by the empire into hopelessness and desperation. Jesus declares them blessed—honored—because to them belongs *God's* empire, the empire that transforms Rome's—and any other empire's— unjust, exploitative, self-benefiting social structures.

This beatitude offers a different vision of human community that clashes with business as usual in Rome's empire. Rome claims divine blessing and sanction for the way of life of the ruling elite. Jesus announces that God's favor extends to all people. The son of Abraham, in whom all the peoples or households of the earth are blessed, says so. That elevation of the nobodies, that dignifying promise of reversal, is as contrary to the ways of empire as one can imagine. And that's the point. Imagining it is the beginning; a whole way of life can be lived that enacts such a vision. That's the identity and role of communities of disciples; enacting life-giving power in a world of self-serving exploitative power. Good preaching of Matthew's Sermon will help us imagine into being that communal way of life.

The poor in spirit are the meek (5:5), the third blessing or beatitude. Jesus promises that they will inherit the earth. Again we must not spiritualize the meek. They are not the wimps, doormats, spineless, nonassertive, humble. We can't fill the term in for what we like. Instead, we follow the clue the beatitude gives us to identify the meek. In promising that the meek will inherit the earth, Jesus cites Psalm 37, where that promise is made at least four times (37:9, 11, 22, 29). Psalm 37 gives us a very clear picture of the meek and the circumstances they endure. It begins, "Do not fret because of the wicked." You can be pretty sure that when that sort of command is given, people are fretting. Why are they fretting? And who is fretting? If we read on through the psalm, we find out what the wicked are up to. They are evil doers (37:1); they prosper and carry out evil devices (37:7); they plot against the righteous (37:12); they kill the poor and needy (37:14, 32); they borrow and do not pay back (37:21); they bring the righteous to court (37:33); they oppress (37:35). Do you hear the terms, the synonyms, for the meek? The meek are the oppressed, the poor, the needy, the righteous, those who walk uprightly. Threatened and endangered by the wicked elite, they fret.

Throughout, the psalm promises God's sustaining and saving presence, God's justice now and in the future (e.g., 37:6, 13, 17, 28, 39–40). That justice will mean adequate resources to sustain life–the return of land, which is the basic means of survival in an agrarian empire (37:9, 11, 22, 29). The psalm offers a classic imperial situation in which the powerful elite control the land, gaining wealth and depriving the poor/meek of this basic life-sustaining resource. God's verdict is clear, as is the exhortation to the community. In the words of the next beatitude, they are to hunger and thirst for justice. That means distributive justice, through which resources and just societal relationships sustain life for all. The beatitude invites disciples to imagine a vastly different world, not "business as usual," but a world with reversal and transformation. And, in imagining, we are challenged to live out the vision. Good preaching will help us do that.

That imaginative work continues in the next four beatitudes: God's blessing–God's favor–is found in the doing of mercy (5:7). Honored in God's view–esteemed in God's perspective–are those who do mercy. God's reign, God's saving presence, creates a world marked by mercy rather than revenge, meanness, selfishness, or exploitative power over others, whether military, political, economic, religious, or personal and relational. Later, in quoting Hosea, Jesus instructs his hearers to go and learn what this means: "I desire mercy, not sacrifice" (9:13; 12:7). One has to learn mercy to survive in a cultural context dominated by destructive and self-serving power.

The story is told of a woman who went to do her Christmas shopping.[34] So she headed off to the mall in her Volvo. Because it was cold, she wanted to park near the mall entrance and not walk far. She circled a few times and saw the lights of a car reversing out of a parking spot near the entrance. She waited for it to leave and was about to pull into the space when a young guy in a little red sports car whipped into the parking space in front of her. Furious, she lowered the power windows and shouted at him, "You can't do that." He said, "Oh, yes you can, when you're young and fast." So, muttering to herself, "I'll show you 'young and fast,'" She backed up, put her Volvo into gear and charged, crashing into the little red sports car. She backed up again, put her Volvo into gear and charged, crashing into the little red sports car. She backed up again, put her Volvo into gear and charged, crashing into the little red sports car. The young guy was beside himself, first in shock and then in rage. He shouted at her, "Hey, lady, what are you doing? You can't do that." She leaned out the window and said to him, "Oh, yes you can, when you're old and rich." Isn't revenge sweet? How do we learn mercy? I will return to that question in the next essay.

In 5:8 the disciples are to imagine a world marked by purity of heart, a phrase that in Psalm 24 denotes both purity in worship and truth in dealings with others. It holds together worship and work, liturgy and living. Moral purity accompanies acceptable worship. It is a world of integrity born from a heart committed to God's purposes and lived out societally for the benefit of, not the destruction of, one's neighbor—as Jesus will describe it in the love commandments of 22:37–39. One has to go and learn to live out the vision. Good preaching will help us do that.

In 5:9 God's blessing, God's favor, is encountered in those who make peace—but not Roman peace, *Pax Romana,* where peace means nothing other than brutal military conquest, subjugation, confiscation of land, religious sanction, and systemic exploitation. The Emperor Augustus erected the Ara Pacis, the altar of peace, in Rome to celebrate his military victories in Spain and Gaul, to celebrate peace based on military strength and comprising subjugation. Peace in the biblical traditions, as described for instance in the kingly vision of Psalm 72, commonly means very different things. In that psalm it means sustaining the weak and needy, not crushing them (72:4, 12–14). It is about wholeness and well-being, about just social relationships and adequate resources. It is about peace based on God's distributive justice, not based on the empire's military power. This beatitude envisions an active process of making peace, of taking apart the unjust structures and the weapons of death, rivet by rivet, computer chip by computer chip. Peace makes wholeness. This is the alternative way of life of the community of disciples.

Such a way of life threatens the status quo. One thing we can be very sure of is that to live for God's justice, to live out this vision, means the empire will strike back. It was true for Jesus, and it is true for his disciples (5:10–12). We should not be surprised that Pilate and his Jerusalem allies take out Jesus by crucifying him.[35] We should not be surprised that presidents order surveillance of citizens opposed to their wars and that officials leak compromising information about those who do not support them.

In the beatitudes, Jesus has the disciples imagine a different world, a different identity for themselves, a different set of practices, a different relationship to the status quo. Why imagine? Not because it is impossible. Not because it is escapist. Not because it is fantasy. But because it begins to counter patterns imbibed from the culture of the imperial world. It begins to form an alternative. It begins to shape a different identity and way of life not based on imitating imperial power but on faithfully enacting and living out God's purposes. Preaching on Matthew's Sermon on the Mount, I am suggesting, takes up the hard work of elaborating, fleshing out, and living such visions.[36]

Conclusion

I have suggested that attention to two contexts of Matthew's Sermon on the Mount—its narrative context as part of Matthew's gospel, and its imperial context as a text emerging from the Roman Empire—can helpfully shape our preaching from Matthew's Sermon. I have suggested that Matthew's Sermon is a work of imagination, helping us envision a community, practices, and a way of life that embody God's saving presence, the reign or empire of God manifested by Jesus. I have suggested that Matthew's Sermon helps us imagine a community that offers a human experience and way of life that differs significantly from the practices of the Roman Empire and the norms of our own age.

Matthew's Sermon on the Mount, I have suggested, begets envisioning sermons. Such sermons help the people of God imagine a different identity for themselves and for this world. Envisioning sermons help people imagine and live into being practices and habits that do not exercise or exploit power over others but are empowering for all. Envisioning sermons help the people of God imagine and live into being a way of life that is not a religious variation of our dominant cultural values but a way of life that enacts God's good and just transforming and redemptive purposes for all people. Envisioning sermons represent God's saving presence, the reign or empire of God. Envisioning sermons help folks develop strategies, formulate plans, and commit to concrete enactments of God's just and good and life-giving purposes for all of creation.

Preaching from Matthew's Sermon is very hard and skillful work, but it is life-changing and world-changing work.

2

Embodying God's Empire in Communal Practices

Matthew 6:1–18

WARREN CARTER

Consider some of the contours of the world in which we live and the context in which we hear Matthew's Sermon on the Mount:

According to the Children's Defense Fund, 37 million U.S. inhabitants in 2004 were "food insecure" and considered poor, including 13 million children.[1] Poverty among children is increasing. In 1973, 14.4 percent of those under 18 were considered poor; in 2000 the figure was 17.8 percent,[2] the increase since 2000 is 12.4 percent.[3] Especially increasing are the numbers in "extreme poverty;" three of five kids who have fallen into poverty since 2000 are in "extreme poverty." "Extreme poverty" means less than half of the poverty level (under $7412 of household income).[4]

The gap between those with wealth and those in poverty is increasing. The average income of the top 20 percent of households is fifteen times greater than the households of the bottom 20 percent. The average income of the top 1 percent of households is fifty times greater than the households of the bottom 20 percent.[5] In 2003, the average compensation for CEOs was 185 times more than a typical worker. In 1965, the figure was 24 times.[6] The wealth of the richest 1 percent of U.S. households was greater than the combined total of the bottom 95 percent. The top 1 percent of income-earners (2.7 million people) received 50.4 percent of the national income, more than the poorest 100 million people combined.[7] There are close links between high poverty levels and poor health.[8] More than 44 million people are uninsured[9] including 9 million children.[10] In 2002 the infant mortality rate rose in the United States for the first time in forty years, to 7.00 deaths per 1,000. The United States is ranked twenty-fifth in industrialized nations for child mortality.[11]

And these are just some U.S. figures, for just a few issues. There's the rest of the world and so many more issues—literacy, homelessness, AIDS, availability of medical care and prescription drugs, unemployment, malnutrition, etc. So, *so* much to do. It is exhausting, isn't it?

In the previous chapter, I noted two contexts for reading Matthew's Sermon on the Mount: its narrative context (the relationship between chapters 5–7 and 1–4), and its imperial-historical context (life in the post-70 C.E. post-temple Roman Empire). I suggested to you that attending to these contexts was crucial for interpreting and preaching from Matthew's Sermon. The Sermon is a contextualized text; it is not free-floating. It comes in the narrative or literary context of Matthew's gospel, specifically Matthew 1–4, in which Jesus has been commissioned to manifest God's saving presence, the kingdom or empire of God in the midst of the Roman Empire.

Matthew's Sermon comes in the context of Jesus announcing his commission to manifest God's saving presence in the language that the kingdom or the empire of the heavens has come near (4:17). Matthew's Sermon comes in the context of Jesus enacting or embodying his commission to manifest God's saving presence, God's reign or empire, in calling disciples to follow him, to fish for people, and to be an alternative community (4:18–22). Matthew's Sermon comes in the context of Jesus' demonstration or enacting or embodying of God's saving presence, God's empire, as he engages Rome's world and rolls back imperial damage in the healings of 4:23–25.

Empires should come with a warning—they are bad for your health! Rome's empire made people literally sick because it deprived people of adequate nutrition by removing food through taxation, forced overwork, and stress, and consigned people to dreadful living conditions where contagious diseases were rife. Jesus' healings in this context roll back imperial damage. They anticipate that world of justice, of physical transformation, and wholeness that prophets like Isaiah depict as they describe God's coming to save the world: "the eyes of the blind shall be opened, / and the ears of the deaf unstopped; / then the lame shall leap like a deer, / and the tongue of the speechless sing for joy" (Isa. 35:4–6; quoted in Mt. 11:2–6). Rolling back, repairing imperial damage is the church's mission.

In these narrative and imperial-historical contexts we encounter Matthew's Sermon. A work of imagination, it offers visions of what life in God's reign, God's empire, looks like. It offers some "for examples"; it envisions enactments of God's purposes; it sets out practices that embody God's saving presence or reign; it trains disciples to see, to act, to live differently. It shapes the identity and way of life of a community that does not imitate the Roman—or any other—Empire, but offers an alternative to it.

Preaching from Matthew's Sermon assists congregations to grasp these visions and be grasped by them. It helps congregations flesh out this imagination in our world and daily lives through practices and words.

But, of course, my analysis thus far is inadequate for preachers. My analysis has named two contexts. It has assumed a third. In this chapter I make explicit that third context, our twenty-first–century context. As we all know, the path from the preacher's study to the pulpit does not go through an underground tunnel. Rather, it goes through the lives of the folks in all their diversities and particularities of circumstances,[12] through the structures of our imperial society, through the values and practices of our culture, through the events of our world. That is, not only do we exegete texts—and of course we do that— but we also exegete congregations, communities, cultures,[13] to re-present the word of the Lord as a word on target.

Contemporary Context

There's much we could say about this twenty-first–century world—and these figures quoted at the outset of the chapter about "health and wealth" crises say so much—but I want to highlight a couple of other things that I think are especially important before taking up chapter 6 of Matthew's gospel.

Of what consequence is it, for example, that we engage Matthew's Sermon on the Mount in an unashamedly consumerist society? You know the doctrines: we live to shop and shop to live; we think that the one with the most stuff wins. We are fixated with the latest gadget, with being self-absorbed and entertained, with pleasure and comfort, with more and more, and with disregard for the environment and for our neighbors in the global village, not to mention our disregard for Jesus' words in 6:24, "You cannot serve God and wealth [mammon]." We think Jesus is just plain wrong about that.

To defend our right to this way of life, in fact to promote it, we live in the most powerful military empire the world has ever seen. This empire extends its economic, political, and cultural influence everywhere. This empire claims religious sanction for its self-benefiting actions. This empire decides to set aside international laws and conventions and opinion when it suits. This empire struggles to recognize the legitimacy of expressions of internal dissent and uses its military power at will. All of this is in defense of a way of life that is unaccountable to the rest of the world and in direct violation of Jesus' command to "not resist violently the evil doer" (5:39)[14] and to love your enemies (5:44). None of that is new. And you can name all sorts of other dimensions. Matthew's Sermon on the Mount does not sustain that way of life; it imagines an alternative to it. Proclaiming that alternative is a great challenge for the preacher for several reasons.

I began this chapter with ghastly figures of our "wealth and health" crises, of poverty, lack of food, lack of adequate healthcare. Just a few figures because in our age of mass media we all have disaster fatigue; but I wanted to name a few, just enough to remind us that our world, with its hierarchies and vast inequalities of wealth and unjust access to resources and multiple casualties of power, shares some of the features of Rome's world. Just a few figures to remind us of the cost of our empire, and of this contemporary context of our engagement with Matthew's Sermon on the Mount.

President Dwight Eisenhower was right in his farewell address in 1961 when he warned about the cost of militarism: "Every gun that is made, every warship launched, every rocket fired, signifies in the final sense a theft from those who hunger and are not fed, those who are cold and are not clothed," and we could add those who are homeless and are not housed, those who are illiterate and are not educated, those who are sick and do not have access to healing or medications.[15] Eisenhower understood the interconnectedness of these things.

What does it mean to be rich Christians in an age of hunger,[16] well fed Christians in an age of poverty, vacation-homed Christians in an age of homelessness, overclothed Christians in an age of nakedness, highly entertained Christians in an age of militaristic violence? Sermon-on-the-Mount–shaped Christians in our age of empire?

My point is this. When we engage Matthew's Sermon and the section that is before us (6:1–18), when we read texts that exhort us to acts of mercy and justice, that exhort us to pray each day for God's empire to come, that exhort us to pray for our daily bread, we must not spiritualize these texts. We must not individualize them. We must not privatize them. We must not gut them by reducing them to "my little interior world." Matthew's reach and God's purposes are so much bigger than that–they are systemic, they are societal. Matthew's Sermon trains us to imagine ways of embodying and living God's reign, not taking us away from the pain and privilege of this world but leading us right into the heart of it to enact God's transforming, saving work *there* as a community of disciples.

Preaching from Matthew's Sermon must help us to do that, as difficult as it is, and as resistant as we as congregants are likely to be.

One Sunday I was leading a study in a church adult Sunday school class. We were looking at the story of the feeding of the 5,000 (Mt. 14:13–21). I was talking about it as a text that enacts the prophetic, eschatological visions of plenty, abundance, fertility, and wholeness for all people that mark the establishment of God's good and just purposes.[17] We had looked at the vision of Isaiah 25:6–10 of an abundant feast for all peoples that Isaiah presents as a sign of the establishment of God's reign. I was suggesting that in the feeding of the 5,000 Jesus was enacting that sort of vision, enacting God's will for hungry people to be fed in anticipation of the time when God's saving purposes are established in full so that all have plenty to eat because all will have just access to adequate resources. And I was suggesting that disciples of Jesus are obligated to participate in that task and to live actively, with actions, toward that goal now. In the middle of discussing the feeding of the 5,000, a man in the group said, "I'm not sure that I am following you. You seem to be saying that Jesus provided these people with real bread." I hesitated, waiting for him to get to his question or comment, but he didn't say any more. There was an awkward silence while I waited. Then he said, as if to prompt me, "Is that so?" Still not getting his point, I said, "I'm not sure what you're asking." So he said it again. "You seem to be saying Jesus gave these people actual bread." And it suddenly dawned on me what he might be getting at. So I said, "Sure, that's exactly what I'm saying. What did you expect that I would say?" He said, "All my life I've heard preachers talk about Jesus meeting all my needs, my emotional and spiritual needs. But I've never heard anyone ever suggest that this scene is about real bread and God feeding real people and disciples feeding real people. That's very different." We agreed on that.

How can we have so privatized, so individualized, so dematerialized, so de-crumbed, so de-breaded this story so badly? Eschatological visions commonly feature at least three themes: physical wholeness in which the sick are healed; abundant fertility in which the hungry are fed; and security in either the overthrowing or conversion of oppressors. They are good preaching in that they help us imagine such a world and live toward it now with appropriate practices that live it into being—not run from it; not reduce it to me and my needs; not privatize it. Preaching from Matthew's Sermon must help us live it into being in a world of imperial power, even when we as hearers are as resistant as we can be.

But there is another challenge for preaching Matthew's Sermon, another challenge that this talk of living the vision into being, that any exegesis of a contemporary congregation must acknowledge: busyness, overcommitment, limited time, limited energy. Folks are busy with all sorts of things, legitimate things, good things. But Matthew's Sermon compels us into a very active way of life focused on enacting God's reign and engaging our culture. It demands our effort, time, energy—precisely those things we don't have any of.

Three Acts of Justice: Matthew 6:1–18

Consider Matthew 6:1–18 with this issue in mind because at least part of what this section of Matthew's Sermon does is to weave together demand with renewal, action with rest, activity with refocusing. It suggests a rhythm of living God's reign that may be helpful for us, that might reframe some of our busyness—perhaps.

This section sets out three acts for followers of Jesus to be about: mercy in 6:2–4, prayer in 6:5–15, and fasting in 6:16–18. These three actions are linked together in some Jewish texts. For example, in Tobit, the first book of the apocrypha, the angel Raphael preaches a wedding sermon to Tobit's newly married son and daughter-in-law, urging them to prayer, fasting, and acts of mercy with justice (Tobit 12:8–9). These actions are not done to earn God's favor but to express it.[18]

The first act in verses 2–4 is usually translated "almsgiving," which for us has a very old and constricted feel. The root of the word means "mercy," as in the beatitude in 5:7, the blessing on the merciful, so I translate it as "acts of mercy." These three actions—mercy, prayer, and fasting—are introduced in verse 1 under the rubric of justice: "Beware of practicing your justice before others" (author's translation). The term, *dikaiosyne*, in verse 1 is unhelpfully translated in the NRSV as "piety." The term has appeared four times previously in the gospel (3:15; 5:6, 10, 20), and in none of these instances does it designate "piety" in the narrow sense we usually understand that term. Rather it indicates living in accord with or doing God's purposes. Jesus tells John, for example, that John should baptize him "to fulfill all righteousness" (3:15), to enact God's will and purposes. The term is about living righteousness, doing justice, much bigger concepts than piety. So the emphasis is on three acts that enact justice—mercy, prayer, fasting—three very different ways of enacting justice, combining activism and retreat, doing and relationship. It is the interaction among these elements through the sequence of these eighteen verses that is very important. I want to highlight eight aspects of these verses.

1. Public enactment

Matthew 6:1 sets out the general warning repeated through the passage, "Beware of practicing your justice before others in order to be seen by them." A life of doing justice is lived for God's glory and not for human show or display. You can be sure a warning about this motivation of public display and approval means someone's doing it. Who are these people enacting such a thing? I think the obvious answer is that they are followers of Jesus. Matthew's Sermon is addressed to disciples (5:1). Matthew's gospel is an in-house document addressed to followers of Jesus in the 70s or 80s, not to the public at large. So some followers are falling prey to this practice of public display and approval.

Why? Why would followers of Jesus be so vulnerable? It is, I suggest, the old problem—not the church in the world but too much world in the church. It's the issue of cultural imitation, of loss of identity. Disciples of Jesus, as are some in the synagogue in the next few verses, are taking their cues for how they live not from following Jesus but from the larger society, particularly elite acts of public beneficence. Let me explain that.

One of the obligations of elites in Rome's world was that of civic good works.[19] This practice of civic benefaction was called *euergetism.* Elites undertook numerous civic good works: building a fountain, paving a road, sponsoring a feast for the imperial cult celebration, sponsoring the meals and meetings of an artisan guild, carrying out the priesthood duties associated with some god or goddess; paying for public games, making a food handout, building a statue or a gate, giving a client a special handout. Elites knew that civic good works were one of the ways of maintaining the status quo. They created dependence and built gratitude among nonelites. They enhanced elite reputations because they provided an opportunity to parade wealth and display status and build power and receive honor. Innumerable inscriptions from the Roman world record such actions, set them in stone to make very sure that everybody's left and right hands knew what this particular set of hands was accomplishing. These actions maintained the hierarchical social structure. Such giving was often "self-regarding," self-rewarding in that it did more for the giver than the recipient. It was calculated and conspicuous public kindness, public acts of "mercy" for one's own benefit. It often indebted recipients to some sort of reciprocal response, such as displays of deference or service. Conspicuous consumption and display were fundamental to elite imperial values and practices.

About as far from this as one can imagine, Matthew's Jesus instructs disciples in a different practice. Acts of justice, says Jesus, are not about impressing other people, not about making us feel good. They are about doing God's saving purposes, because that is who disciples are, that is our identity, committed to glorifying God by enacting God's empire, by living it into being. Preaching on Matthew's Sermon will help us identify appropriate acts of justice and will remind us of their origin and their purposes.

2. Learning mercy (6:2–4)

Again the focus is on doing. Jesus assumes the practice—"*When* you *do* acts of mercy"—and warns—"don't blow your horn about it." The language is metaphorical and polemical, not literal and factual, so we don't need to use it to feed Christian anti-Jewish attitudes and prejudices by generalizing it to claim that all Jews were trying to earn God's favor. They weren't; they already had it by being born into the covenant.[20] Matthew 6:3–4 offers the alternative to self-benefiting actions: do it in secret. Instead of self-serving public display, acts of mercy are to be done in secret, life-giving works for another, focused on the well-being of another, not the elevation of one's self.

Doing mercy is a big theme in Matthew's gospel. The blessing in 5:7 is on the merciful, not the revengeful. Twice, in 9:13 and in 12:7, Jesus quotes Hosea 6:6, "I desire mercy, not sacrifice." In 23:23 he complains that the elite Jerusalem leaders ignore the big matters of the tradition: justice, mercy, and faithfulness. In 9:13 he leads into the citation from Hosea about desiring mercy by instructing them: go and learn what this means.

That is, while acts of mercy are assumed, they are not assumed to be natural. In an imperial society that majors on domination, exploitation, military power, self-serving interests, submission, owning stuff, and nonelite deprivation—our world—mercy is not a given. Not surprisingly, in the alternative community that enacts God's purposes, it has to be learned. At least most of Matthew's community was part of the nonelite. Life in a city such as Antioch was pretty desperate for most in the late first century. Generally there is little surplus; often there is shortage. Squalor, dirt, disease, deprivation, and death define normalcy. Jesus' words are a tough message of not hoarding the little we have, but mercifully making it available to one another, trusting that others will do the same for you. It's a community practice, sharing from need to need. Preaching on Matthew's Sermon has to help us do mercy.

3. How do we learn to do mercy?

That is an important question. But for most of us—not all—for most of us the question is perhaps a little different because of our social location. How do we rich Christians learn acts of mercy? How do we rich Christians who have bought into our cultural values of entitlement that more is better, that we deserve what we have, that it defines our success and identity, etc—how do *we* learn mercy in an age of hunger, poverty, and homelessness? What does mercy look like?

A scene later in Matthew's gospel is very disturbing because I think it offers us a master class in doing mercy. In 19:16–22 a rich man, a man defined in verse 23 by the amount of stuff he possesses, a member of the elite, one of the folks who knows wealth, power, and status, asks Jesus about inheriting eternal life. He mentions his careful observing of the commandments, including not stealing and loving his neighbor. But Jesus gives him three big commands in 19:21 about learning mercy.

The first is, "Sell your possessions," or, if you prefer, "Liquidate your assets." Interestingly, Jesus does not order all disciples or disciple-wanna-bes to do this. Peter leaves the fishing business, but he is not commanded to sell his house, which Jesus later visits (8:14). So wealth itself is not the evil, but it does have enslaving power. It does possess people; it does define them. The "lure of wealth," as Jesus warns in 13:22, can turn people from the gospel because it costs too much. This man is defined by his wealth—he is a rich man—so Jesus commands him to get rid of it. Jesus' command means nothing other than dismantling his whole identity as a rich man, nothing other than dismantling his participation in an elite hierarchical system. That seems to be the first step in learning mercy.

The second step involves transfer: "Give to the poor," the nonelite, those without resources, the powerless, the broken, the needy, the 97 percent of society. This is an act of restoration and restitution. The rich man had declared that he had not broken the command to steal, but that's not exactly true. In Jesus' world, people did not think of the ancient economy as an ever-expanding one as we think ours to be. It was understood to be a limited-goods economy.[21] There was a certain quantity of goods to go around. If a wealthy person had more, he had deprived others of their goods by owning too much land, consuming too many products, transferring too much wealth through rents and taxes and tribute. The whole system was designed to transfer wealth from the bottom upward. Jesus commands the rich man to restore to poor folks what should have been theirs, to reverse the flow of products from nonelites to elites. His divestment means redistributing his resources more equitably, without reciprocity, without creating new obligations and indebtedness, without gaining honor or power. Jesus' instruction means collapsing elite economic hierarchy. This is not just a momentary act; this is nothing other than systemic attack, systemic change, systemic collapse. That is, Jesus exposes the systemic damage of the rich man's acquisitions and gives him a way to reverse the damage and to live God's just world into being. Doing restorative work, divestment, is a second step in learning mercy.

The third command is, "Come, follow me." He is to join the alternative community of disciples, to be resocialized with different visions of being human with different practices, take up new social relationships with a new societal vision of God's mercy. This is very practical learning. Jesus identifies for him a project, spells out the steps that will end the world as he knows it, and offers him a new community, a new social experience. But he rejects a new identity shaped by God's saving presence, God's empire, and chooses to remain a rich man.

Preaching Matthew's Sermon means bravely and wisely helping folks learn mercy in a self-absorbed indulgent age. That's a huge and very difficult task with no easy or quick answers. I co-taught a preaching class last fall in which we thought about preaching Matthew's gospel in contexts of empire. I posed this question of how we might learn mercy. One of the strategies that several students devised involved providing their congregations with numerous and repeated opportunities, some small, some more challenging, to divest their wealth and reinvest their time, energy, and resources. Part of the message was that one of the crucial ways in which you belong to a Christian community is by being committed to such works of societal mercy—not sitting on a committee, not imitating the ways of empire—but repairing, rolling back their damage by employing one's assets.

4. Centrality of prayer (6:5–15)

Interestingly in 6:5–15, after emphasizing doing justice (6:1) and mercy (6:2–4), we now move into a section on prayer. Here we run right into the problem of so many twenty-first–century churches: busyness, limited time, limited energy.

The sequence from justice to prayer is not accidental. I suggest that it gives us insight into a rhythm that is fundamental to the way of life that Matthew's Sermon offers us. Envisioning and living God's reign into being is hard work. The prayer suggests it is only possible in a rhythm of engagement and renewal, of activism and retreat, of doing and imagining.

Commentators have noticed that structurally this section of prayer, and especially the Lord's Prayer, comes in the middle of Matthew's Sermon.[22] That is, the material in chapter 5 and 6:1–6 leads into the Lord's Prayer and the material from 6:14 or 6:16 leads out from it. This structuring underlines a key point about living the Sermon, namely that prayer is central to the identity and practices created by Matthew's Sermon. That is, to live the practices envisioned by Matthew's Sermon up to this point in chapter 5 and 6:1–4 leads one to prayer, and in turn prayer provides the foundation for doing the practices envisioned in the Sermon and in Jesus' prayer. That's a circular rhythm. To do justice in 6:1, to do mercy in 6:2–4, leads into prayer in 6:5–15 that in turn leads one to do justice.

How does this work? The content of Jesus' prayer—right at the center of the Sermon—reiterates central aspects of the identity of followers of Jesus:

- The Lord's Prayer reasserts our relationship with God our Father;
- It refocuses us on the presence of God's empire, God's saving presence, as the basis of discipleship;
- It renews focus on the doing of God's life-giving purposes and will;
- It expresses reliance on God for daily bread since the earth is the Lord's no matter what Rome claims;
- It seeks God's release from and protection against forces that oppose God's purposes and this way of life.

The Lord's Prayer functions to center, to refocus, to renew the vision of disciples who have been about doing justice and mercy. It provides a means for disciples to align themselves again with God's just purposes, in order to live them into being. It's a cyclic pattern.

5. Side-tracked

Reenvisioning is necessary because numerous things get us off track. I have mentioned Mammon, our imperial context, and the ever-present struggle with busyness, overcommitment, and shortages of time and energy. The prayer names three more powers that threaten God's purposes:

a. Disciples pray for forgiveness from debts or sins (6:12);

b. Disciples pray not to be brought to the test or time of trial (6:13a). I do not think this refers to temptation in general but to a particular temptation that especially besets those who actively try to live God's justice into being, who actively live the practices of chapters 5 and 6. All that hard work, all the effort, and does anything ever change? The vocabulary used here for the time of testing is the same vocabulary that appears in the account of the incident at Massah or Meribah during the wilderness wanderings in Exodus 17. That incident refers to testing God, doubting God's power, faithfulness, and saving activity in the world.[23] In that episode, the people in the wilderness need water and complain to Moses about being brought out of Egypt only to die of thirst along with their children and livestock. Moses responds, "Why do you quarrel with me? Why do you test LORD?" (Ex. 17:2). Moses then turns to God, demanding help and action. God tells him to strike the rock, making water appear, and the folks survive. A few verses later, the narrator sums up the incident, "The Israelites quarreled and tested the LORD, saying, 'Is the LORD among us or not?'" (Ex. 17:7).

Israel did not see signs of God's saving purposes at work in their world. They doubted God's power and will to do anything to effect any change. Is the Lord among us or not? Doubting God's effectiveness happens because of God's apparent inactivity or powerlessness in being unable to change the world. "Is the Lord among us or not?" As the world of injustice, distraction, and greed stays the same, disciples know despair, paralysis, futility, burnout. "Arise, O Lord," as the psalmist demands; or, "How long, O Lord, how long?" Or, in psalm 37, "Fret not because of the wicked," where you can be sure the meek and oppressed poor are fretting because of the wicked and paying the price for the wicked's actions. God's response seems to be inaction. Anyone who has struggled actively for justice in this world, anyone who has officiated at the funeral of a young person, anyone who has watched the network news, knows this temptation of despair and the paralysis it brings. The prayer names it: "Do not bring us to the time of trial." Do not remain inactive so long that we give up expecting you to do anything, O Lord. But not only does the prayer name it; ironically, it seeks God's help in resisting such fatalism and despair.

c. The third power that threatens God's work is identified in verse 13b. Disciples pray to be rescued from the evil one—the one who controls all the empires of the world (4:8).

These are opponents of God's purposes that God's people confront in living God's purposes. The prayer does not shirk from them but names them head-on. We could add others. It prays against them in order to re-find focus, to be renewed, to reenvision. Good preaching will help us do the same thing.

6. Communal identity

Communal language—"we," "us," "our"—appears throughout the prayer. It is the prayer of a community of children of "our Father." Father was a common form of address for the supreme god Zeus or Jupiter and, of course, for the emperor who was known as "Father of the Father land," a title that imaged the empire as a household presided over by the emperor as its father.[24] "Our Father" is not Zeus and is not the emperor. Our Father is the God of Jesus. This community wants God's will, not the emperor's, done on earth. This community yearns for the completion of God's purposes because this is not yet the world that God intends. It asks that God forgive us and rescue or deliver us. That is, we experience renewal in knowing that we are in this together and that failure is not the end. We receive refreshment knowing that no one of us is charged with saving the planet single-handedly. We seek God's justice together, community by community by community.

7. How is this prayer answered?

Does God answer prayer while disciples remain passive, or does God answer prayer through disciples? Or are both true? And a second question: When is the prayer answered? Is it the future, is it fundamentally an eschatological prayer that God answers in the eschaton at the completion of God's purposes? Or is it answered in the present? Or is it answered in both the present and future? I would suggest the answer both times is the last option, "both." While the prayer does implore God to complete God's purpose—that is, it has a future dimension, it is eschatological in asking God to hallow God's name, establish God's reign, and do God's will—these realities are not reserved only for the future in Matthew's gospel; they are already under way in Jesus' ministry (4:17). While they are God's role, they are not the sole prerogative of God, as we have seen in the commissioning of disciples. Jesus manifests God's reign now. Disciples do God's will now.

That is, to pray this prayer is both an act of trust and an act of commitment, an act of piety and one of justice. It is an act of trust in that it recognizes that only God can and will establish God's reign and will among us. But to pray it is also an act of commitment to be a human participant in God's work now. To pray for God's empire to come is to commit to live out God's reign now. To pray for God's will to be done is to commit to live it now. To pray for daily bread is to commit to a different human community in which all have enough, which means the end of hoarding and depriving. That is, acts of piety (prayer) and acts of justice (enactments of God's purposes) belong together. Trust in God exists along with a commitment to participate. One without the other won't work. Preaching on Matthew's Sermon must help us to see these two as both/ands, as complementary, as necessary to each other.

8. Fasting emphasized (6:16–18)

Two observations are in order. First, fasting is affirmed: "*whenever* you fast." My hunch is that this is not the most popular or widely practiced spiritual discipline among contemporary followers of Jesus. Fasting seems so contrary to our overindulgent and distracting society, yet it offers a crucial means of being centered on God and God's purposes.

Second, the biblical tradition is quite critical of fasting when it is separated from a life of justice. Isaiah criticizes those who fast while they serve their own interests, oppress their workers, quarrel, and fight (Isa. 58:3–4). Instead, God says, "Is not this the fast that I choose: / to loose the bonds of injustice, / to undo the thongs of the yoke, / to let the oppressed go free, / and to break every yoke? / Is it not to share your bread with the hungry, / and bring the homeless poor into your house, /

when you see the naked, to cover them, / and not to hide yourself from your own kin?" (Isa. 58:6–7). Preaching from Matthew's Sermon on the Mount must help us hold these dimensions of piety and justice, worship and work, activism and renewal, together in living into being the Sermon's visions of God's reign, God's empire.

Conclusion

These eighteen verses identify three acts of justice—doing mercy, praying, fasting. If Matthew's Sermon is about offering visions of life as shaped by, as enacting, God's empire or reign as I have claimed, we have here dimensions that embrace both activity and rest, both hard work and retreat, both reaching out and inner renewal, justice and piety. Living Matthew's Sermon requires both together. It drives us to prayer, and prayer propels us into acts of justice. Preaching Matthew's Sermon will keep the vision of God's reign before us. It will help us imagine and formulate concrete steps, strategies, practices, and projects, even when we as congregants don't want to know about it. Preaching will motivate us not only to work hard, but it will also permit us to find renewal and refreshment as we live Matthew's Sermon's vision into being.

3

The Way of the Church

STANLEY HAUERWAS

In a sermon entitled, "A Sermon on the Sermon on the Mount," I argued that Matthew's Sermon on the Mount presupposes the existence of a community constituted by the practice of nonviolence, and is unintelligibly divorced from such a community.[1] I want to use this occasion to develop that suggestion by providing a reading of the last third of Matthew's Sermon. I do so because I think the ecclesial implications of the Sermon are in the climactic ending of the Sermon. Just as the content of the Sermon is unintelligible when separated from the One who preached it, so is the Church unintelligible when she is not shaped by the Sermon—a shaping that begins by learning not to judge.

No teaching of Jesus seems more paradoxical than his prohibition against judging. Any attempt to avoid judging is defeated by the judgment against those who judge. Moreover, Jesus obviously is in the business of judgment, particularly judgments against the scribes and the Pharisees who "sit on Moses' seat" (Mt. 23:2). So any attempt to avoid judging seems self-defeating. Yet the paradoxical character of Jesus' admonition against judging is the result of our attempt to separate Jesus' teaching from the teacher and the community he has come to establish.

To become a disciple of Jesus is to learn to see and accept the world as God's world. We are not called to be God, but rather we are called to learn to be creatures of God. Should we criticize birds, for example, for not sowing or reaping? Should we think lilies are any less than what God created them to be because they neither "toil nor spin" (6:28)? Rather than remake God's good creation, our task is first to learn why we persist in ways of life that deny that we are God's good creation.

Dietrich Bonhoeffer observed an essential connection between chapters 5 and 6 of Matthew, the first two thirds of the Sermon on the Mount, and sees that these climatic admonitions conclude the Sermon. According to Bonhoeffer, the fifth chapter describes the extraordinary character of being a disciple of Jesus. To be a follower of Jesus entails nothing less than becoming a visible alternative to the world. Chapter 6 displays the simple and "hidden" character of the life to which the disciples are called. Both chapters were designed to help us see that to be a disciple of Jesus requires separation from the community to which we had belonged, for we now belong to Jesus. Accordingly, the boundary between those who would follow Jesus and those who would follow the world is unmistakably apparent, although it is permeable. Chapter 7 consists in Jesus' instructions on how to negotiate that permeability.

The disciples have been called from the "crowd," but does their being set apart mean they have special rights? Does it mean the disciples have special powers, standards, or talents that give them power over those who have not received these gifts? All this might have been the case, according to Bonhoeffer, if Jesus' disciples had assumed they were to separate themselves from the world by sharp and divisive judgments. If they had done so, Bonhoeffer noted:

> People could have come to think that it was Jesus' will that such divisive and condemnatory judgments were to be made in the disciples' daily dealings with others. Thus Jesus must make clear that such misunderstandings seriously endanger discipleship. Disciples are not to judge. If they do judge, then they themselves fall under God's judgment. They themselves will perish by the sword with which they judge others. The gap which divides them from others, as the just from the unjust, even divides them from Jesus. Why is this so? Disciples live completely out of the bond connecting them with Jesus Christ. Their righteousness depends only on that bond and never apart from it. Therefore, it can never become a standard which the disciples would own and might use in any way they please. What makes them disciples is not a new standard for their lives, but Jesus Christ alone, the mediator and Son of God himself.[2]

The disciples are not to judge because any judgment that needs to be made has been made. For those who follow Jesus to act as if they can, on their own, determine what is good and what is evil is to betray the work of Christ. Therefore, the appropriate stance for the acknowledgement of evil is the confession of sin. We quite literally cannot see clearly unless we have been trained to see "the log" that is in our eye (7:3). But it is not possible for us to see what is in our eye because the eye cannot see itself. That is why we are only able to see ourselves through the vision made possible by Jesus–a vision made possible by our participation in a community of forgiveness that allows us to name our sins.

In his *Confessions,* Augustine describes his struggle with the problem of evil. Augustine came to understand, paradoxical though it may sound, that evil does not exist, because "existence" names all that is created and everything created is good. He observes that there are separate parts of God's creation, which we think of as evil because they are at variance with other things. But there are other things with which they are in accord and so they are good. For example, the sky, which can be cloudy or windy, suits the earth for which it exists. Augustine observes, therefore,

> It would be wrong for me to wish that these earthly things did not exist, for even if I saw nothing but them, I might wish for something better, but still I ought to praise you for them alone...And since this is so, I no longer wished for a better world, because I was thinking of the whole of creation and in the light of this clearer discernment I had come to see that though the higher things are better than the lower, the sum of all creation is better than the higher things alone.[3]

Augustine had learned not to judge the birds of the air or the lilies of the field. But he tells us that this was but the beginning of his lesson in not judging. He had yet to come to terms with his pride. To find that "log" required that he encounter the stories of Victorinus and Anthony. Their stories led him to face the humiliation of the cross of Christ. Only then was Augustine able to confess that evil was "not out there," but rather resided in his will. Augustine confesses:

> I began to search for a means of gaining the strength I need to enjoy you, but I could not find this means until I embraced the mediator between God and men, Jesus Christ, who is man, like them (1 Timothy 2:5), and also rules as God over all things, blessed for ever (Romans 9:15). He it was who united with our flesh that food which I was too weak to take. For I was not humble enough to conceive of the humble Jesus Christ as my God, nor had I learnt what lesson his human weakness was meant to teach.[4]

Augustine learned that judging makes us blind because, as Bonhoeffer puts it, "when I judge, I am blind to my own evil and to the grace granted the other person. But in the love of Christ, disciples know about every imaginable kind of guilt and sin, because they know of the suffering of Jesus Christ."[5] Following Christ requires our recognizing that the one I am tempted to judge is like me—a person who has received the forgiveness manifest in the cross. The recognition that the other person is like me—in need of forgiveness—prevents those who would follow Jesus from trying to force others to follow Jesus. We must, like Jesus, have the patience necessary to let those called deny that call. It means the disciples are not called to be effective, to make the world conform to the gospel, but rather the disciples are schooled in nonviolence. That means the gospel is not a "conquering idea" that neither knows nor respects resistance. Rather, "The Word of God is so weak that it suffers to be despised and rejected by people. For the Word, there are such things as hardened hearts and locked doors. The Word accepts the resistance it encounters and bears it."[6]

Therefore, not to judge is to be schooled by the humility of the Son. That schooling begins through learning to confess our unwillingness to live as creatures that have been given all we need to live at peace with ourselves and with one another. It does no good, therefore, to try to force what we have been given on others. Jesus tells us we are not to give what is holy to those who have no capacity to receive what they are being given. Jesus does not deny there will be those who are too afraid to receive the life he has come to offer. This fear is precisely why he has come into the world—that the world may know it is the world.

This makes it all the more remarkable that Jesus would have a people exist who have received the forgiveness made possible through the new age begun in his life, death, and resurrection, to live eschatologically. John Howard Yoder observes that the central affirmation of the New Testament is that Jesus Christ was sent to exercise dominion over the world. Before Jesus' ministry, our existence was dominated by powers and principalities that had revolted against their Creator, but through Jesus' ministry the powers and principalities have been again restored to service in God's kingdom (1 Cor. 15). That Jesus has been victorious means the time of the church, the time constituted by those called by Jesus into his kingdom of forgiveness, is characterized by the coexistence of two ages or what the New Testament calls "aeons."[7]

According to Yoder, the two ages coexist but represent different directions. "The present aeon is characterized by sin and centered on man; the coming aeon is the redemptive reality which entered history in an ultimate way in Christ. The present age, by rejecting obedience, has rejected the only possible ground for man's own well being; the coming age is characterized by God's will being done."[8] The new age has yet to reach consummation, but it has clearly already begun to supersede the old. Jesus' admonition to his disciples not to judge, his charge not to give what is holy to those who will not receive what they are given, presupposes that the kingdom has come.

That Jesus expects and requires some to respond to his call to follow him creates a division between church and world. Crucial, though, is that this division not be understood as an ontological given, a dualism that frustrates the witness of the church. The difference between church and world is not a given, but rather a difference between agents. The difference between church and world is not that of realms or levels, but of response.[9] Therefore, Christians believe that all people can live the way Jesus would have us live. The world is merely the name for those who have chosen to use this time of God's patience not living the way Jesus has given us in the Sermon on the Mount. The only advantage the disciples have is that they are able to acknowledge their sinfulness, and in that acknowledgment they are able to embody, through community, the life of forgiveness.

We should not, therefore, be surprised that Jesus tells his disciples not to give what is holy, what is of great value, to those who will only profane what they have been given. Again Jesus recognizes that the kingdom he has begun can be rejected. Instead, those capable of receiving the kingdom are those able to ask. Just as Jesus needed to teach us to pray, so he must teach us to ask that the door be opened. We can do so with the full confidence that the door will be opened. Even those who are evil know how to give appropriate gifts to their children. Therefore it is surely the case that those who follow Jesus can ask the Father to give the good things that only he can give. The trick, of course, is to learn how to live on the basis of gift. We fear receiving, requiring as it does the acknowledgment of our dependence and our need for forgiveness.

To be forgiven, to ask for forgiveness, forges a space that makes possible a community that has learned to live by receiving. John Milbank observes that before a gift can be given it must have already started to be received.[10] For the life to which Jesus calls us through the Sermon is a life of renewed communion with God. The Father has refused to let our refusal determine our relationship with him. We are, therefore, being trained to ask through the Sermon Jesus delivers, and the asking is part of the way of life that makes it possible for us to be befriended by God and one another. Sacrifice may well be part of what such a life entails, but sacrifice is in service of the gift of mutuality otherwise unattainable.[11]

The so-called "golden rule" is an expression of the mutuality discovered through forgiveness. Oddly enough, however, when the rule is isolated from the eschatological context of the Sermon, indeed when the rule is abstracted from Jesus' ministry in order to ground "ethics," it is made to serve a completely different narrative than the one called the kingdom of God. For example, Jesus' admonition that everything we do to others should be done as we would have them do to us, is often thought to have been given more exact formulation in Kant's famous statement of the categorical imperative: "Act only according to that maxim by which you can at the same time will that it should become a universal law."[12]

Yet Kant's statement of the categorical imperative is an attempt to free us of the need to rely on forgiveness and, more critically, a savior. Kant's hope was to make us what our pride desires, that is, that we be autonomous. To be free in Kant's sense requires that we rely on *reason qua reason*. To rely on any resource other than reason is to abandon ourselves to irrational authorities. According to Kant, no reasonable person should believe his or her sins can be forgiven without that person doing the work necessary to transform his or her life. To be forgiven by another would force us to acknowledge that our lives depend on being capable of receiving a gift without reparation. But from Kant's perspective such a capacity for reception makes the moral life impossible.[13]

Jesus knows nothing of a realm Kant called "ethics." That we are to do to others as we would have others do to us is not "ethics." According to Jesus it is the summation of the law and the prophets. Kant sought to free "ethics" from historical particularity. Jesus calls us to live faithful to the particularity of Israel's law and prophets. Jesus does not say, now that we know the golden rule–and the rule was known prior to Jesus–we no longer need to know the law and the prophets. On the contrary, we *must* know the law and the prophets if we are to know how to act toward others. Let us not forget that this is the same Jesus who told us earlier in the Sermon on the Mount that he has not come to abolish the law and the prophets, but to fulfill them.

> "You shall love the Lord your God with all your heart, and with all your soul, and with all your mind." This is the greatest and first commandment. And a second is like it: "You shall love your neighbor as yourself." On these two commandments hang all the law and the prophets. (Mt. 22:37–40)

Love is the fulfillment of the law. But this is not a sentimental love, rather it is a radical politic fundamentally counter to the world's misappropriation of God's good gift. Christ's being the embodiment of God's love means disciples cannot know love apart from loving one's enemies. For that is precisely what God has done regarding us; we are God's enemies, yet God would still love us–even coming to die for us. We are, therefore, not surprised when, tested by the lawyer concerning which is the greatest commandment, Jesus offered a twofold answer.

Jesus makes explicit what is implicit in the statement of the golden rule in the Sermon, namely, that the love of neighbor and the love of God are interdependent. If we are to know how to love our neighbor, we must love God as God has loved us. This is the animating presumption that is the law and the prophets. The law and the prophets are now to be seen in the ministry of Jesus where God's love for us is most intensely present. And yet we fear such intensity. We fear the intimacy of God's love, desiring instead to believe we are separated from God by vast space. But in Christ, God has drawn near to us and our neighbor. As a result we discover we do not have a long journey to undertake to get to God; rather the long journey is the rigorous path necessary to accept our own, and our neighbor's, reality.[14]

That journey takes place on the road called discipleship. Jesus does not try to entice us to undertake that journey by telling us it will be easy or that many will join us along the way. The gate is narrow, and the road is hard. Moreover, the journey is made even more difficult by false prophets who are quite good at disguising themselves as fellow travelers. Bonhoeffer bluntly tells us:

> To give witness to and to confess the truth of Jesus, but to love the enemy of this truth, who is his enemy and our enemy, with the unconditional love of Jesus Christ—that is the narrow road. To believe in Jesus' promise that those who follow shall possess the earth, but to encounter the enemy unarmed, to prefer suffering injustice to doing ill—that is the narrow road. To perceive other people as being weak and wrong, but to never judge them; to proclaim the good news to them, but never to throw pearls before swine—that is a narrow road. It is an unbearable road.[15]

We are only able to walk such a road, Bonhoeffer suggests, because we can see Jesus walking ahead of us and with us. If, however, we begin to consider the threats along the road, if we fear losing our way and keep our eyes to the ground rather than on Jesus, we can be sure we will lose our way. We must keep our eyes on him because he is the gate and the way. How could we expect anything different, given Jesus' calls for us to abandon the world for the kingdom of God? Surely, Bonhoeffer rhetorically asks, we could not have expected a wide road to run between the kingdom of heaven and the world.

Jesus clearly does not expect that many will follow him on the road he must walk. Moreover, he has already suggested that some who will follow him will do so falsely, and they will not be easily identified. Indeed, they may even, for a time, fool themselves. Jesus, however, suggests to his disciples that the only way to discover those who are false is to judge them by their fruit. Of course, if we know ourselves and others by our fruit, we must have learned what constitutes good fruit. Jesus' Sermon provides the outline for the discernment of those who are true.

Jesus' recommendation for discernment has important implications for what it means to believe that what we believe as Christians is true. In recent times, Christians have found themselves unable to explain to themselves or their neighbors why they believe what they believe to be true. Too often these attempts to establish the truth of what we believe try to separate the truth of our beliefs from how we live. But if we are to follow Jesus, that is exactly what we cannot do.

The temptation is to separate the truth of what we believe from our lives because we fear holding ourselves accountable. Moreover, the idea that we can separate what we believe from how we live is a habit deeply rooted in culturally established Christianity that assumed the coercive character of Christianity or the church was justified because what Christians believed was "true." But Jesus claims it is by our fruits we will be known, making impossible any attempt to separate the content of the Christian belief from how we must live. To believe that this man Jesus is the Christ requires that we become his disciples. Christology and discipleship are mutually implicated, which entails that no account of the truthfulness of Christian belief can be abstracted from how lives are lived.

Therefore, it is not enough to call him Lord. It is not enough to prophecy in his name. It is not enough to do deeds of power in his name. Rather, only those who do the will of the Father will enter the kingdom of the Son. This means during this time between the times we will need to be patient, often unable to identify the false prophets from the true. But Jesus has not left us without resources. We know that the poor, those that mourn, the meek, those who hunger and thirst for righteousness, the merciful, the pure in heart, the peacemakers, those persecuted for righteousness' sake, are signs of what it means to live truthfully.

Moreover, a community constituted by such people has no reason to fear the truth. Nor would such a community need constant reassurance that what they believe is true. If they live confidently and joyfully, the truth will be seen for what it is, that is, a witness to the One alone who is the Truth. For the truth of the gospel cannot be known without witnesses because it is not a truth separable from lives lived according to Jesus' life. But Jesus alone is the One who can be the Truth because he shares his life with the Father.

There is no other foundation for the truth than the call to follow Jesus. Those who hear his words and act on them have lives founded on the only foundation capable of weathering the world. Jesus does not promise that those who follow him, those who become his people, will not experience difficulty. The exact opposite is the case. He tells us that we will be persecuted for his sake. Indeed, those who follow him will necessarily be exposed to dangers that those who are not his disciples can avoid. For his disciples offer the world an alternative to the violence of the world based on the lies thought necessary for people to survive in a world governed by mistrust. In such a world, a people of truth cannot help but be in danger because the world does not want its lies exposed.

Yet those who hear Jesus' call to follow him can do nothing else, even if their response exposes them to danger. But they may take comfort in knowing they are not alone, because Jesus calls us to be part of a people who have learned to need one another. Jesus does not call us to be heroes. He calls us to be disciples who have learned by living lives described in the Sermon on the Mount that to so live makes them dependent on God and on one another. It should not be surprising, therefore, that such a people have lives capable of surviving good and bad fortune.

Matthew reminds us at the end of the Sermon that the crowds have also been listening to Jesus' Sermon. They are, moreover, astonished because he has taught, unlike the scribes, as one having authority. Scribes, it seems, exercise authority by citing another authority. In contrast, Jesus teaches as one who has the authority to determine what is authoritative. What he says cannot, therefore, be separated from who he is and how he says what he says. His life is but a commentary on the Sermon, and the Sermon is the exemplification of his life. What he teaches is not different from what he is.[16] Is it any wonder that the crowds are astonished at his teachings?

And yet astonishment is not the response Jesus would have from those who hear him. He does not want our admiration. What he has taught, what he is, requires nothing else than our lives. We cannot serve two masters. Like those Athenians who heard Paul preach, we would like to respond to Jesus by saying, "We will hear you again about this" (Acts 17:32). But Jesus refuses to let us determine our relation to him. He teaches as one having authority. That authority, moreover, extends to asking us to be willing to lose our lives for his sake (Mt. 16:25). Only the Son of God has the authority to ask for our lives, and that is the authority behind every word of the Sermon on the Mount.

Dare We Live in the World Imagined in the Sermon on the Mount?

Three Case Studies

RICHARD HUGHES

The question at the heart of this volume is this: "Dare we live in the world imagined in the Sermon on the Mount?"

Dare we? Indeed!

The truth is, many who work in the pulpit find it difficult to preach faithfully from the texts that describe that world, simply because we find that world so alien and so threatening.

Part of the problem we encounter in Matthew's Sermon on the Mount is the fact that if we take it seriously, we will find ourselves radicalized beyond measure. In his recent book, *What Jesus Meant,* Gary Wills writes, "For creating radicals, there is nothing like a reading of the gospels" because they "constantly inveigh against the rich, the powerful, [and] the exploiters."[1]

But the American church does not wish to be radicalized, precisely because, more often than not, we *are* those rich and powerful exploiters whom the Sermon on the Mount both indicts and convicts. So we ignore the Sermon on the Mount or transform it into something it is not, often reshaping its message into our own image.

So, I want us to begin at this point—with a confession that we stumble and stumble badly—when we come to the Sermon on the Mount. How, then, can we preach it more effectively? I have been asked to explore this question with reference to Christians who have gone before and who have genuinely grasped and faithfully responded to the meaning—and to the challenge—of the biblical text and of the Sermon on the Mount in particular.

While there are many Christians to whom we might look as exemplars in this regard, I want to consider a single Christian from the twentieth century, a single Christian from the nineteenth century, and an entire movement from the sixteenth century.

William Stringfellow

Our single Christian from the twentieth century is William Stringfellow (1929–1985). Of Stringfellow, Karl Barth once told an audience, "You should listen to this man."[2] Stringfellow was an Episcopal layman, not a preacher. Still, he offers stunning insights into the Bible—insights that are indispensable if we hope to understand and to implement the challenges of Matthew's Sermon on the Mount.

A veteran of the United States Army, Stringfellow attended Harvard Law School; but then, instead of establishing a practice in an affluent setting, he set up his practice in a Harlem slum where he worked for many years among the poor. Over the course of his career he published numerous books on Christian theology and ethics, but none was more important than the book that bore the title *An Ethic for Christians and Other Aliens in a Strange Land*—a book he completed just as the United States was withdrawing the last troops from Vietnam. And, indeed, we cannot fully understand that text apart from that context. In the opening pages of that book, Stringfellow makes a statement that few American preachers—or Christians—seem inclined to grasp. He makes that point in five short words: "The biblical topic is politics," he wrote. And then he enlarged on that statement in the following way:

> The Bible is about the politics of fallen creation and the politics of redemption; the politics of the nations, institutions, ideologies, and causes of this world and the politics of the Kingdom of God; the politics of Babylon and the politics of Jerusalem; the politics the Antichrist and the politics of Jesus Christ; the politics of the demonic powers and principalities and the politics of the timely judgment of God as sovereign; the politics of death and the politics of life; apocalyptic politics and eschatological politics.

Stringfellow lamented the fact that so many Christians "denounce the truth that the Bible is political" when "so many of the biblical symbols are explicitly political—*dominion, emancipation, authority, judgment, kingdom, reconciliation* among them."[3] But what does Stringfellow mean when he writes, "The biblical topic is politics"? He explains himself like this: "Biblical ethics, when all is said and done, concerns…[God's] dominion on behalf of human life over time and history or, in other words, the doctrine of Christ as Lord of time and history. Biblical politics[, therefore,] has to do with acting now in anticipation of the vindication of Christ as judge of the nations and other principalities, as well as persons."[4]

This statement means three things. First, it means that God alone is Lord of time and history. Second, it means that Christians are called to pledge allegiance to the kingdom of God and to no other kingdom or nation on earth. And third, to borrow Timothy Weber's memorable phrase, it means that we live "in the shadow of the second coming."[5] In other words, we live as if the fullness of the kingdom of God is present in the here and now, even though we know its consummation is yet in the future.

If you still doubt that the biblical topic is politics, let me ask you to reflect on statements made by the current president of the United States in light of the biblical truth that God alone is the Lord of history. On September 7, 2003, the president spoke of terrorists who "grew bolder, believing that history was on their side." However, he said, because "America put out the fires of September the 11th, and mourned our dead, and went to war, history has taken a different turn."[6] Then, in his 2003 "State of the Union Address," the president categorically proclaimed, "Free people will set the course of history."[7]

In 2004, a senior advisor to President Bush went well beyond the president's declarations and argued that the American government will set the course of history. In a statement to reporter Ron Suskind, the advisor said,

> We're an empire now, and when we act, we create our own reality. And while you're studying that reality—judiciously as you will, we'll act again, creating other new realities, which you can study too, and that's how things will sort out. We're history's actors…and you, all of you, will be left to just study what we do.[8]

These kinds of statements illumine beautifully Stringfellow's contention that "the Bible is about…the politics of the nations…and the politics of the Kingdom of God." The point is simply this: when someone tells you that "free people are in charge of history," or "the nation is in charge of history," or "the empire is in charge of history," that person has posed a direct challenge to God's assertion that God alone is in charge of history. And you are telling me that the Bible is not political?

War and Peace

But is the Bible—and is the Sermon on the Mount—really about politics, as Stringfellow contends? We can test that claim by making this simple observation: all nations—including our own—seek to shape history by force and by war. As our president said, because "America...went to war, history has taken a different turn." But Jesus offers a radically different proposal. His kingdom is a kingdom of peace, and that kingdom will finally triumph over all the nations of the earth since he is the lord of history. Jesus makes this point abundantly clear in John 18:36. "My kingship is not of this world," Jesus told Pilate. "If my kingship were of this world, my servants would fight."[9]

The Sermon on the Mount is an extended commentary on this point. "Blessed are the peacemakers," Jesus says to the assembled crowds, "for they shall be called the sons of God" (Mt. 5:9). "You have heard that it was said to the men of old, 'You shall not kill, and whoever kills shall be liable to judgment.' But I say to you that every one who is angry with his brother shall be liable to judgment" (Mt. 5:21–22). "You have heard that it was said, 'An eye for an eye and a tooth for a tooth.' But I say to you, 'Do not resist one who is evil. But if any one strikes you on the right cheek, turn to him the other also'" (Mt. 5:38–39). "You have heard that it was said, 'You shall love your neighbor and hate your enemy.' But I say to you, 'Love your enemies and pray for those who persecute you, so that you may be sons of your Father who is in heaven'" (Mt. 5:43–45).

A great irony has characterized many American churches in their relation to the Sermon on the Mount: regardless of what Jesus clearly says on the topic of love and hate and war and peace, many Christian preachers have urged Christians to support the nation in its quest to control history through the use of force and war. The pastor of the First Baptist Church in Atlanta is a case in point. "We should offer to serve the war effort in any way possible," he counseled his congregation. "God battles with people who oppose him, who fight against him and his followers."[10]

Even more common are preachers who have never seen the Sermon's implications for bringing the kingdom of God to bear on the politics of the nations. Or, if they have seen those implications, they shrink from addressing those issues for a variety of reasons. First, many pulpit preachers erroneously imagine that proclaiming the politics of the kingdom of God is in some sense taking sides between Republicans and Democrats, when—in point of fact—nothing could be further from the truth. And no doubt other pulpit ministers' concern for their popularity or perhaps even for their jobs prevents them from proclaiming the politics of the kingdom of God as we find that vision elaborated in the Sermon on the Mount.

I want to say again—and I cannot emphasize this point too strongly—that proclaiming the politics of the kingdom of God in opposition to the politics of the nations is radically different from taking sides between Democrats, Republicans, or Independents. In truth, the kingdom of God stands in judgment on them all. Likewise, one cannot oppose certain wars and favor others and still embrace the kingdom of God. To pick and choose the wars we like and the wars we don't like is hardly the same as siding with Jesus when he says, "You have heard that it was said, 'You shall love your neighbor and hate your enemy.' But I say to you, 'Love your enemies and pray for those who persecute you, so that you may be sons of your Father who is in heaven'" (Mt. 6:43–45).

The failure of the pulpit in this regard has borne some bitter fruit. In an article with the appalling headline, "Conservative Christians Biggest Backers of Iraq War," Jim Lobe reported in 2002 that "some 69 percent of conservative Christians favor military action against Baghdad; 10 percentage points more than the U.S. adult population as a whole."[11] Charles Marsh wrote in *The New York Times* that by April of 2003, "An astonishing 87 percent of all white evangelical Christians in the United States supported the president's decision [to launch the war against Iraq]." Marsh, a believer, then asks the anguished and soul-searching question, "What will it take for evangelicals in the United States to recognize our mistaken loyalty?"[12] One might rephrase Marsh's question to read, "When will Christian preachers begin to proclaim the values of the kingdom of God as Jesus spelled out those values in the Sermon on the Mount?"

Charles Reed, a Southern Baptist deacon and the former mayor of Waco, Texas, sums up the tragic situation we face today:

> Christian values tell us to love our enemies, love our neighbors as ourselves, and do unto others as we would have them do unto us. The secular ruling ideology, on the other hand, cultivates hate, fear, violence, greed and exploitation…
>
> The polls now show that, the more often people go to church, the more they support the anti-Christian goals and values of the secular ruling ideology.
>
> Who would have dreamed that Christians would support military invasions to build a secular corporate empire…?[13]

Wealth and Poverty

We can also test Stringfellow's claim that the Bible is about politics by exploring Jesus' teachings on poverty and wealth. In the first of the beatitudes, Jesus proclaims, "Blessed are the poor in spirit, for theirs is the kingdom of heaven," a statement Luke renders as, "Blessed are you who are poor, for yours is the Kingdom of God" (Luke 6:20). But there is so much more on this theme in the Sermon on the Mount. Listen!

> Do not lay up for yourselves treasures on earth, where moth and rust consume and where thieves break in and steal, but lay up for yourselves treasures in heaven, where neither moth nor rust consumes and where thieves do not break in and steal. For where your treasure is, there will your heart be also. (Mt. 6:19–21)

> No one can serve two masters; for either he will hate the one and love the other, or he will be devoted to the one and despise the other. You cannot serve God and mammon. (Mt. 6:24)

> Therefore I tell you, do not be anxious about your life, what you shall eat or what you shall drink, nor about your body, what you shall put on. Is not life more than food, and the body more than clothing?...Therefore do not be anxious, saying, "What shall we eat?" Or "What shall we drink?" Or "What shall we wear?" For the Gentiles seek all these things; and your heavenly Father knows that you need them all. But seek first his kingdom and his righteousness, and all these things shall be yours as well. (Mt. 6:25, 31–33)

Why is this teaching from the Sermon on the Mount so political? It is political because the nations of the earth strive against one another for access to food and water, for access to raw materials from which we can make our clothes and build our houses, and for access—dare we say it?—to energy. And it is political because the American economic system would collapse without continued expenditure of money for more and more things. Perhaps this is why many government officials—including the president of the United States—advised Americans following 9/11 that the most patriotic act they could undertake would be to "go spend money."

But Jesus tells us that the lust for money and goods—so central to the kingdoms of this earth and so central to our own capitalist society—are not to be our concerns. Instead, he tells us to "seek first his kingdom." If we ask what it means to seek first the kingdom of God, a quick look at scripture will reveal the answer. In almost every instance where the phrase, "the kingdom of God," is used in the New Testament, it appears in connection with outreach to the poor, the dispossessed, the sick, the blind, and those in prison. The kingdom of God, therefore, is that realm in which God, and those who have pledged their allegiance to God, reach out to those in greatest need.

No wonder, then, that the second most prominent theme in the Hebrew Scriptures is God's concern for the poor—a point Jim Wallis makes in his marvelous book, *God's Politics*. That very same theme consumes one of every sixteen verses in the New Testament, one of every ten in the synoptic gospels, and one of every seven in the gospel of Luke.[14] But in keeping with the mandates of our culture, we are so concerned with spending money on ourselves that we seldom notice those whom Jesus called "the least of these." And because we have been so captured by this mandate of our culture, many of us who preach find it difficult to speak in a faithful and meaningful way about Jesus' teachings on wealth and poverty in the Sermon on the Mount.

When Jim Wallis was in seminary, he and his friends made a thorough study of what the Bible teaches regarding our obligations to the poor. When they concluded their study, he recalls,

> We all sat in a circle to discuss how the subject had been treated in the various churches in which we had grown up. Astoundingly, but also tellingly, not one of us could remember even one sermon on the poor from the pulpit of our home churches. In the Bible, the poor were everywhere; yet the subject was not to be found in our churches.[15]

The struggle I want to highlight by offering these examples is not a struggle between capitalism and socialism, or between capitalism and communism, since all these systems are ultimately doomed and belong to that reality the Bible describes with the term, "the fall." Rather, the struggle is between "the politics of the nations" and "the politics of the kingdom of God." The question we must ask ourselves is simply this: Are we willing to speak and act on behalf of the politics of the kingdom of God, or have we been so captured by the politics of the nations—and especially by the politics of our own nation—that we cannot speak as faithful servants of the one who spoke these words: "But seek first his kingdom and his righteousness, and all these things shall be yours as well"?

David Lipscomb

I want now to turn to the second in our list of faithful Christians who lived out the values of the Sermon on the Mount and spoke on behalf of the coming kingdom of God that Jesus described in that text. David Lipscomb was clearly the single most influential figure among Churches of Christ from the close of the Civil War until his death in 1917. And he was a faithful student of the Sermon on the Mount. He regularly proclaimed the principles of that Sermon both in his preaching and in the editorials he wrote for the *Gospel Advocate,* the paper he edited on behalf of the Churches of Christ.

Lipscomb understood that in the Sermon on the Mount, Jesus called his disciples to embrace the politics of the kingdom of God, and Lipscomb understood that the kingdom of God stood in judgment on the politics of the nations, including the politics of the United States. So he sought to live his life in faithful service to that kingdom, even though he knew its consummation was yet in the future.

He regularly voiced his conviction that "the mission of the kingdom of God is to break into pieces and consume all these [other] kingdoms, take their place, fill the whole earth, and stand forever...How [then]," he asked, "could the individual citizens of the kingdom of God found, enter into, and become part and parcel of–upbuild, support, and defend...[those nations] which God's kingdom was especially commissioned to destroy?"[16] Clearly, Lipscomb understood the political dimensions of the Sermon on the Mount.

But there is more. Lipscomb argued, "All human government rests for authority upon the power of the sword; its mission has been strife and bloodshed." He claimed, "Every act of alliance with or reliance for aid upon the human government on the part of the church or any of its members, is spiritual idolatry."[17] As a result, Lipscomb refused to fight in America's wars. He refused even to vote, and he counseled members of Churches of Christ to do the same.

Lipscomb regarded the biblical teachings concerning the kingdom of God and the Christian's singular allegiance to that kingdom as the very "key notes...of the Old and New Testaments." Without them, he said, the Bible was "without point of meaning."[18] In 1881, Lipscomb reflected on the Civil War that had concluded some sixteen years earlier, and, in that context, spoke on the brutal nature of civil governments in comparison with the peaceable kingdom of God. "In the beginning of the late strife that so fearfully desolated our country," he said,

> much was said about "our enemies." I protested constantly that
> I had not a single enemy, and was not an enemy to a single
> man North of the Ohio River. I had never been brought into
> collision with one–but very few knew such a person as myself
> existed...Yet, these thousands and hundreds of thousands who
> knew not each other...were made enemies to each other and
> thrown into fierce and bloody strife, were embued with the spirit
> of destruction one toward the other, through the instrumentality
> of human governments.[19]

In 1889, Lipscomb published a little book–a compilation, really, of some of his earlier articles on the kingdom of God and its absolute priority in relation to the politics of the nations. He called that book, simply, *Civil Government,* and of that text he said in 1890, "Nothing we ever wrote affects to nearly the vital interest of the church of Christ and the salvation of the world as this little book."[20]

Lipscomb grasped Jesus' teachings in the Sermon on the Mount regarding the sword, violence, war, and peace. He also grasped Jesus' teachings regarding poverty and wealth. In his view all aspects of the church—its hymn books, its meeting places, and its customs—should be adapted "to the necessities of God's elect—the poor of this world, rich in faith toward God." The church, he suggested, "is the special legacy of God to the poor of the earth." Or again, "Christ intended his religion for the poor, [and] adapted it to their necessities."[21]

Lipscomb lived out these principles on many occasions. In 1873, a cholera epidemic struck Lipscomb's home city of Nashville, Tennessee. During the month of June alone, 500 people died. People with means to do so left the city in any way they could—by horse, carriage, or train. But the poor had no way to leave and therefore bore the full brunt of this disease. The hardest hit was the impoverished African American section of Nashville—a scenario that eerily echoes our contemporary Katrina tragedy in New Orleans.

At the time of this epidemic, the South was still caught in the grip of Reconstruction, and white hatred toward blacks during this period knew no bounds. Few whites, therefore, would even consider ministering to blacks, whose intense suffering was only a prelude to death itself. But Lipscomb believed that his allegiance to the kingdom of God required him to enter the houses where the plague had struck, to clean and feed the victims, and to do everything in his power to help restore their health, regardless of their race or their poverty.

He urged Churches of Christ to follow suit: "It is a time that should call out the full courage and energy of the church in looking after the needy," he said. "Every individual, black or white, that dies from neglect and want of proper food and nursing, is a reproach to the professors of the Christian religion in the vicinity of Nashville."[22] This is how David Lipscomb interfaced with the Sermon on the Mount.

Sixteenth-century Anabaptists

I want now to turn our attention to a group of believers who stand in many ways as the signal paradigm of Christians who both preached and sought to live by the politics of the kingdom of God as they found those principles espoused in the Sermon on the Mount. We know these believers as the Anabaptists of the sixteenth century—forerunners of today's Mennonites, Amish, and Hutterites. The Anabaptists inherited a world in which everyone without exception received baptism shortly after birth. That act alone made one a Christian. One might very well grow up to be a murderer, an adulterer, a thief, or a liar; but none of this made any difference. One was still a Christian by virtue of one's baptism as an infant.

The political dimensions of this arrangement are obvious; for if everyone were Christian, then the church and the state were coterminous. And indeed, everyone answered both to the church and to the state, since everyone was inevitably both citizen and Christian. The job of the church was to honor and sanctify the state, even as the state insured the preeminent status of the church and favored it with special privileges. In such a context, the church inevitably adopted the worldly values of the state, and therefore embraced and defended violence, war, and materialism. Likewise, the church paid homage to the rich and the powerful and, for the most part, had little time for those Jesus called "the least of these."

This arrangement was a dramatic departure from the early church when Christians often suffered imperial persecution. In those days, no one became a Christian for gain, power, or privilege. Indeed, no one became a Christian lightly, for that choice could very well cost one one's life. But all that changed in the fourth century when the Emperor Constantine legalized Christianity and when another emperor later in that century, Theodosius, made Christianity the official religion of the Empire. At this point in time, mandatory infant baptism invaded the church so that every citizen would also be a Christian. It no longer cost to be a Christian; it paid. In that atmosphere of favor and privilege for the church of Christ, the moral integrity that had characterized the early Christian communities began to ebb away.

At that time, something else that had been vital to the health of the early church also began to disappear. That was the commitment of the early Christians to nonviolence and their rejection of war. Every text we have from the first three centuries of the church testifies to this commitment. After all, Christians claimed to follow the One they called "the Prince of Peace."

But once the Empire bestowed its favor on the Christian religion, leaders of the church quite naturally felt they owed something to the Empire in return. So Augustine, one of the most honored thinkers in Christian history, worked out for the church what we now call the just war theory. That theory was a sop to the Constantinian compromise, since it clearly said that there were times when Christians could fight for the state since—after all—the state had honored the church and freed it from persecution. So the church essentially turned its back on its earliest commitments. With respect to violence, at least, the kingdom of God had now become almost indistinguishable from the kingdoms of this earth.

This was the world the Anabaptists inherited in the early sixteenth century. In the beginning, those who would soon become Anabaptists were followers of the great Protestant reformer, Ulrich Zwingli, in the city of Zurich, Switzerland. But as they tracked with Zwingli's reform, these young people paid close attention to the gospels and especially to the Sermon on the Mount. On the basis of that reading, they soon began to see vast differences between the demands of the gospel and the all-too-worldly norms of the medieval church. While Jesus had required his followers to be agents of peace, medieval Christians often served as agents of violence and war. While Jesus had called his followers to lives of service to the poor, medieval Christians—and especially the hierarchy of the church—devoted themselves to the shameless acquisition of greater and greater wealth at the expense of the poor.

From the perspective of these soon-to-become Anabaptists, the heart of the problem was infant baptism, a practice that made everyone a Christian, even though many of these so-called "Christians" utterly rejected the teachings of Jesus and the values of the Sermon on the Mount. These young people, therefore, began to call for a church composed exclusively of those who had committed themselves to the teachings of Jesus and to lives of radical discipleship. The symbol of entry into that church—and of one's commitment to serve as a disciple of Christ—would be the baptism of adults—adults who were prepared to risk even their lives, if that's what it took to follow Jesus.

Precisely at this point these would-be Anabaptists crossed into the world of politics. For to reject the baptism of infants in favor of baptizing only believing adults would erase the bond that made the church the vassal of the state. When these young people proceeded to baptize one another as believing adults and as radical disciples of Jesus Christ—and when this revolutionary movement began to spread beyond the borders of Zurich into other parts of Europe—the authorities derisively labeled them with the term "Anabaptists," or re-baptizers.

By using this designation, the authorities made these people eligible for the death penalty since the Empire had prescribed death for re-baptizers some thousand years before. Now, having labeled these people as "Anabaptists," the princes, the pope, and even the Protestant reformers came down on these people with violent force. They hunted them down and executed them—by drowning, by burning, and with the sword. Thousands died in what can only be described as an imperial act of genocide.

But the Anabaptists stood fast and, indeed, the movement grew. For these people understood from the gospels and from the Sermon on the Mount the political nature of the kingdom of God. They understood that their allegiance to the kingdom of God would inevitably pit them against the kingdoms of this world. So they resisted violence, warfare, and the sword and emptied themselves of their goods so they could relieve the needs of those less fortunate than themselves.

They counseled one another–and preached to others–with words like these:

> The worldly are armed with steel and iron, but Christians are armed with the armor of God, with truth, righteousness, peace, faith, salvation, and the word of God. –Michael Sattler, 1527[23]

> Rather than wrong any man of a single penny, we would suffer the loss of a hundred gulden; and sooner than strike our enemy with the hand, much less with the spear, or sword, or halberd, as the world does, we would die and surrender life. We carry no weapon, neither spear nor gun, as is clear as the open day…We would that all the world were as we are, and that we could bring and convert all men to the same belief; then should all war and unrighteousness have an end. –Jacob Hutter, 1534 [24]

> Always and everywhere I have said as follows…: that each man should have regard for his neighbor, so that the hungry might be fed, the thirsty refreshed, and the naked clothed. For we are not lords of our own property, but stewards and dispensers. Assuredly no one could say that we claim that one should take his own from anybody and make it common property; rather we would say: if anyone would take your cloak, give him your coat also. –Balthasar Hubmaier, 1526/27 [25]

In these ways, the Anabaptists of the sixteenth century both preached and lived the principles of the Sermon on the Mount.

Conclusions

I want to suggest that the Constantinian compromise that dominated the world of the sixteenth century is not as far in the past as we might think. Even though we have no state church in the United States, there has emerged in the United States a Christian civilization that is deeply corrupted, a civilization that claims the label "Christian" only by virtue of its history, though if we would be honest, we must admit that America's history has never been Christian in any biblical sense.

Just as the church in the medieval period promoted one liturgical rite–the baptism of infants–as the essence of a Christian civilization, many preachers in the United States today place only two issues–abortion and gay marriage–at the center of their efforts to transform America into a "Christian" nation. Somehow they never seem to mention the issues that were closest to the heart of Jesus—our addiction to violence and the plight of the poor.

Here's an example of how Constantinian Christianity plays itself out in American life. Progressive evangelical leaders recently issued "An Evangelical Call to Action" regarding global warming and carbon dioxide emissions. From the perspective of these progressive evangelicals, global warming is an issue that bears directly on poverty and war and peace—issues that were close to the heart of Jesus. Indeed, they understand that global warming ultimately is a matter of life and death.

But some very powerful evangelicals see things differently. What is most important, these Christians are especially concerned to enhance what they view as the Christian character of the United States. Thus, Tom Minnery, director of James Dobson's political action group, called this concern for the environment "a distraction...when abortion continues as a great evil."[26] James M. Inhofe, a United States Senator from Oklahoma, the chair of the Senate's Environment and Public Works Committee, and a fervent evangelical Christian, also opposed the evangelical summons to care for God's earth on the grounds that such an initiative is "inconsistent with a conservative agenda that...includes opposition to abortion and gay rights."[27] In ways like this, the meaning of Christianity in the United States has been perverted almost beyond recognition.

But the Constantinian dimensions of American Christianity go far beyond the effort to restrict the meaning of Christian faith to one or two issues while ignoring Jesus' concern for the poor and his prohibitions against violence. In my judgment, Cornel West accurately describes the problem Constantinian Christianity poses in America today. "Most American Constantinian Christians," West writes,

> are unaware of their imperialistic identity because they do not see the parallel between the Roman Empire that put Jesus to death and the American Empire that they celebrate. As long as they can worship freely and pursue the American dream, they see the American government as a force for good and American imperialism as a desirable force for spreading that good. They proudly profess their allegiance to the flag and the cross not realizing that just as the cross was a bloody indictment of the Roman Empire, it is a powerful critique of the American empire...[28]

In the 1970s, William Stringfellow captured a similar critique of Constantinian Christianity in America when he wrote:

> In the United States, the Constantinian Accommodation has been marvelously proliferated. Practically all churches and

sects are, in effect, established and, in turn, conformed to the dominant social philosophy or secular ideology or civic religion. Biblical faith, here, in consequence, is strenuously distorted and persistently ridiculed—in the name of God—of course.[29]

This is precisely why Stringfellow argued that the politics of the kingdom of God is a summons to resist the politics of the nations, including the politics of the United States. "The biblical lifestyle," he wrote,

> is always a witness of resistance to the status quo in politics, economics, and all society. It is a witness of resurrection from death. Paradoxically, those who embark on the biblical witness constantly risk death—through execution, exile, imprisonment, persecution, defamation, or harassment—at the behest of the rulers of this age. Yet those who do not resist the rulers of the present darkness are consigned to a moral death, the death of their humanness. That, of all the ways of dying, is the most ignominious.[30]

That is why we must catch a vision of the Sermon on the Mount. And that is why we must preach the Sermon on the Mount. Without that message, our preaching may conform far more precisely to the politics of the kingdoms of this world than to the politics of the kingdom of God.

The Folly of the Sermon on the Mount

CHARLES CAMPBELL

Nobody wants to be called a fool. In our society, being a fool won't get you anywhere. In our homes, our workplaces, and even our churches, foolishness is not highly valued. "What a fool!" is one of the most demeaning comments we can make about someone. Certainly things were no different in the Roman Empire when the New Testament was written. The philosophers valued reason, and the divine was sometimes equated with rationality. In that context, being called a fool might have been even more devastating than in our own.

In much of the biblical witness, the fool also has extremely negative connotations. The fool is the one who says in his or her heart, "There is no God" (Ps. 14:1a). Therefore the fool is cut off from God. As a counter to such folly stands an entire section of the Bible known as the Wisdom literature, though even that literature contains interesting tensions and contradictions within it. In the Sermon on the Mount itself, Jesus speaks at times from within this thread of the biblical tradition. He teaches, "If you say, 'You fool,' you will be liable to the hell of fire" (Mt. 5:22d). Calling someone a fool involves claiming that the person has no relationship with God; he or she is cut off from God and outside the covenant. Making such a judgment is not the prerogative of human beings. In our individual lives, in our society generally, and even in the biblical witness, "the fool" carries extremely negative connotations. Foolishness is something to be avoided.

All of this makes what happens in the New Testament, particularly in the Pauline literature, quite extraordinary. The language of folly gets inverted and becomes something positive. This inversion or subversion of language is not limited to the language of folly. Early Christian writers do this all the time. Take, for example, the imagery of king or kingdom. It runs throughout the gospel narratives. But in the course of the narratives, within which the language takes its meaning, the imagery of king or kingdom gets turned on its head. Consider two scenes from the beginning and end of the Passion narrative.

At the beginning of the Passion narrative, Jesus triumphantly enters Jerusalem riding humbly on a donkey.[1] In this carefully orchestrated piece of "street theater," Jesus enacts a parody of kingship, which is also a parody of the religious community's expectations about the Messiah.[2] He begins at the Mount of Olives, the traditional location from which people expected the final battle for Jerusalem's liberation would begin. From this traditional location, Jesus begins his "final campaign." When he sends out for provisions, however, things begin to get rather strange. The provisions he seeks are not the weapons of war, but a donkey and a colt. Jesus goes to take possession of Jerusalem unarmed and on a donkey.

When Jesus does finally enter the city, he enjoys all the trappings of a great military procession for a triumphant national hero. The people get caught up in the event and do all the things a victorious military leader would expect. They spread palm leaves and cloaks before Jesus as a symbol of honor and acclaim. They shout, "Hosanna! Blessed is the one who comes in the name of the Lord." "God saves." "Long live the King!" And Jesus rides through the midst of the adoring crowds.

The whole time, however, he is turning the world's notions of power, rule, and kingship on their head. His theater is a wonderful piece of political satire. In his "triumphal entry" Jesus lampoons all the powers of the world and their pretensions to glory and dominion, and he enacts an alternative to the way of domination. He comes, not as one who lords his authority over others, but as one who rejects domination and comes as a servant. He comes, not with pomp and wealth, but as one identified with the poor. He comes, not as a mighty warrior, but as one who refuses to rely on violence. Jesus enacts the subversive, nonviolent "kingdom" of God in the midst of the city. Jesus in fact comes close to being a kind of jester here—a "fool"—who enacts in a humorous, disorienting way a totally different understanding of "rule" and invites people to see the world in a new way. The event takes on the air of a carnival, where those on the bottom of society festively unmask and challenge the dominant social order.

At the end of Jesus' passion, in some of the most ironic moments in the narrative, the soldiers, following Jesus' trial, dress him up as a king, complete with a robe and a crown of thorns, and bow down to him. Later, when he is crucified, they hang a sign above Jesus on the cross, which reads, "King of the Jews." The actions are all done in mockery. But they are profoundly true; they contain a deep, hidden meaning, which is the character of irony. Here the king is the one who eschews domination and violence—and suffers the consequences of that decision. Here is a kingdom of peace, which, unlike the *Pax Romana* (Peace of Rome), is not coerced and enforced by military power and occupation.

In these narratives the language of king or kingdom is taken up, but thoroughly inverted. When one considers the context of empire in which the gospels were written, this use of language represents a politically subversive act.

In Paul's letters to the Corinthians a similar thing happens with the language of foolishness. Paul proclaims the cross, the crucified Christ—a message the world rejects as foolish (1 Cor. 1:18–25). Religiously, it was simply unimaginable that the Messiah—the Christ—would be crucified. Philosophically, it was unimaginable that the Divine could hang on a cross. Messiah—cross. Divine—cross. These were incommensurable realities. Neither the religious nor philosophical imagination could entertain such a thing—it was foolishness. Indeed, according to some scholars, the translation "foolishness" is actually too tame. It was rather "madness."[3]

What seems like madness to the world, Paul proclaims as the wisdom and power of God. In the process Paul inverts the language of foolishness; it becomes something positive. So he will speak of the foolishness of preaching, which proclaims the cross and announces this odd, new world—a world shaped, not by domination and violence, but by a God of self-giving solidarity and love. The core content of Paul's preaching—Christ crucified—is precisely this foolishness. "We proclaim Christ crucified, a stumbling block to Jews and foolishness to Gentiles…" (1 Cor. 1:23). Through these extraordinary words, Paul announces a new creation that can only appear foolish in the eyes of the old. So the term "fool" becomes a positive name for Christians who live in this odd new world. As Paul writes to the church in Corinth, "God chose what is foolish to shame the wise" (1:27a). He even speaks of the apostles, including himself, as "fools for the sake of Christ" (4:10), language that will be taken up in fascinating ways in the Christian tradition of the holy fools. The fool becomes, not the one who thinks he or she doesn't need God, but the one who is actually closest to God.[4]

Just as with the language of king or kingdom, so through the language of foolishness, Paul subverts the presuppositions, rationalities, and myths of the world. This is the sense in which I understand gospel foolishness: it is that which subverts the presuppositions, rationalities, and myths of the world, which often constitute the "air we breathe" and prevent us from even imagining any alternatives. "Foolishness" captures the dislocating and disorienting nature of the gospel. Foolishness characterizes a gospel that shatters commonsense presuppositions to help us glimpse the odd new creation that is breaking into the world. Before this foolish gospel, we stand in a moment of decision. Is all of this *just* foolishness, as those enamored with the wisdom and power of the world would argue? Or is it *holy* foolishness—the wisdom and power of God for life?

In this sense, Matthew's Sermon on the Mount should also be considered a kind of folly. Although Jesus obviously does not preach "Christ crucified" in the same way as Paul, the content of his Sermon is just as foolish as Paul's. It is just as subversive of the world's presuppositions, rationalities, and myths. Too often, many of us read the Sermon on the Mount as a kind of legalistic book of rules for the Christian life. Of course, the Sermon does give directives and delineate particular practices for the Christian community. Nevertheless, if we read the Sermon on the Mount as a rulebook, we may miss the deep dimensions of its folly.

At the deepest level, the Sermon is not primarily a list of rules. Something bigger—and indeed more startling—is at work. The Sermon on the Mount offers a vision of an alternative world.[5] It is an odd world that runs counter to the presuppositions, rationalities, and myths of Jesus' day—and of our own. Within this vision, Jesus delineates suggestive practices for what life in this strange, new world looks like. In this new community, reconciliation takes priority over vengeance (5:21–26); women are no longer treated as objects or property (5:27–32); love of enemies and nonviolent resistance replace violent domination of the "other" (5:38–48)[6]; religious practices do not become the source of superiority and competition (6:1–18); the desire for wealth is not the driving motivation of life (6:19–34). Socially, politically, religiously, and economically Jesus subverts a world driven by domination and violence. The Sermon seeks to disorient and dislocate the hearers; it shocks us out of our commonsense, taken-for-granted assumptions so we might see the world differently, and possibly glimpse the new creation that has come in Jesus himself.

In this regard, we might think of Jesus as a kind of jester—or fool—in the Sermon. We often read the Sermon so seriously that we may miss its startling craziness. Thinking of Jesus as a jester may help us get at this. Throughout history, the jester is a figure who fundamentally sees the world differently; he or she has a different perspective on the world. Through often-comical antics, the jester seeks to startle and dislocate people so that they too might be released from their commonsense presuppositions and see and live in the world in new and creative ways.[7] As I noted earlier,

Jesus engages in this kind of activity in his entry into Jerusalem. Certainly in his parables Jesus does this as well; he tells stories that begin familiarly enough, but then have extravagant, odd, dislocating elements. Indirectly, and often humorously, the parables seek to disorient us, shake us up, and invite us to see and live in the world in new ways.

A similar kind of thing happens in the Sermon on the Mount, though the Sermon is usually not as indirect and humorous as some of Jesus' other actions and words. As the Sermon crashes up against the presuppositions, rationalities, and myths of the world, Jesus' words do indeed sound foolish: "Blessed are the poor in spirit..." (5:3). "Blessed are those who mourn..." (5:4). "Blessed are you when people revile you and persecute you..." (5:11). "If anyone strikes you on the right cheek, turn the other also" (5:39). "Love your enemies and pray for those who persecute you..." (5:44). On and on it goes–foolishness worthy of a jester.

At times Jesus even employs comedy. Consider the way he pokes fun at–even lampoons–those who display their righteousness before others: "So whenever you give alms, do not sound a trumpet before you, as the hypocrites do in the synagogues and in the streets, so that they may be praised by others" (6:2). What an image: a person sounding a trumpet before himself as he gives alms. However, this is not a literal description of the way people behaved; almsgivers did not really carry around trumpets. Jesus here uses hyperbole, creating a comical image.[8] He doesn't stop there; he continues, "When you are praying, do not heap up empty phrases as the Gentiles do; for they think they will be heard because of their many words" (6:7). Most of us know exactly what Jesus is talking about. We've slept through those kinds of prayers. I imagine the people to whom Jesus was speaking were at least snickering beneath their breath at his images of the publicly righteous people. In Jesus' culture, in which receiving honor from others was in many ways the highest value, these humorous depictions of those who gain honor from their acts of righteousness were radical indeed. What had been the source of great status now comes in for the worst kind of critique: laughter and lampooning.[9]

Or consider Jesus' words, "If anyone wants to sue you and take your coat, give your cloak as well" (5:40). This response is not an act of generosity or passivity, though it has often been interpreted in these ways. Rather, as Walter Wink persuasively argues, the situation is one in which the economic powers have so milked the poor that all they have left to be sued for are their garments.[10] When their outer garment is claimed in court, Wink argues, Jesus counsels them to give the inner one also. That is, the victim of the economic system, who has no other recourse, takes off the inner garment and walks out of court stark naked. In this way the victim not only retains his or her status as a moral agent, but also exposes the system's essential cruelty and "burlesques its pretensions to justice, law, and order."[11] As the person walks out of court naked and people begin to ask what is going on, the economic system itself stands naked and is exposed for what it is: a system that treats the poor as "sponge[s] to be squeezed dry by the rich."[12] Jesus here presents a kind of homiletical burlesque of the economic system. It is really a hilarious image—that person walking out of court stark naked. People surely would have been laughing.

Preachers can learn from Jesus here. Challenges to the "powers that be" need not always be earnest and serious tirades against "capitalism" or "consumerism" or "injustice." Burlesque and lampooning will often work just as well. Like Jesus, preachers can simply carry the system to its logical, absurd (even hyperbolic) extreme and unmask its pretensions and destructiveness in comical ways.

Several years ago in Atlanta, the City Council passed an ordinance that basically made homelessness illegal. Virtually every activity required for a homeless person to survive on the street—from sleeping in public to urinating to asking for money—became a violation of the law. The ordinance became known as the "Urban Camping Ordinance" because in the legislation homelessness was euphemistically called "urban camping"—reminding us that we should always pay attention to the language used by the powers!

Following the passage of the ordinance a couple of organizations distributed thousands of flyers inviting people to come to Atlanta and enjoy urban camping. "Don't go to the National Parks this year!" the flyer read in big, bold letters. "Forget about the beach or the mountains. This year, come to Atlanta and enjoy URBAN CAMPING! Have the unique experience of sleeping on concrete and shivering through the night! Meet new people as you stand in line for hours waiting to receive an unhealthy meal! Participate in the adventure of the hunt, as you try to avoid arrest by the police! Come to Atlanta and enjoy urban camping! For more information call…"—and here the flyer gave the names and phone numbers of organizations that had supported the urban camping ordinance. Like these pamphleteers—and like Jesus in the Sermon on the Mount—preachers can employ lampoon in similar ways to unmask the powers in their sermons.

Much "gospel foolishness" appears in Jesus' Sermon—and much of it is comical. Like a jester, Jesus repeatedly subverts the presuppositions, rationalities, and myths that constituted the very air people breathed. It's almost as if nothing remains the same by the time Jesus finishes speaking. One particular myth comes in for special attention throughout the

Sermon. This myth is what Walter Wink calls the "myth of redemptive violence."[13] This myth comes to shape not only the activity of nations and institutions, but also human interactions as well. This myth all too often constitutes the air we breathe today, just as it constituted the air people breathed in Jesus' day.

According to this myth, which traces itself back to the Babylonian myths of creation, the way to bring order out of chaos is through violence, the way to deal with enemies is to violently defeat them.[14] Violence becomes the ultimate solution to human conflicts. As Wink writes, "Ours is neither a perfect nor a perfectible world; it is a theater of perpetual conflict in which the prize goes to the strong. Peace through war, security through strength: these are the core convictions that arise from this ancient [myth]."[15]

One does not have to look far to see this myth at work; it pervades American culture. The old, almost archetypal Popeye cartoons present this myth in its most unabashed form. Do you remember those cartoons? Popeye and Olive Oil are having a wonderful day, enjoying an outing on a picnic. The sun is shining, the birds are singing, and all is right with the world. Then Bluto comes along, disrupts the picnic, tries to steal Olive Oil's attention, physically pounds on Popeye, and throws the world into chaos with his bullying. Predictably, the only way to restore order is for Popeye to eat his spinach and beat the tar out of Bluto, a pattern repeated time after time in the cartoon. The myth of redemptive violence permeates our earliest memories, even the cartoons on which many of us were weaned.

This same pattern continues in children's comics and video games and popular movies (even such an innocuous movie as *The Lion King*, in which violence finally wins the day and order is restored).[16] This myth becomes more serious when we turn to national and world affairs, from the war on terrorism, to the Middle East, to the death penalty. This myth is profoundly at work in the seemingly unending Israeli-Palestinian conflict. On a larger scale, it shapes both acts of terrorism and the United States' responses to those acts. Indeed, it seems to me that the one thing terrorists and the United States have in common is this myth of redemptive violence: the way to bring order out of chaos is through violence; the way to deal with enemies is to violently defeat them. This myth runs so deep that we can hardly even imagine an alternative. As a result, the cycle of violence seems unending.

Time and again in the Sermon on the Mount, Jesus pointedly challenges this myth—and the violence and domination it embodies. It is not the only myth he challenges, but it is one of the most important. I've come to suspect that the deepest folly of the Sermon on the Mount—that which disorients us and dislocates us most radically—grows out of Jesus' subversion of this myth. When Jesus begins to subvert the myth of redemptive violence, the Sermon starts sounding not just foolish, but like sheer madness, possibly because at these points Jesus exposes the depth of our own captivity to this myth.

We cannot avoid this dimension of the Sermon, for Jesus' challenge to the myth of redemptive violence confronts us directly or indirectly at every turn.[17] Jesus opens the Sermon with the beatitudes (Mt. 5:3–12), which announce a new order that provides the context for the practical instruction in the rest of the Sermon. Notice how many of the beatitudes envision an alternative to the myth of redemptive violence:

"Blessed are the merciful..."

"Blessed are the meek..."—those who renounce retribution and revenge and live faithfully and expectantly.[18]

"Blessed are the peacemakers..."—those who pursue not the peace of Rome, established through military domination, but the peace of God, in which all things are in just relation to each other and their Creator.[19]

"Blessed are you when people revile you and persecute you and utter all kinds of evil against you falsely on my account. Rejoice and be glad, for your reward is great in heaven, for in the same way they persecuted the prophets who were before you." (5:11–12)

According to the myth of redemptive violence, the "normal" response to persecution would be retaliation. But not here. Here the "foolish" response is to rejoice and be glad—and possibly to disorient the persecutors and even change the situation.

Consider just a couple of the practices that follow the beatitudes:

You have heard that it was said, "An eye for an eye and a tooth for a tooth." But I say to you, do not [violently] resist an evildoer. But if anyone strikes you on the right cheek, turn the other also; and if anyone wants to sue you and take your coat, give your cloak as well; and if anyone forces you to go one mile, go also the second mile. (5:38–41)

The original commandment—an eye for an eye and a tooth for a tooth—was actually intended to limit revenge.[20] One was to respond "in kind" when harmed by an enemy, rather than engaging in more extreme forms of vengeance such as killing. The law really meant, "*No more* than an eye for an eye. *No more* than a tooth for a tooth." It was a piece of progressive legislation. But Jesus subverts even this limited form of revenge. "Do not [violently] resist an evildoer," he says. Unfortunately, as my use of brackets suggests, the *New Revised Standard Version's* translation of this verse is horrible. Actually, the word translated "resist" is a military term for violent resistance.[21] Jesus is not telling people to be passive in the face of evil; Jesus himself certainly wasn't passive when faced with evil. Rather, Jesus is saying, "Do not *violently* resist an evildoer." Do not resort to the ways of the world governed by the myth of redemptive violence, which simply perpetuate the cycle of violence.

Instead, Jesus counsels creative, imaginative *nonviolent resistance.* We get extraordinary examples of turning the other cheek, giving the cloak also, and going the extra mile, which are not acts of passivity, but rather ways of resisting evil nonviolently. Remember what I noted earlier about the cloak: the person gives the undergarment and walks out of court naked, exposing the injustice of the system without resorting to violence. It is an act of nonviolent resistance. The same is true of the other two actions.[22] Jesus here suggests ways to resist evil, while still breaking the cycle of violence and living free from the myth of redemptive violence.

Then, in possibly his most extreme words, Jesus says, "You have heard that it was said, 'You shall love your neighbor and hate your enemy.' But I say to you, Love your enemies and pray for those who persecute you, so that you may be children of your Father in heaven" (5:43–45a). It is easy to discern the foolishness of these words. Can we even fathom a president of the United States (Democrat or Republican) going on TV after an event like 9/11 and saying, "Love your enemies and pray for those who persecute you. We will not respond to violence with more violence." It's unimaginable. The public reaction to such a comment, however, is not at all difficult to imagine. Maybe here we can see most clearly the incredible foolishness of Jesus' Sermon and the foolishness of our calling as the church. Possibly we may also be confronted by our own captivity to the myth of redemptive violence.

Such is the strange new world–the "foolish" new world–envisioned by the Sermon on the Mount. It is a world that runs counter to the myth of redemptive violence, which so drives our world even today. It is the same new world embodied on the cross. Fundamentally, Jesus is crucified for two reasons. First, he challenges the "powers that be," so they have to get rid of him. Second, Jesus explicitly and consistently refuses to respond to those powers on their own violent terms. Jesus refuses to take the military option; he refuses to combat violent domination with more violent domination–even if it costs him his life. Jesus lives out the Sermon and *breaks the cycle of violence.* He exposes the myth of redemptive violence for what it is–not the way of life, but the way of death. To preach

"Christ crucified" is in many ways the same as preaching the Sermon on the Mount because Jesus' words and deeds are one. Both Paul and Jesus offer a new vision of the world, that runs counter to the myth of redemptive violence.

So, at the end of his Sermon Jesus, like Paul, challenges us to reconceive wisdom and foolishness:

> Everyone then who hears these words of mine and acts on them will be like a wise man who built his house on rock. The rain fell, the floods came, and the winds blew and beat on that house, but it did not fall, because it had been founded on rock. And everyone who hears these words of mine and does not act on them will be like a foolish man who built his house on sand. The rain fell, and the floods came, and the winds blew and beat against that house, and it fell—and great was its fall. (7:24–27)

The preaching of Jesus, which the world calls "foolish," is now called wisdom. Jesus reverses the world's understanding of wisdom and foolishness just as radically as Paul does when the apostle claims that the foolishness of the cross is in fact the wisdom and power of God.

This is the foolish word we are called to preach today. We are called to preach a disorienting and dislocating word that exposes the presuppositions, rationalities, and myths that hold people captive, and from which they often ache to be set free. We are called to envision a new creation so people might see and live in the world in new ways. We are called to invite the community of faith to become an odd people whose life together bears witness to the way of Jesus, a way that breaks the cycle of violence and embodies God's shalom in the midst of a violent world. We are called to invite the community of faith to live in such a way that our life together makes no sense if Jesus is not who he says he is.[23]

Many people—even people in our churches—will call such a word "foolish," crazy, mad. But as Paul notes, this is part of our calling as preachers: to be "fools for the sake of Christ." This is part of the great risk of preaching—being called foolish. At times we may even wonder ourselves if what we are proclaiming is holy foolishness or just plain foolishness. We're way out on a limb. But we do have a promise: "The message about the cross is foolishness to those who are perishing, but to us who are being saved it is the power of God" (1 Cor. 1:18).

6

Great in the Empire of Heaven

A Faithful Performance of Matthew's Sermon on the Mount

DENNIS DEWEY

The winds gusted and howled the day of my first visit to the natural amphitheater of the Mount of the Beatitudes, the site overlooking the Sea of Galilee where tradition says that Jesus spoke the words commonly known as "The Sermon on the Mount." I had to strain against the fury to hear but a few of the words our tour guide spoke. I imagined Jesus on a day like that day sitting atop the hill, opening his mouth to teach, "Blessed are the...Blessed are the...Let's come back and do this tomorrow!" We who attempt to perform these words two millennia later face no less daunting challenges as we approach the task of learning and telling[1] this text. In the face of the blustery winds of church tradition and cultural currents, my present task is to examine what is entailed in the learning and performing of the text that we call "The Sermon on the Mount." But first I must provide some context for this enterprise from my personal experience and in the art of performing biblical texts.

I came to the task of learning Matthew's Sermon on the Mount as a professional biblical storyteller, one who for fourteen years has performed the texts of scripture.[2] This ministry has been nurtured in the Network of Biblical Storytellers (NOBS),[3] an organization whose mission is "to encourage everyone to learn and tell biblical stories." My first text telling came about when, as a newly ordained Presbyterian pastor, I determined to perform the passion narrative from Mark's gospel (Mk. 14–15) in lieu of scripture reading and sermon. Some parishioners greeted me after worship with the astounding question, "Where did you get that script?" The experience awakened me to two realities: (1) the power of faithful performance of biblical texts and (2) my vocation to continue in this practice. I did not yet think of this as "biblical storytelling." In fact, I was not even familiar with the term at the time. With a background in theater, I naturally conceived of the performance of this text as "dramatic monologue." But the following year I took part in a seminar in biblical storytelling led by Thomas Boomershine,[4] a seminar that was to change my understanding, my nomenclature, and my life.

Tom helped me reconceptualize my performance experience as storytelling, not theater/drama. He taught me that the art form of ancient Israel and of the early church was not writing (at least not the silent composition of words by a solitary author) but the performance art of storytelling–the lively, out loud extemporization of the narrative tradition in community. This epiphany launched me on a journey of research and practice that has captivated me for a quarter century. I regard the written texts of the Hebrew Scriptures as something like the "fossil record" of the lively storytelling tradition that was Israel's, and the written gospels as transcriptions of communities' collective audience memories of performance events no less "inspired" than the writing that "transmediatized"[5] them.

Some may doubt that much power or creativity can be involved in just telling the text. The silent text tradition has normalized, even prescribed, a flat delivery of the text that renders it dead on arrival. But hearing is believing. As a musician performs scores, I perform the scriptures. No one ever walked out of a symphony concert demanding a refund because the orchestra played only the notes Beethoven wrote. Nor would anyone confuse listening to that performance with perusing the orchestral score. This kind of biblical storytelling attempts to stay close to the text as "a spiritual discipline which entails the lively interpretation, expression and animation of a narrative text of the Old or New Testaments which has first been deeply internalized and is then remembranced,[6] embodied, breathed and voiced by a teller/performer as a sacred event in community with an audience/ congregation."[7] The Sermon on the Mount, although situated squarely within the Matthean community's story and clearly marked by narrative elements, is not narrative per se. Something can be learned from the process of engagement with narrative texts for the performance of non-narrative texts.

We relate differently to a text when it is inside us, part of us. Words that are sounds in the memory of the heart are different from the unvoiced ink on the silent, printed page. Internalized, the stories are de-objectified and take on life. As literate people, proud to be identified as "people of the book," we forget that for much of Israel's history books were rare, that the word of God was carried in the heart, that the written scripture was secondary to the remembered, breathed, voiced, text. When Jesus walked with the disheartened, unseeing companions on the road to Emmaus, "He interpreted to them the things about himself in all the scriptures" (Lk. 24:27b, emphasis mine). Did he then carry a half ton of scrolls with him? No, Jesus retrieved them from the memory of the heart. After all, this is the same Jesus of whom it was said as a twelve-year-old, "Everyone who heard him was surprised how much he knew and at the answers he gave" (Lk. 2:47, CEV), that is, how much he had stored in his heart and how he was freely able to access it. The pedagogy that instilled such remarkable "random access memory" in the boy-Jesus is hinted at in Deuteronomy 6.

Most pastors can remember the last four of the five "corollaries" to the Shema (Deuteronomy 6:4ff): catechize (teach these things to your children), theologize (talk about them continually), symbolize (wear them on your wrists and foreheads), publicize (inscribe them on your doorposts and gates). But few can remember the important corollary that follows immediately upon the commandment to love God with heart, soul, and strength: "Keep these words that I am commanding you today in your heart" (6:6) (internalize). Ironically, we do not need to; we have downloaded them to paper. Although the word *spirituality* is nowhere to be found in the First Testament, this notion of carrying the word of God in the memory of the heart is suggested throughout. We may even go so far as to say that the heart (of the individual and community's) is understood to be the primary repository for the text, while the writing is understood to be secondary, back up, storage. This metaphor of keeping the word in the heart holds the key to the fundamental understanding of ancient Israel in their experience of and relationship to the text. Furthermore, the metaphor implies a pedagogical model for our process of internalizing the text.

I am careful to distinguish between what is commonly called "memorization" and what I call "learning by heart." The former is largely a mental process, often bypassing the emotions altogether, focusing on the words alone as data, as bits of information strung together by sheer force of repetition for recitation of print text, which, when performed, sounds very much like ink on the page: a kind of sing-song, robotic stream of words. Understandably, many regard memorization not only to be egregiously difficult, but unsatisfying for performance purposes; it entails too much work for the monotonous product at the effort's end. In contrast, heart-learning requires the engagement of the whole person, a kind of "St. Ignatius meets Stanislavsky" Ignatian spirituality joined to the understanding of emotion suggested by the great teacher of "method" acting. Heart-learning is different from head-learning. It is not merely rote memorization, but entails the creation of deep, embodied memory. Daniel Goleman observes:

> The emotional/rational dichotomy approximates the folk distinction between "heart" and "head"; knowing something is right "in your heart" is a different order of conviction somehow, a deeper kind of certainty than thinking so with your rational mind.[8]

Of course, what Deuteronomy means by "heart" and what Goleman intends are two different things; the heart is not primarily an organ of feeling in the ancient scheme of things. Nonetheless, its function includes feeling as well as thinking and willing. To love God "with all your heart" means "with your whole person." What we experience with deep emotion, we tend to remember. Aquinas observed that a learner "should apply interest and emotional energy to the things [s/]he wants to remember because the more deeply something is impressed upon the soul, the less does it drop out of the soul."[9] One technique of the pedagogy of Greco-Roman rhetoric was literally to beat students so that the emotional pain would serve as an emotional "hook" for the memory's retrieval.[10]

Furthermore, the text that is remembered in the heart is a spoken word, a word that resounds in the imagination, a word that is voiced. Just as Judaism regards the written text of Torah as incomplete without the oral Torah, the unvoiced scripture is incomplete. The ink is "black fire," but all around it on the page is what Judaism calls the "white fire," the oral context of the written word. The rabbinical term is *arichat sfatayim,* literally, "arrange it on the lips." Rabbi Noah Weinberg observes of this principle:

> It bridges the gap between lofty notions of the soul and the world of reality. In other words, you'll find out if you really believe what you say. We come from a "quiet learning" society where "shhhh" is the rule. If you drop a book in a university library, people jump as if a bomb went off. Contrast this with a rabbinic study hall, where you're greeted by a rippling sea of sound. The uninitiated often ask: "How can these people learn with so much noise?!"[11]

My storyteller's hunch is that Jesus' education would have involved just such a noisy "rabbinic study hall," each student repeating more loudly than those around in order to speak the words into residency in the heart. Orality's pedagogy is different from that of the emerging high-literate academy. The tension between these respective pedagogies erupts in

Jesus' clashes with the literate power structures of his time. Each gospel contains stories in which surprise is expressed that Jesus demonstrates such learning without being educated ("literate"). But what has the culture of orality to do with our age?

The post-literate world in which we live is secondarily oral, says Walter Ong.[12] The gap between the "then" of long-silent scripture and the "now" of postmodernism is bridged by an experience of the text that is akin to the way it was experienced in the oral culture from which it emerged: as lively performance that once again captures imaginations, moves hearts, engages listeners at their deepest levels, and feeds the spiritual hunger of a fast-food culture. My typical workshop begins by reading a biblical story and then performing that same story word-for-word as a telling. A participant once aptly observed, "The reading is like there and then, but the telling is like here and now." Richard Lischer argues that the performance of the text is an answer to the preacher's problem:

> And what is the dilemma of interpretation? It is not the question of "what the text meant"; we have shelves of commentaries to tell us [that]...The problem is the "movement" from past to present and the use of ancient materials for contemporary purposes. The notion of "performance" as a metaphor for the interpretive move from exegesis to proclamation recommends itself to all preachers as one possible means of resolving the hermeneutical dilemma.[13]

Some find the term "performance" puzzling or offensive. For much of our early history, however, scriptures ("writings") were experienced not as silent ink read in solitude, but as lively, communal performances. Even the rare, personal reading was almost never done silently.[14] In contemporary American culture, the verb *perform* has come to connote "showing off" or "hamming it up." But the word's etymology suggests its appropriateness in the present context: "to form fully, completely." We do not think that the doctor is "showing off" when she performs open heart surgery, nor that the priest is "hamming it up" when he performs a marriage ceremony. As a professional biblical storyteller, I have advocated reclaiming this worthy word and have advanced the performance of the scriptures as a spiritual discipline whose roots go deep in the oral cultures from which the Bible sprang.

David Rhoads calls attention to the deficiencies of the historical-critical method in biblical studies:

> When you think of the Second Testament writings as performance literature—either as transcriptions of prior oral compositions or

as written compositions designed for oral performance—you wonder why Second Testament scholars do not function more like musicologists or dramatists. Interpretation of music and drama is done primarily by both performers and music/drama specialists. Can you imagine a musicologist who does nothing but sit in libraries and study the score of a composition without ever hearing a performance of it? Would it not seem strange for interpreters of drama, including ancient Greek drama, to analyze a play apart from interpretations of it in performance? Similarly, does it not seem odd that biblical critics interpret writings that were composed in and for oral performance—as gospels, letters, and apocalypses were—without ever experiencing performances of them and without giving some attention to the nature of the performance of these works in ancient and modern times?[15]

With these compelling rhetorical questions, I conclude this brief attempt to reframe the understanding of "biblical text," no longer as silent ink on paper but as transcription of past performances and as script for contemporary re-performances. I now turn to the specific challenges presented by Matthew's Sermon on the Mount, asking, what is entailed by learning *this* text by heart, and what clues may be found within the text itself for its performance?

At the outset we should avoid conceiving of any "original text" (singular) of Matthew's Sermon on the Mount, whether as oral performance or as written transcription. More helpful is to think of "original texts" (plural) as a gestalt of the collective memory of a number of performances. In whatever fashion the sayings of Jesus coalesced from "Q" and other tellings into their present form, they have been reshaped repeatedly on many tongues and in the hearing of many audiences. Clearly, the material in its Matthean form is instruction and is so identified in the introduction, "[Jesus] sat down…and taught." We may safely assume that the Sermon on the Mount was readily performable in antiquity. Although the length of Matthew's gospel as a whole renders its performance at one sitting somewhat difficult, the entire text does "fall within the length of texts for which we find oral performance in the first century."[16] Understanding the present text as an approximation of many tellings can also serve to liberate us from "verbatim fright," anxiety about reciting the text word-for-word.

The first step in learning a biblical story is to read it out loud. The second step is to read it out loud. The third step is to read it out loud. Words that are to be heard finally as oral performance must be listened to with the ear that shares the same head that speaks them. Putting the words of the text on the lips is critical for moving the text from "out there" to "in here." Often the third telling begins to lift to the consciousness an awareness of the structure of the text and to identify its "arc," the rise and fall (or series of rises and falls) characteristic of all works of art. When I began to learn the Sermon on the Mount, perhaps too eager to discern its basic structure, I found myself challenged after repeated readings. The arc remained elusive even as I was beginning to internalize the text. As I was mentoring a Doctor of Ministry course in biblical storytelling at the time, I did what any teacher so challenged would do: I assigned the task to my students, selfishly anticipating that they might help me find a shortcut to discerning the text's shape. In the end, each of the students who learned the text by heart identified a different point as the text's apogee.

The best way to come to know a challenging text is to keep performing it, to live with it over time, to breathe with it. This is especially true of non-narrative texts such as the Sermon on the Mount. My rule of thumb for learning any text by heart is to allow a minimum of six weeks. One can memorize the words of a text in a few hours, but learning by heart requires living with it, sleeping with it, ignoring it, letting it work on us even while we are unaware. Fallow time is an essential ingredient in the "growing" of a text in the heart. I often recite portions of the text in my mind's ear in the moments before falling asleep each night, so that my unconscious mind may absorb it, that my dreams might be shaped by it.

What emerged over the nearly four months that I lived with the text before performing it for the Rochester Sermon Seminar was a mnemonic macro-structure that I sketch as follows:

    I. Narrative Introduction (5:1)

    II. The Upside-Down Blessings of the Community (5:2–12)

    III. Who You Are As Community (5:13–16)

        A. Salt (5:13)

        B. Light (5:14–16)

    IV. The Fulfillment of Righteousness in the Community (5:17–48)

        A. Introduction (5:17–20)

            1. Purpose (5:17–18)

            2. Warnings (5:19–20)

        B. Murder (5:21–26)

        C. Adultery (5:27–30)

        D. Divorce (5:31–32)

        E. Swearing (5:33–37)

        F. Evildoers (5:38–42)

G. Love of enemies (5:43–47)

H. Conclusion (5:48)

V. The Sincere Practice of Piety in the Community (6:1–18)

    A. Introduction (6:1)

    B. Alms (6:2–4)

    C. Prayer (6:5–15)

    D. Fasting (6:16–18)

VI. Attitudes about Wealth/Security in the Community (6:19–34)

    A. Antitheses (6:19–24)

    B. Worry (6:25–34)

VII. Living in Relationship in the Community (7:1–12)

    A. Judgment (7:1–5)

    B. Stewardship (7:6)

    C. Seeking (7:7–11)

    D. Doing (7:12)

VIII. The Community Anticipates Judgment (7:13–29)

    A. The narrow gate (7:13–14)

    B. False prophets (7:15–20)

    C. Rejection (7:21–23)

    D. Hearing and acting (7:24–27)

IX. Narrative Conclusion (7:28–29)

An early step in the process of internalizing the text involves a typographical re-presentation, the rearrangement of the text on the page in a learner-friendly format: the production of a "script." The way the text lies on the page in print Bibles is not particularly conducive to the learning process—neat columns of words with double-justified margins, page after page, the same. Visual uniformity is pleasing to the eye, but poses a challenge to one who is learning a text to speak it. I follow Boomershine's method of dividing texts into episodes of about three lines each. Each line is typically a breath. Each line ends at an appropriate, sensible place—not, for example, in the middle of a phrase or thought. Additional manipulation of the text to enhance the visualization of patterns is sometimes employed. Several episodes scripted in a way helpful for internalizing, then, might look something like this:

When Jesus saw the crowds, he went up the mountain;
and after he sat down, his disciples came to him.
And he began to speak, and taught them, saying:

Blessed are the poor in spirit, because theirs is the empire of heaven.

Blessed are those who mourn, because they will be comforted.

Blessed are the meek, because they will inherit the earth.

I might further rearrange the text to show patterns on the page as follows:

Blessed are	**the poor in spirit,**
	because theirs is the empire of heaven.
Blessed are	**those who mourn,**
	because they will be comforted.
Blessed are	**the meek,**
	because they will inherit the earth.
Blessed are	**those who hunger and thirst for righteousness,**
	because they will be filled.
Blessed are	**the merciful,**
	because they will receive mercy.
Blessed are	**the pure in heart,**
	because they will see God.
Blessed are	**the peacemakers,**
	because they will be called children of God.
Blessed are	**those who are persecuted for righteousness' sake,**
	because theirs is the empire of heaven.
Blessed are **you**	when people revile you
	and persecute you
	and say all kinds of evil things against you
	falsely on my account.
Rejoice and be glad,	**because your reward is great in heaven,**
	because in the same way they persecuted
	the prophets who were before you.

The repetitions are evidence of the orality of this unit. My experience as a biblical storyteller is that episodes (units of a few lines that "hang together") typically are three lines long. "Three-ness" is a characteristic feature of narrative structure. Sayings material, however, is more frequently characterized by "two-ness," i.e., doublets and parallelisms. For mnemonic purposes, three groupings of three-line episodes is a memory-friendly way to format the nine beatitudes. I look for all kinds of cues, patterns, "hooks," and structures—whether conceptual/thematic or aural/linguistic. Although I study the text in Greek, I learn it in translation.

Some of my hooks have nothing to do with the Greek text, but are purely accidental to the English translation. The acrostic "MAD SEL," for example, helps me remember the order of the antitheses (Murder, Adultery, Divorce, Swearing, Evildoers, Loving enemies).

Beyond structure mnemonics, conceptual affinities help one remember the groupings. A performance understanding of the text often rescues it from an accepted, familiar interpretation. Hearing this text as somewhat bland, cliché words of comfort, for example, can inure us to the radical quality of their shocking assertion that in the community associated with "the empire of heaven" (the rendering that Warren Carter suggests and that I have come to prefer),[17] the truly happy (*makarioi*) are not those who are rich and well fed, strong and self-confident, those who do not suffer, those who are powerful and aggressive, those who can get their way in this competitive world, but exactly the opposite.

The role of the fool in Roman theater and evidence of the surprising pervasiveness of the theater around the Mediterranean at the beginning of the Common Era may well have implications for understanding what I refer to in my structural analysis of the Sermon on the Mount as "the upside-down blessings" (i.e., "the beatitudes"). Lawerence Welbourne points to the long-standing tradition in Greco-Roman culture of "the comic-philosophic tradition" whose "hero is the 'wise-fool'...who is allowed to utter critical truths about authority."[18] What Matthew's Sermon has preserved and shaped is akin to this upside-down wisdom tradition, wisdom that is not so much orthodox as it is paradox in which Jesus is the wise fool. As a teacher of biblical storytelling, I often encourage tellers to push the envelope, to treat the text with what I call "reverential risk," to test a range of interpretations of the text.[19] The question for the performer is, then, what does a wise fool sound like?[20]

I decided to perform "the beatitudes" with an imploring energy, a kind of radical pointedness that is suggested by the rhetoric and is revisited in the antitheses ("you have heard that it was said...but I say to you..."). The text is suffused with shocking, unconventional wisdom, from not worrying about money to turning the other cheek. So why not perform it as the rhetoric of shock, building on that rhetoric as the foundation upon which various arcs are found? If, as I believe, on several levels the teller/performer in some sense becomes the incarnation of the word in the time and space of the performance, the question of tone is no minor matter. The gravity of this assertion is suggested by the title of Richard Horsley and Jonathan Draper's landmark work on Q as oral performance, *Whoever Hears You Hears Me*. The performer of Matthew's Sermon on the Mount not only speaks the words of Jesus, but embodies, bears, represents Jesus in the act of the telling. The greatest compliment that can be paid to a performer of a text such as this is to have a listener say (as one said to me at the Rochester Sermon Seminar), "I felt as if Jesus was talking to me."

An imploring rhetoric with an intent to shock may be the entree to the performance of this text. Whitney Shiner notes that first-century performances were noisier, more audience-involving than we might imagine. Moreover, he notes a certain fluidity that marked the performance of texts, including gospel texts:

> Oral performance...tends to be much more audience specific than the written word...Moreover, it is far from certain that the text would have been considered sacrosanct in the early years of its existence. As we will see, speakers were often quite free with their texts. There is certainly no reason to believe that a speaker would adhere to a text word for word.[21]

For a number of reasons I frequently use the NRSV as my "base translation." I "massaged" the translation for my script of the Sermon on the Mount. Most translations are not guided primarily by oral performance considerations. Like a jazz musician's performance of a "chart," biblical storytellers render a sense that accurately corresponds to the original. For example, the "polish" of most translations is guided more by *literary* considerations than by those of oral performance. And so the NRSV occasionally removes the Greek oral punctuation, "and" (*kai*), especially from the beginning of a sentence. The result is a more literate translation, but a poorer performance script. Where "ands" are removed or replaced, I often restore them.

In addition, I often massage the rendering of the Greek terms *oti* and *gar* not as the more formal "for," but rather as "because." (When was the last time you uttered something as stilted as, "Honey, I'm running out to the mini-market for we are out of bread"?) Using "because" instead of "for" as a translation of *oti* and *gar* has the effect of lessening the distance between the text's discourse world and that in which we live. In the present case then, the poor in spirit are blessed *because* they will inherit the empire of heaven. Whit Shiner observes, "In oral presentation the words of the narrative exist simultaneously in two worlds. The first is the imagined story world of the narrative. The second is the social world in which the narrative is taking place."[22]

Although the implications of Shiner's assertion go far beyond issues of diction, we must address this gap between ancient rhetorical forms (as they are preserved in translations influenced by a kind of "religious-speak") and the aural world that lies outside liturgical praxis and popular piety. To close that gap I freely prefer to use contractions, for example, where the translation is more formal. On some occasions, however, the form "do not" may be preferred to the terser "don't." Admonition is often amplified by the more formal form, as when a parent seeks a more authoritative voice to declare, "Do not enter this house with mud on your shoes!" So I may keep the formal form for, "You cannot serve God and wealth," but use the familiar form in the clearly comedic put-downs of the hypocrites ("Whenever you fast, don't look dismal") and to reinforce what is expressed as commonplace ("Don't even the tax collectors do the same thing?").

I sometimes modify the text where the translation has obscured a "verbal thread," a word or phrase that recurs. So, for example, instead of accepting the translation of *lampei* as "give light," I will retranslate it as "shine on" to make clear the verbal thread with *lampsato* in the next line:

> No one lights a lamp and puts it under a bushel basket, but on a lamp stand, where it shines on *(lampsei)* everyone in the house. So let your light shine *(lampsato)* before others that they may see your good works...

Of course, the pronunciation of the English word *blessed* presents us with an immediate performance issue. Does the performer adopt the Elizabethan two-syllable pronunciation ("blessèd") or stay with the contemporary monosyllabic version ("bless'd")? Sometimes pastoral issues take priority in such a decision. For example, because anyone who has any passing knowledge of scripture will recognize the traditional (from KJV to NRSV) English of John 3:16 ("For God so loved the world..."), I choose not to massage *gar* into the more contemporary rendering "because" to avoid jarring the sensibility of the listening audience. But, as I have already indicated, with the Sermon on the Mount I want to jar the listening audience. I want to rescue the words of the beatitudes from comfortable familiarity. Matthew's text presents Jesus as establishing a new covenant community in this teaching—one marked by a very different ethos, a stunning ethic, a radically different worldview from that of the empire of Caesar. These words can only comfort the community when the community has seen where they lead and what it means to walk through that narrow gate and down that narrow road.

The value of inclusive language in the NRSV is one that I welcome as being true to the Spirit of Jesus. But sometimes the gyrations required by inclusive language result in drawing more attention to the circumlocutions than to the gist of the text. So rather than employ "brother and sister" consistently to translate *adelphos* in 5:22 and 5:23f, I will do so in the first two (proximate and parallel) instances in verse 22 to establish the antecedent but then substitute the word "someone" in verse 23 and "that person" or "that one" in verse 24 to say:

So when you are offering your gift at the altar, if you remember that someone has something against you, leave your gift and go; first be reconciled to that person…

Similarly, I appreciate and observe the NRSV's substitution of "neighbor" for "brother" (*adelphos*) in 7:3ff.

The two questions of how we learn the text and how we perform it are really interrelated. We answer both simultaneously in a dialectic of praxis and reflection. That reflection must take into account the contextual realities of the original performances of this text to the extent that these can be surmised. I am constantly mustering the energy to overcome what I was taught about this text by the scholarship of my day, a scholarship suffused with theological interpretations that render them aphorisms for personal piety completely divorced from the economic and political dimensions of life in the community of the empire of heaven.[23]

As my structural outline of the passage attempts to suggest, the Sermon on the Mount represents a prophetic, covenantal vision for the life of the community in the new empire of heaven. As such, its performance tone must be heraldic of the foolish wisdom that characterizes the community of Jesus' followers over against the values of Caesar's empire. I appreciate the wisdom of one of my denomination's statements of faith to the effect that peacemaking and the reconciliation of enemies is to be commended to the nations "as practical politics,"[24] an assertion that some of my fellow Presbyterians must surely scorn as utter foolishness. My performance register will attempt to hold together these two realities before me as I perform this text: that the instruction is for the community and that it represents real political-economic challenges.

In the salt/light passage, the audience is invited to *become* that community envisioned, perhaps more implored than invited, but addressed as already constituted ("You are the salt of the earth"). Next comes an explication of what this means in practice, the antitheses ("You have heard that it was said/but I say to you"), which flesh out the contours of the ways in which the law is to be fulfilled. This is no mere, dry "how-to" instruction. There are moments of humor, hyperbole, admonition, and shock along the way. We may well wonder about a world in which saying, "You idiot!" and looking at another with lust are tantamount to capital crimes. The culmination in the call to perfection leaves the audience mystified if not shell-shocked.

What follows, aesthetically speaking, is like that moment in the final movement of Beethoven's Ninth Symphony, when chorus and orchestra have come to a fever pitch climax from which there is nowhere to go. After a grand pause, Beethoven introduces in genius *pianissimo* the laughable entrance of a German "oompah band." Having assaulted the audience with the hyperbole of perfection, the turn now is toward comic relief. All three of the explications of practical piety (almsgiving, prayer, and fasting) poke a bit of fun. Hypocrites lend themselves to it. The puncturing of the pompous is comedic tradition as old as story itself. How can a performer of the text resist doing a face-scrunching while saying, "When you fast, don't look dismal like the hypocrites"? Tension resumes with the mention of money. It always does. The audience is put on the defensive. But then comes the reality check: Don't worry about tomorrow; leave it in God's hands. This is life in community in the reign of heaven. A series of admonitions and rhetorical questions follow about judging others, being stewards of what is sacred, living the life of a seeker, building toward and culminating in the articulation of the "rule" for the life of the community, an ethic of mutuality: "Do to others as you would have them do to you." The final section builds in intensity as the audience is introduced to the difficulties of approaching what the future holds for those who take the road less traveled, the one gated by a narrow entrance that leads to a hard way—a way where wolves dressed as sheep lurk, a way at the end of which some of our traveling companions will be found deficient, a way that entails more than going through the motions.

This exploration merely skims the surface of the questions that are raised as we consider the challenge and opportunity presented by the performance of this text. But, performing the text is one way of fulfilling the instruction of Jesus to teach his commandments (5:19). Biblical storytellers are fond of asserting, "The text well-told is the sermon mostly preached." To perform these words in order that they may be heard again as though for the first time (especially when they have already been heard many times over) is to teach them in a way that they may be "inwardly digested."

My summary advice to tellers of the text is (1) know the text, (2) love the text, (3) trust the text. Observing these three "commandments" is a recipe for a successful performance. As biblical storytellers, as faithful text-performers, we are not merely mouthing words. Nor do we "make texts come alive." We start from the belief that they already are alive; our job is not to kill them. Faithful telling is that which both honors the text and springs from faith for faith. We are not actors mouthing someone else's words but Word-bearers acting out our lives through and in the Word.

The question posed by the theme of the Sermon Seminar ("Dare we live in the world imagined in the Sermon on the Mount?") clearly implies that courage is required to live in such a world. Indeed, courage is required even to imagine such a world. In the rhetorical system of ancient Rome the faculty of memoria included imagination. To construct a text from memory is an act of imagination. We human beings are storytelling creatures, homo narrans,[25] who live in a storied world. Story stores memory and shapes our reality even as it shapes us. Recent studies of memory suggest that we do not so much remember events themselves as the act of imagining the events,[26] that any account we give of an experience is fictive (i.e., "constructed") in the telling. Anyone who seriously attempts to perform this text must at some point find the courage to imagine the world it presents in order to tell it faithfully. Good biblical storytelling is based, not on the memorization of the words of text alone, but rather in a creative act of assembling and reassembling the text from patterns and elements of its sensory images, feeling tones, and narrative contours—what we storytellers refer to as the story's "geography." To perform the Sermon on the Mount is to have been to the mountaintop and to have glimpsed in the imagination what lies beyond. Having been there, there is no turning back. The experience changes us. The question for us then becomes, "Dare we live in any other world but the one imagined in the Sermon on the Mount?"

The final measure of the success of our telling will entail, as the text itself tells us, the relationship between word and deed, offering life-service in place of mere lip-service. If we speak the words only and do not seek to live them, then, we are like those Corinthians whom Paul warns away from the table lest they eat and drink condemnation on themselves. If we build our telling on sand, all the greater will be its fall. The teller of this text must see him/herself as a prophet and do so in the knowledge that nearly always a prophet is not welcome. To give breath and voice to the vision articulated by Matthew's Jesus is to re-present him. To embody the text is to incarnate the Word. Our challenge and our consolation will be the admonition and the promise of the text itself: that to do these commandments and to teach them to others is to be called great in the empire of heaven.

PART TWO

Sermons on the Sermon on the Mount

7

The Surprising Blessing
of the Beatitudes

Matthew 5:1–9

RONALD J. ALLEN

Compositional Comments

This sermon was prepared for a middle-class congregation of the Christian Church (Disciples of Christ) located in a county seat town with a population of about 10,000. A generation ago, the town was supported by several assembly plants for a major United States automobile company. The plants paid well and provided excellent benefits. The local high school was named for the automobile company. However, the plants closed as that manufacturer moved those jobs to other countries. While the community has made something of an economic recovery, wages and benefits are much less now; and many households have adjusted to lower lifestyles. Many people who invested their vocational lives in the automobile industry now scramble to make ends meet, and feel betrayed. This community has been brutalized by latter day principalities and powers that Charles Campbell interprets so insightfully and powerfully in his epic book *The Word before the Powers: An Ethic of Preaching*.[1]

I filled the pulpit while the minister of the congregation was out of town (the Fourth Sunday of Epiphany). I selected the text because it was assigned by the Revised Common Lectionary. I did not have a significant relationship with the congregation, so did not try to relate the sermon to the community in a detailed way. I did try loosely to correlate the beatitudes as exemplifications of the realm of God with feelings of loss and betrayal that the minister sees and feels at work in community. As Warren Carter points out in "Power and Identities," the realm of God is a leading theme in the gospel of Matthew, which looks forward to a world in which the exploitative and violent Roman Empire is replaced by the empire of God with its economic justice and supportive community. In the spirit of Charles Campbell's essay, I hoped that the sermon would encourage the congregation by helping them recognize that God is present and seeking to help their community more fully embody qualities of the divine realm.[2] I hoped that the message would help them imagine everyday ways they might live toward the realm and thus help create an alternative social world.[3]

When preaching on the beatitudes previously, I have focused on one beatitude as representative of the group. The following sermon is my first attempt to deal with all the beatitudes in a single sermon. On the one hand, this approach allows the sermon to sketch in a broad way a world shaped by some core values of the realm of God. On the other hand, the sermon barely scratches the exegetical, theological, and ethical surfaces of the individual beatitudes. This message needs to be preceded or followed by an extended Bible study to explore the beatitudes in greater depth.

Sermon

➢ For the longest time, when I heard someone mention the beatitudes, I got a warm feeling. In part I think this feeling came from seeing them printed on elegant book marks, on impressive wall hangings, or in glowing stained-glass windows. A famous congregation in Phoenix is called the Church of the Beatitudes. I would like to have a dollar for every time I have heard someone say that the beatitudes summarize Christianity.

But I began to be puzzled. Each of the nine beatitudes begins with the word *blessed*. Some of the beatitudes seem logical enough. "Blessed are the peacemakers." Sure. It makes sense to think of peacemakers being blessed. But some of the beatitudes are almost contradictory. "Blessed are those who mourn?" "Blessed are you when people revile you and persecute you." How are people blessed when they are crying their hearts out? Or when they are abused or run out of a community or kicked by a soldier's boot?

Blessed is the key word here.[4] So I take the Bible dictionary off the shelf and start to read. In the period of the First Testament, the notion of blessing typically referred to fullness of life. To be blessed was to be aligned with the purposes of God. Blessing often, though not always, included material security–a warm and dry house, nourishing food, clothing, land, family. Peace. Shalom. Joy. Abundance.

Shortly before the time of Matthew, some Jewish thinkers added a dimension to the idea of blessing. To be blessed was to be included in the realm of God. Like many other Jewish people, Matthew believed that history was divided into two periods—the present age and the age to come. From that point of view the present is an evil time disfigured by sin, hunger, demons, sickness, violence, and death. The principalities and powers, especially Caesar and the Empire, brutalized the world.[5] But to be faithful to the divine promises, God would destroy this old age with a massive historical interruption—an apocalypse—and create a new world called the realm of God or the realm of heaven. The realm is a renewed world in which everything takes place according to God's purposes—forgiveness, abundance, freedom, health, peace, and Life with a capital L: unending, eternal. Now here's the connection to blessing: to be blessed is to know you have a place in the realm.

According to Matthew, the first words from Jesus' mouth in his public ministry are, "Repent, for the [realm] of heaven is at hand" (Mt. 4:17, KJV). The ministry of Jesus is the signal that the turning of the ages is taking place. Matthew invites us to believe that we have a place in this realm when we repent of complicity with the powers of the old age and join the movement toward the time when everyone will live in peace, love, joy, and abundance.

So when Matthew says, "Blessed are...the poor in spirit...those who mourn...the meek...,"[6] Matthew does not mean that life will be a continuous party nor that we will necessarily feel the emotions of happiness and joy—"Hey, let's get some spritzer and confetti." To be blessed in Matthew's world is to recognize the limitations of the world as it is and to live in the confidence that God is at work to bring about a realm of peace and love and joy and abundance.

So far, so good. But when I dig into the individual beatitudes, more surprises come. In almost every case, I have a preconceived idea of what the beatitude means; but when we dig into how these ideas functioned at the time of Matthew, I come away surprised. If I were a PowerPoint preacher, I would have a series of paired screens. On the first I would have a picture of what I thought the beatitude meant, and on the second screen a picture of what I found.

Blessed are the poor in spirit. First screen: I thought of people who are quiet, humble, and not arrogant. Second screen: In the world of Matthew, the phrase "poor in spirit" probably referred to people to whom God gives courage when they are poor and beaten-down by evildoers and forces of injustice.[7] If you are crushed, you are blessed not because you are happy right now but because God is acting to restore the world.

Blessed are those who mourn. First screen: Blessed are those who sorrow over the deaths of family and friends, and who suffer other kinds of losses. Second screen: In the world of Matthew, the word for "mourn" often referred to those who recognize how far the world is from the way God would like for it to be. Such mourning is the first step toward longing—and living toward—the realm of God.

Blessed are the meek. First screen: The meek are quiet, humble people. Second screen: In the world of Matthew, the meek are the poor who have lost their land to the wealthy. The meek are blessed because the realm will have plenty of land for all.

Blessed are those who hunger and thirst for righteousness. First screen: Those hungering and thirsting for righteousness are people who are "Serious Believers." You know who I mean? Folk who can't get to church enough for Bible study. Far be it from a preacher to pour cold water on getting to church, but second screen: In the world of Matthew, *righteousness* is a word that describes the quality of life in the realm—when all relationships are right—that is, the way God wants them to be. You are blessed when you hunger and thirst for right relationships.

Blessed are the merciful. First screen: Mercy is not giving people what they deserve but what they want or need. "Please, mama," the child pleads, "have mercy." Second screen: In the world of Matthew, the Greek term "mercy" translated the Hebrew word *hesed,* that towering notion of covenantal loyalty. To be merciful is to be faithful in covenant within the community of the realm even as God relates to Israel. You are blessed when you express *hesed,* the values of the covenant, toward others. Indeed, in one of those odd turns, by expressing *hesed* in community, you experience that very thing.

Blessed are the pure in heart. First screen: The pure heart is the one that never thinks a dirty thought. Second screen: In the world of Matthew, the pure heart is one that is undivided, the heart that wills one thing, and that thing is the realm. In the old age, the heart is divided and is pulled so many directions—the nation, the family, achievement on the athletic field or in the workplace, the latest perfume, the latest shoe. You are blessed when your heart wills one thing: for all the pieces of the world to fit together in the realm.

Blessed are the peacemakers. First screen: Peacemakers wear sandals and loose-fitting shirts with embroidery, and meet on Tuesday nights to write letters to the President protesting the current war in which the United States is involved. Second screen: In the world of Matthew, the peacemaker is one who seeks *shalom,* the cessation of conflict, yes, but much more: the growth of community in support and in all the things that make for blessing. You are blessed when, in the midst of conflict, you have the security not only to resist the immediate violence but to press for a change of social conditions that point to a world of shalom.

Blessed are those who are persecuted for righteousness' sake. Blessed are you when people revile you and persecute you and utter all kinds of evil against you falsely on my account. First screen: Someone with a suffering neurosis. Second screen: In the world of Matthew, persecution probably referred to social rejection by your community, perhaps even your family because you witness to the values of the realm. You are blessed when you recognize that even though you are no longer welcome in your old group, you have the support of the community of the realm.

For almost twenty years, our family sat behind Win and Joe Smith in Sunday worship. Win and Joe were unusual in that each had gone to seminary in the late 1930s. Both pacifists, they had gone to China as missionaries. In 1941, the Japanese aggression in China threatened their safety, so they moved to the Philippines. In late 1941, the Japanese invaded the Philippines, and on the day after Christmas, the Japanese interned Win and Joe, their five-year-old son, and a large group of missionaries.

Soon after they were placed in their first camp, they speculated with other internees about how long they might be interned before liberation. Some predicted one year, others two. Joe thought it would be three. "But," Win replied in tearful horror, "We can't last three years living like this." Joe replied, "We don't have to live three years at once. We live one day at a time."[8] That became their working philosophy for the more than four years they were in concentration camps: "Doing what came to hand," Joe says, "taking advantage of every opportunity in the present."[9]

Almost always living in limited space, conditions grew worse as the war went on. Often surrounded by barbed wire and segregated by gender, they had less and less to eat. Sometimes, they found weevils in their thin soup. Many of their missionary friends were brutalized when they were questioned. One was tortured to death.

Yet they continued "taking advantage of every opportunity in the present" to love and support one another and to express such respect and concern for their captors as the situation allowed. Joe, for instance, voluntarily learned to bow in a traditional Japanese form of respectful greeting.

After the war, someone in their group received a letter from the commandant of one of the camps saying that he, the commandant, had learned much from the way the internees lived together and with their captors—such things as "fusion of religion into life, courtesy and order, collective life." He was impressed with how "five hundred persons were united together as if they had been members of a family." This commandant was himself imprisoned after the war during which time someone described him as "a kind man, a gentleman." He said in his letter, "If I was so, I am sure it was what I learned from you."[10] A few years later, Win and Joe welcomed this commandant to their home in the United States, and they maintained a friendship to the end of his life.

I never heard Win or Joe use the word *blessed* in connection with their experience. But I have never known two people who better embodied the beatitudes—who mourn the violence of the world, who hunger and thirst for righteousness, who have deep passion for peace. Indeed, they themselves radiated peace. I liked to sit close to them in worship because through the aura of their life, I could feel the realm. I could feel it. Sitting behind them, I want to live more like they do. I want to live in a world in which violence ends and commandants and internees become friends. I want to work for such a world.

As I think about it now, the beatitudes themselves are not the puzzle. The puzzle is why we do not live out of them all the time.

In a few moments we take the bread and the cup. Among the many dimensions of the sacred meal is this one: it is a week-by-week assurance in touch and taste that God is present, seeking to lead the world toward the realm. Come, eat and drink, and feel God say over your life, "Blessed are you."

8

Salt and Light, Salsa and Tortillas

Matthew 5:13-16

LEE C. CAMP

Compositional Comments

The "salt and light" text is, in many ways, a fundamental text for many of the themes articulated by Carter, Hauerwas, Campbell, and Hughes. Shaped more deeply by our Sunday school songs–"This little light of mine, I'm gonna let it shine"–Jesus' admonition regarding salt and light can be quickly reduced to a lesson about the importance of setting a good personal, moral example. But in light of the background studies that cast the Sermon in its historical and sociological context, "salt and light" quickly becomes more an issue of the clash of two (or more) cultures: that is, if the Sermon is a description (as Matthew 4 suggests) of life in the now present and coming *kingdom of heaven* (as opposed to a new personal morality, or set of mental attitudes), then the salt and light text calls us to a mode of cultural transformation quite different from the mode and methods employed by the powers-that-be discussed at length by Carter and Campbell. Moreover, being "salt and light" becomes a bit more edgy, a bit more "sketchy" when we read this text through those stories of Lipscomb and Stringfellow that Hughes recounted.

In that light, I employed first an astute observation by John Yoder, in which he suggests that the varied histories of minority cultures shaping and transforming their host cultures is an important sociological note through which we should read the gospel. And second, my own experience of late in the American South informs the concrete particulars of this sermon.

This sermon was preached at the North Boulevard Church of Christ in Murfreesboro, Tennessee on August 30, 2006.

SERMON

I'm not sure when I first ate chips and salsa, or enchiladas, or chimichangas. It was either my late teens, I suspect, or my early twenties. Much has changed since then. For one, my wife has learned to prepare quite a few Tex-Mex dishes, those exquisite enchiladas with sour cream sauce not being least among them. Beyond our homemade dishes now peppered with black beans and tortillas, *El Palenque* is my favorite weekday lunch spot, and Sunday lunch finds us, more often than not, at our sons' favorite restaurant, *Mazatlan.*

While our children will have no memories of life prior to chips and salsa and queso, I do remember it not being too many years past when the aisles in my neighborhood grocery store began carrying bilingual labels. In fact, my own children attend a "Spanish immersion" elementary school, in which a bulk of their standard curriculum is taught in Spanish. I know little Spanish myself, other than cursory greetings and polite exchanges, how to order my favorite menu items, and how to count to ten. But my six-year-old will have developed basic Spanish literacy by the time he completes fourth grade.

That Hispanic culture has so swept into the southern United States is, of course, an issue of great political significance these days. However, those hotly debated issues argued on the front page of our newspapers do not relate as directly to our text as do salsa, enchiladas, and my children's Spanish elementary school curriculum. In fact, the spread of Hispanic culture in the United States is a classic case study in the way one culture intermingles with and changes its host culture.

This notion that a minority subculture can profoundly shape and reshape its host culture is an important observation about our text. It is very important for you to know that a great litany of theologians and exegetes have found ways to explain away the force and authority of our Lord's Sermon on the Mount. It has been explained away, for example, as a so-called "interim ethic," a reasonable way of life only if one presupposes that Jesus was mistaken in thinking the "end of the world" was to come very soon. If "the end of time" has come, then it's all very fine to love your enemies rather than war against them, because God will sort out the good guys from the bad guys real soon. If the "end of time" is right around the corner, it's all very well not to seek mammon and trust God to provide—it's simply good economic advice, like knowing that you should only buy a four-roll package rather than a twenty-four double roll package of bathroom tissue, if you know the world will end tomorrow.

If the apocalypse is now, then we can put up with being persecuted for a little while, knowing that our persecutors will be burning in hell tomorrow. But, now that we know Jesus and the early church was wrong on the timing, then the Sermon loses its moral force.

Another way of setting aside the Sermon runs like this: Jesus' Sermon on the Mount is not providing an ethic for how we Christians should live out in the "secular world," but only how we should interact with other individuals. The Sermon is not political, or social, but spiritual and individualistic. This is the way the great Protestant Reformer Martin Luther taught us to read the Sermon: Do you want to know what kind of ethic you should have in your job? Well then, don't read the Sermon on the Mount. Instead, read the job manual, and it will tell you what you should do. The Sermon on the Mount, this way of reasoning goes, is not telling us what we should actually *do* (that is, to love our enemies, or trust God to provide, or pray for those who persecute us), but the attitude we should have in our hearts. If you're an executioner, then you have to kill the poor chap, but you can love him in your heart while you're cutting off his head.

There are other ways of setting aside the Sermon—but you get the idea. One of the presuppositions undergirding these sorts of attempts at setting aside the moral authority of the Sermon is that if we really obey, if we really *do* what Jesus teaches us, then we will have no relevance to the real world. If we actually obey Jesus, then we will get run over, be irrelevant, and not be able to change the world for good.

But this is the great irony of the Sermon, and why salsa has anything to do with our text: Jesus is teaching us a *different way* of "making a difference." Jesus is teaching us the way *the church is to make a difference* in the world, not the way the powers make a difference. It's not the way the mighty make a difference. It's not the way the wealthy make a difference. But it is the way of the kingdom of God.

What is most obvious about Hispanic culture and its host "American culture" is the way in which Hispanic culture has so rapidly infiltrated "American culture."[1] That is, not by power, not by might, not by wealth (at least to this point in our history) have salsa, queso, and green chili sauce changed American culture. Hispanics have changed, are changing, American Southern culture with such rapidity simply by coming, and being, and doing. That is, through their labor, their marrying, their cooking, they are changing the South.

Hispanics in contemporary America—most often laborers, most often low-income, too often the butt of jokes—are much closer to the sociological status of those whom Jesus addressed on the mountain than are we white children of privilege. Indeed, much recent biblical scholarship increasingly points out that most of the hearers addressed by Jesus and the early church were very aware of their status as subjects under empire. Those blessed ones who mourned the injustice and oppression of human history; those blessed hearers who were meek in the face of imperialistic might and pretense; those blessed peasants who desired above all the reign of God's righteousness to overcome the arrogant purveyors of the right made right only by might–all these were keenly aware of the forces of empire that bore down upon their lives, that bore down upon the lives of their neighbors and children and kith and kin.

Yet the powers-that-be try to convince us that simply being the kind of people Jesus calls us to be–chaste, truthful, peacemakers, lovers of enemies, seekers of justice and righteousness first and foremost–that this kind of people does not give us much. At best, they are dangerous because they refuse to support the powers. At worst, such folk are depicted as parasites, living off of blessings and wealth and rights that come not by meekness or mercy or service, but through power and wealth and the sword. This was one of the characteristics of the early church that provoked great hostility: that the early Christians would not try to employ or support or prop-up the powers of the empire to "bring about good," but instead believed that their most important task was to be the church. Such a vantage provoked such hostility that Celsus, a second century pagan critic of the church, insisted that such a stance was unbelievably arrogant. Christians thus reminded him of maggots in a dunghill saying, "Look at us! Look at us! God has revealed all things to us!"

Jesus was no utopian idealist; he knew quite well that proclaiming and living according to the reign of God means trouble. Thus immediately prior to the "salt and light" sayings, Matthew places the beatitude for the persecuted. To live according to the kingdom will cost us something, and often that cost will come as some folks think of us as fools.

Little has changed since the time of Celsus, except a whole lot–that is, the critique is the same, but it is now the Christians who speak the words of the pagan. That is, many Christians–white, American, privileged Christians–believe that it is not through being salt and light, but through being powerful and mighty, that Christians are supposed to "change the world." Thus a popular southern senator, who publicly professes his Christian faith, recently proclaimed:

It has been said so truthfully that it is the soldier, not the reporter, who has given us the freedom of the press. It is the soldier, not the poet, who has given us freedom of speech. It is the soldier, not the agitator, who has given us the freedom to protest. It is the soldier who salutes the flag, serves beneath the flag, whose coffin is draped by the flag, who gives that protester the freedom he abuses to burn that flag.[2]

For the minions of the powers, all good ultimately comes from those who wield force and might. Jesus had the audacity to address this paltry band of followers, this paltry band of poor, oppressed people, and suggest that *they* were the "salt of the earth," the "light of the world." Note that Jesus does not tell them to "be salt" or "be light," but that they *are salt,* they *are light*: these ones who follow him, his disciples, they are salt and light. When Jesus called the disciples "salt," they would have been well aware of the multiple and necessary purposes of salt: a preservative, a cleansing agent, a seasoning for bland food. Salt was indispensable in their daily lives. Thus, Jesus in effect says that disciples of Jesus—those who embody the kind of life depicted in the Sermon—are to the world what salt is to life.

As Gerhard Lohfink says, "The radiant city on the hill is a symbol for the church as a contrast-society, which precisely as *contrast-society* transforms the world. If the church loses is contrast character, if its salt becomes flat and its light is gently extinguished . . . it loses its meaning."[3] The way we make a difference is by being and doing what we do, those ways of life to which Jesus calls us. This is not, as some theologians tell us, a way of life that is irrelevant to the way the world works; this is not a withdrawal strategy; this is not trying to keep our own little hands clean so we can observe our religious scruples. Instead, this is precisely about embodying the kingdom that Jesus proclaimed in the gospel.[4]

Another presupposition undergirding the explaining away of the Sermon lies, it seems to me, in fear. Indeed, to live the way of the Sermon requires the practice of trust—and thus the Sermon at length treats the issue of fear, anxiety, and worry. To mess with the way of the powers, to suggest that our task is steadfast, obedient discipleship, this may indeed arouse suspicion and quiet dismissal. Anticipating our fear, the Sermon reminds us, "Do not worry." Indeed, a recurring refrain throughout scripture is simply this: "Do not be afraid."

Still, to make even feeble steps toward living in the world imagined in the Sermon on the Mount is frightening to us, for the Sermon on the Mount does not envision a utopia, in which all are living according to the reign of God. Quite to the contrary, the Sermon envisions a world in which there is "the world," and there is the church. The church is called to live according to the Lord's teachings. It is precisely this vision that gives rise to the teaching about persecution.

In other words, the fear that often arises in response to the Sermon is this: if we do what Jesus commands, we will get walked all over, stomped on, thrown out, cast out as fools. Here lies again a great irony: Jesus casts precisely *this* judgment on those who fail to be the salt and light they are called to be. That is, we *will be walked over,* or *cast out,* or *trodden under the foot of man,* or be *fools*—not by living according to the vision of the Sermon, but by *failing* to live according to that vision.[5]

Thus here near the beginning of the Sermon stands both the calling and the warning: the calling to be God's salt and light in a world so desperately in need; and— with the calling—the warning that if you refuse your vocation, then you *will be* cast out, useless, insipid, to be thrown out and walked on. Of course, the Sermon ends with this same warning. Will we obey, and build our house upon the rock? Or disobey, and build our house upon the sand, a structure sure to fall, and be demolished?

9

Fulfilling the Law

Matthew 5:17–20

JOHN SIBURT

Compositional Comments

Warren Carter asserts that Matthew's Sermon on the Mount "sets about enabling disciples to envision life shaped by God's empire" and "to imagine life created by God's saving presence." This sermon seeks to perform such world construction by employing Charles Campbell's image of the jester. According to Campbell, the jester used comical antics "to startle and dislocate people so that they, too, might be released from their commonsense presuppositions and live in the world in new and creative ways." Campbell identifies ways that Jesus played the role of jester and used folly to subvert the presuppositions and myths that constituted the worldview of his hearers.

This Sermon employs the jester's use of folly to offer hearers a fundamentally different world than the one they are used to inhabiting. The Sermon playfully debunks common suppositions regarding God's law and relocates hearers into a world in which God's law is a gift of grace. The playful tone of the Sermon allows for some prophetic lampooning of the contemporary church as well. The playfulness of the Sermon is most fully experienced when heard orally, but it is still detectable in the written manuscript.

I preached this sermon on the first anniversary of Hurricane Katrina as the guest preacher for another congregation's Wednesday night summer series. I incorporated the memory of Katrina into the sermon manuscript because I believe it puts flesh on the sermon. The church hearing this sermon was very active in Katrina relief and has continued to develop a more socially active ministry focus since the tragedy. Thus, I chose to include Katrina in the sermon as both a symbol of the chaos that comes from life as ordered by the powers and as an image of hope for disciples of Christ wanting to see how God's empire imagined becomes God's empire embodied.

SERMON

It weighs 5,280 pounds. It weighs roughly 500 pounds per commandment. I am talking about the monument of the Ten Commandments that Judge Roy Moore fought unsuccessfully to keep from being removed from the courthouse of the Alabama Supreme Court. Judge Moore now hauls the monument around the country on the back of a flatbed truck making appearances. I cannot think of a more fitting metaphor for how the church views the Old Testament law: a heavy burden that no longer governs God's people, but serves as a great exhibition piece for remembering days gone by.

The Law of Moses, or Torah, conjures up memories of a Santa-like God who used to point a finger at us and say, "You better not kill, you better not steal, your better not covet; I am telling you why." When God came to town, he made a list and checked it twice. Anyone seen to be less than perfectly obedient to the law was found to be naughty instead of nice. Thankfully, Jesus finally came to town, too, and removed the burden of the law once and for all. To be honest, 5,280 pounds looks a lot better on the back of a flatbed truck than on the backs of the people of God.

At least that is the story as I heard it growing up in a faith tradition focused on restoring "New Testament Christianity." But something tells me that my tradition was not the only one that thought God nailed the law to the cross along with sin and death. I have met Christians from other faith traditions whose Bibles were divided into "Old" and "New" Testaments. I have encountered other Christians who were taught by the church that "law" was a four-letter word. The myth that Jesus came to abolish the Law of Moses is a prevalent storyline defining the life of the contemporary church.

The problem is that this myth is not true. It does not faithfully articulate the mission and message of Jesus Christ. The longer it remains our dominate storyline, the longer the church will remain disconnected from the inbreaking of God's reign in the world. Matthew understands this, and so he invites us to imagine a new world. In Matthew's world, Jesus comes not to abolish the law, but to fulfill it. Jesus says so in Matthew's Sermon on the Mount:

Do not think that I have come to abolish the law or the prophets; I have come not to abolish but to fulfill. For truly I tell you, until heaven and earth pass away, not one letter, not one stroke of a letter, will pass from the law until all is accomplished. Therefore, whoever breaks one of the least of these commandments, and teaches others to do the same, will be called least in the kingdom of heaven; but whoever does them and teaches them will be called great in the kingdom of heaven. For I tell you, unless your righteousness exceeds that of the scribes and Pharisees, you will never enter the kingdom of heaven. (Mt. 5:17–20)

In our world, such a proclamation sounds like pure legalism. Making sure not one stroke of a letter passes away? Not breaking even one of the least of the commandments? Exceeding the Pharisees? But this is Matthew's world, not ours. In Matthew's world God's law is not a heavy burden but a gift of grace. Matthew's world does not separate an "Old" Testament from a "New" Testament. Matthew's world has only the word of God promised and the word of God fulfilled.

For Matthew, the word of God fulfilled is Jesus Christ. He will enact the promises of God. He will confirm the intentions of God. He will fulfill the law of God. But he will not do it without a fight. At each step of the way Jesus is opposed by religious people who choose to live according to a different understanding of God's law.

Take a trip with me through Matthew's world and visit a few of the spots where Jesus reinterprets the law in the face of opposition. At our first stop Jesus and his disciples are criticized for eating with tax collectors and sinners. Jesus responds, "Go and learn what this means, 'I desire mercy, not sacrifice'" (Mt. 9:13). He repeats this charge when criticized for healing a man with a withered hand and allowing his disciples to pick grain on the Sabbath (Mt. 12:7).

A little further down the road Jesus encounters a man who asks him, "Teacher, what good deed must I do to have eternal life?" Jesus responds, "Why do you ask me about what is good? There is only one who is good. If you wish to enter into life, keep the commandments." When the man wants even more instruction, Jesus invites him to sell all of his possessions and follow him (Mt. 19:16–21). Later, Jesus is challenged, "Teacher, which commandment in the law is the greatest?" (Mt. 22:36). He responds, "'You shall love the Lord your God with all your heart, and with all your soul, and with all your mind.' This is the greatest and first commandment. And a second is like it: 'You shall love your neighbor as yourself.' On these two commandments hang all the law and the prophets" (Mt. 22:37–40).

Even further down the road, Jesus criticizes some for neglecting the weightier matters of the law. He says, "Woe to you, scribes and Pharisees, hypocrites! For you tithe mint, dill, and cummin, and have neglected the weightier matters of the law: justice and mercy and faith. It is these you ought to have practiced without neglecting the others. You blind guides! You strain out a gnat but swallow a camel!" (Mt. 23:23–24).

While we could visit other destinations in Matthew's world, we have traveled enough to gain a new perspective about God's law. We have encountered a world in which God's law is more about mercy than sacrifice. A world in which God's law *is* a four-letter word: L-O-V-E. A universe in which God's law serves the interest of justice, mercy, and faith. We have discovered a world in which real life is experienced in righteous adherence to the ways of God.

This new world offers much to admire. In fact, some things here we might want to take home with us. We better stop by Matthew's gift shop on our way home. Perhaps you would like an "I Desire Mercy, Not Sacrifice" coffee mug? Maybe an "I Have Come Not to Abolish the Law, But to Fulfill It" T-shirt? Or perhaps a postcard portraying the nearness of God's kingdom? Some kind of keepsake that can remind us of what we have seen and heard while traveling through Matthew's world. But Matthew says, "Sorry. I don't run that kind of gift shop." Sure enough, we do not see any T-shirts, coffee mugs, or postcards. Neither do we find 5280-pound stone renditions of the law.

What we find in Matthew's gift shop is a sermon, the Sermon on the Mount. It is a gift of imagination, not in the sense of reality-denying fantasy, but in the sense of envisioning the world as God intends for it to be. It is also a gift of embodiment providing the community of faith with tangible, flesh-and-blood ways of putting God's vision for the world into practice. It is a gift from the mouth of Jesus Christ, the Son of God, who has come not to abolish God's law but to fulfill it through a community that seeks first the kingdom of God and God's righteousness.

It strikes us that Matthew's gift is a timely offering for an American church that already has quite an impressive collection of T-shirts and coffee mugs, but is in desperate need of both imagination and embodiment. We learned that lesson one year ago as Hurricane Katrina ravaged the Gulf Coast. Katrina revealed some painful truths about our society and about the church's role in it. Katrina forced Americans to face the racism that still informs the geography of most of our cities. We were forced to admit that our cities are divided into rich and poor, black and white, haves and have-nots. And so are our churches.

Katrina awakened Americans to the immense poverty present in our cities, and the American church to its own laryngitis regarding it. We face the painful truth that the American church is so accustomed to the status quo we no longer have a vision for what God might intend for our cities. We have stopped imagining the world of Matthew's Sermon on the Mount in which the poor in spirit, the mournful, meek, those starving to be righteous, the merciful, pure in heart, peacemakers, and persecuted are called blessed. We have stopped embodying God's vision of justice, mercy, and faith. Instead, we have set our sights on achieving the American dream.

Still, by the grace of God, whatever the church lost in pursuit of the American dream it may have found again in the midst of an American nightmare. Amid the wind and waves of Katrina, the church recovered its imagination and began to envision a world in which God's law was not abolished but was fulfilled. The church discovered embodiment again by loving neighbors, feeding the hungry, getting the thirsty a drink, welcoming the stranger, clothing the naked, and visiting the sick. With no time to swat at religious flies like worship preference, doctrinal nuance, or denominational hot buttons, the church jumped into the weightier matters of God's law: justice, mercy, and faith.

At a time when the leaders of the American empire seemed embarrassingly powerless, the ordinary citizens of God's empire lived into Jesus' call to be salt and light in the world. We had no time to worry about what tomorrow might bring. The people of God simply put their trust in God to provide for them as they provided for others. For a moment the world caught a glimpse of the kingdom come and God's will done on earth as it is in heaven.

I am catching such a glimpse looking at you tonight. I can tell just by looking at you that some of you have visited Matthew's world before. Some of you have already brought the Sermon on the Mount home with you. It is already gifting you with imagination and embodiment. You exhibit all the signs of being a church, a people gathered by Christ to join Christ in inaugurating his kingdom in the world.

So tonight, let us put Judge Moore's monument in storage, for God's law is not a heavy monument; it is an easy yoke. Let us dispel the myth of God as bad Santa. Tell the children God as Santa really does not exist. Tonight, let us receive Matthew's gift, this Sermon on the Mount; and let us join together in imagination and embodiment until God's kingdom comes and God's will is done on earth as it is in heaven.

The Power of Anger in an Imperialist America

Matthew 5:21–26

KENNETH R. GREENE

Compositional Comments

Based on Charles Campbell's view that anger has two distinctive characteristics,[1] this sermon was delivered to the Metro Church in Dallas, Texas, in September, 2006. First, anger is intimately related to love. Anger is not a deadly sin. Anger is not the opposite of love. Anger is better understood as a feeling that signals that all is not well in our world around us. Anger is a mode of connectedness to others, and it is always a vivid form of caring. The church, just like the God it serves, regularly becomes angry over the injustices in the world. The church becomes angry at the powers that oppress marginalized human beings and becomes an expression of that love, just like the God whom it serves.

Second, anger can be directed at "the principalities and powers" rather than at individuals. Anger is a critical virtue for resistance; it is a sign of resistance in ourselves to the moral quality of social relations in which we are immersed. In the face of the 'principalities and powers,"the fundamental ethical task of this sermon involves building up the church as a *community of resistance.*

I believe that modern pulpits that turn to human experience have written Jesus Christ out of the sermon. This kind of preaching has become captive to world and culture. Postliberal homiletics raises important cautions for a pulpit that has grown too cozy with culture. Yet it would be foolish for the church to assume that it is now time to renounce our commitment to the world.

The Sermon on the Mount is heard in the context of "principalities and powers," and only by confronting the spirituality of an institution and its physical manifestations can the total structure be transformed.

SERMON

"Principalities and powers" are everywhere around us; their presence is inescapable. Matthew's Sermon on the Mount challenges Christians to unmask these "principalities and powers" and call them to justice. But Matthew's Sermon on the Mount teaches that this can scarcely be accomplished by individuals; a group is needed—what Jesus calls an *ekklesia* (assembly) in Matthew 16:13, an assembly that exists specifically for the task of calling these "principalities and powers" to divine justice and righteousness. That is the church's task, "so that through the church [in Greek, *ekklesia*] the wisdom of God in its rich variety might now be made known to the rulers and authorities [or "principalities and powers"] in the heavenly places" (Eph. 3:10). In this new community, reconciliation takes priority over vengeance (Mt. 5:21–26), and Jesus subverts the "principalities and powers."

"Principalities and powers" ignore God's humanizing purposes and speak rather of oppression. The church's task is to remind "principalities and powers" that as creatures of God our divine vocation is the achievement of human well-being (Mt. 5–7; Col. 1:20). They do not exist for themselves; they belong to the God who ordains sufficiency for all.

Anger in Matthew

What did Malcolm X mean when he said, "by any means necessary?" He didn't mean that we initiate violence, just go out and beat up somebody. He meant that when someone bombs your house, you have a *right* to retaliate. He did not mean to turn the other cheek to violence. He meant for us to practice "self-defense."

Christian leaders can call for calm and nonviolence, but it will be a vain appeal. When justice fails, anger is the only, and inevitable, recourse of the disenfranchised. Anger marks an end to the numbness—the demoralization—the powers seek to instill in people. It signals a stirring of the moral sense that the powers want to extinguish to maintain their domination. Such anger is a signal that change is called for, that transformation is required. No wonder the powers seek to make human beings numb! Once anger arises, the powers begin to lose their grip; their deadly ways have been discerned, and human resistance has begun.

Preaching that seeks to resist the "principalities and powers," will be empowered by the virtue of anger.[2] The L.A. riots were a response to the jury's incredible acquittal of those who beat Rodney King, which was the last straw in five and a half centuries of obscene inhumanity. The riots that shocked America were an inevitable response to a nation's history of judicial injustice. The spiral continues in the absence of fundamental change. Any fundamental long-term change will have to result in political and economic empowerment for the powerless in the community. Without power there will be no solution, without strength there will be no justice, and without justice there will be no peace.

Rap Singers

Rap singers saw their neighborhoods devastated long before the Los Angeles uprising. The riots' devastation continued the destruction. Surely, it is important for rap singers to creatively express what happens to people who have to deal with such assault. Their courage and commitment can be supported and expanded in a message of empowerment. The message in the song "Cop-Killer," for example, is not nearly as threatening as its message of personal and community empowerment.

"COP KILLER! Yeah!...This s***'s been too long...but tonight we get even... Die, Die, Die Pig, Die!" So go some of the lyrics to "Cop Killer" by the rapper Ice-T on the album *Body Count,* which was released by Warner Bros. Records, part of the Time Warner media and entertainment conglomerate, in 1992.

The album was by a rap and heavy metal band named Body Count, which Ice-T had been fronting. They had been playing a version of it in concert for a year, including it as part of the 1991 Lollapalooza tour. The recorded version includes references to Rodney King, a black motorist whose beating by Los Angeles Police Department officers had been caught on videotape. Shortly after the record came out, a suburban jury acquitted the officers, and riots broke out in South Central LA. Soon after that outbreak, a Dallas police group called for a boycott of the Ice-T record. Said Ice-T, who actually played a cop in the 1991 movie *New Jack City* and now plays a detective on *Law and Order: SVU,* "I'm singing in the first person as a character that is fed up with police brutality. I ain't never killed no cop. I felt like it a lot of times. But I never did it."[3]

The potential for that expression is the real fear of the "principalities and powers." The police who represent the establishment on the front line are mobilized. You heard their public relations message. They maximize their impact by taking the message out of context, boycotting everything associated with it, and personalizing it. Remember, the message of "Cop Killer" is not the real threat, but it can more easily be manipulated. The real threat is what happens if this message should evolve into more wholesome and powerful liberation.

At this point, "Cop-Killer" captures the language and frustration of an occupied community of the oppressed. It reflects rage and disengagement from the rules of the system. This is preliminary to a broader movement toward liberation and empowerment. The tendency to prematurely negate anger makes it harder to dissect the issue of violence in America. The analysis remains biased against the victims of violence. The perpetrators of violence in America are the American establishment. The cop-killers in reality are not the community of the oppressed who kill police. The cop-killers are the cops who kill people in the oppressed community.

Jesus teaches that we stop the violence by facing this reality and correcting it (Mt. 5:21–26). We stop the violence by looking beyond the police frontline in the community to the controlling sources of power. Violence is not power. Anger is often directed at the individual self or the community self, instead of the "principalities and powers," the establishment. This misdirected focus makes it harder to challenge the wrong or the racism, because the problem is erroneously placed. When Los Angeles burned, the problem quickly returned to the victims. Condemning the riots was easier than condemning national policies of racial abuse. Recognizing true power and accepting the responsibility that goes with it subordinates violence to its appropriate role and place in God's kingdom.

Liberal-thinking Christians blame the establishment for creating a dysfunctional community. Their energy is focused on correcting the actions of the power structures, such as securing more money to restore the riot-torn areas. Conservative thinking Christians blame the victims for their inadequacies, focusing energy on correcting the actions of the victims, such as teaching more law-abiding behavior. Both orientations are limited and can delay liberation for the oppressed. Jesus shows that neither adequately challenges the very existence of the oppressed condition. This blame of liberal and conservative is almost always a remnant of damage caused by racist oppression. It reflects a self-defeating damage by restricting strategy.

Reconciliation

Because any form of oppression is a sin, it is a moral and spiritual issue; only the supernatural love of God can change our hearts in a lasting way and replace hatred and indifference with love and active compassion. Only the church can bring people together. Of all people, Christians should be the most active in reaching out to the oppressed, instead of accepting the status quo of division and animosity. Systems of injustice in society and in the church exact a heavy cost on those outside the centers of power and effectively block reconciliation. Declaring that we are equal without repairing the wrongs of the past is cheap reconciliation.[4] Reconciliation is not just about the change of individual hearts as much as it is dealing with the "principalities and powers" that are devastating people of all races.

Jesus teaches us that the gospel at once works with the individual and the individual's society: to change one, we of necessity must change the other. Jesus teaches us that sin is not limited to individuals. Jesus teaches us that poor relationships are the result of social structures, such as laws, the ways institutions operate, and forms of segregation.

Riots result from such a limited impetus. This in no way acknowledges that the people needing help have been prevented from becoming productive by identifiable barriers. At some point, the emphasis has got to be on removing the barriers of discrimination, drugs, crime, poor education, and the other social scars, which are inflicted by establishment "principalities and powers."

Conclusion

"A riot is the language of the unheard," said Dr. Martin Luther King, Jr. Violence already exists.[5] Christians do not decide between violence and nonviolence, evil and good. They decide between the lesser and the greater evil. They must ponder whether revolutionary violence is less or more deplorable than the violence perpetuated by the "principalities and powers." No absolute rules can decide the answer with certainty. Christians must make a choice.[6]

Matthew's Sermon on the Mount is not a message about the salvation of individuals from the world, but news about a world transfigured, right down to its basic structures—its basic structures being "principalities and powers," which are in fact the actual spirituality at the center of the political, economic, and cultural institutions of the day. These disciples understood that these demons, these spiritual forces of evil, emanated from actual institutions; and that demons could have no impact on them unless they were able to embody themselves in people or political systems.[7]

Matthew's Sermon on the Mount must be preached in the context of "principalities and powers," and only by *confronting* the spirituality of an institution and its physical manifestations can the total structure be transformed. The Christian story of the cross, as Saint Paul tells it, is about the defeat of the "principalities," the "powers," and "the rulers of the darkness of this world." God has not demonstrated nonresistance toward the antihuman powers of disintegration: *God has destroyed them.*

For Saint Paul, victory has been won, and this victory defines the good news as the victory over death, not death's veneration or its masochistic embrace.

Many may disagree with my belief about nonviolence, but the strategy of nonviolence is worn out. It has not brought significant benefits to an oppressed people since its heyday in the 1960s. Even at that time, it was not the only strategy of the civil rights movement. People have forgotten that Dr. King's methods would not have been as effective were it not for the threat of violence articulated by leaders such as Malcolm X. Malcolm's insistence that African Americans respect themselves and stand up against injustice seems especially relevant today. It is not a question of choosing between violence and nonviolence. It is a matter of realizing that if we hope to achieve real progress, we cannot have too much of one strategy without the other.

Just as anger maintains the imbalanced distribution of wealth, so anger is needed to institute change. After decades of persistent agitation against repression, it is evident that economic change for the masses will come no other way. Until the "principalities and powers" are confronted, violence, doublespeak, and repression will continue. Police beatings and judicial injustice will persist as solutions are explored within a framework constructed and maintained by the perpetrators of the problems.

Matthew's Sermon on the Mount places the church in an uncomfortable position. It separates those who have ignored community pain from those who have confronted it. It is important for all Christian churches to play their roles in leading the way to the peace and freedom that they teach.

Christians struggling for the liberation of the oppressed must determine their own means of resistance, and anger remains a live option. Knowing God means being on the side of the oppressed, becoming one with them, and participating in the goal of justice. This concern with human freedom from "principalities and powers" must become the central premise of Christian preaching and living. The church must take part in this mission and once again become God's tool for freedom and justice.

11

Heads without Eyes and Arms without Hands

Matthew 5:27–30

CHARME ROBARTS

Compositional Comments

After months of agonizing on where to land the plane in the vast field of possibilities for this sermon, I settled on two issues: (1) the problem of women being held solely responsible for male sexual behavior, an attitude which is insulting to both men and women; and (2) the relationship of lust and power and the attendant communal problems and limitations we perpetuate when people objectify each other. Especially for the sake of the young people who are just beginning the journey of managing their sexual appetites, I gave a small amount of attention to defining the word *lust* as I understand it. I decided to leave off discussions of modest dress and the fashion industry that sexualizes clothing for both men and women, and I chose not to address the growing problem of pornography. Though obviously related, I had to land the plane.

In the face of this convicting text about sexual lust, the encouragement of Warren Carter and Stanley Hauerwas to consider the Sermon on the Mount contextually helps me. Hauerwas notes that the Sermon presupposes a community that Christ came to establish. Carter encourages us to remember the one who spoke the words—introduced to us in chapters 1–4 of Matthew as Immanuel, God with us. Both these points shape the sermon, each giving hope and providing impetus for staying the course of purity. The one who saves us from our sins and who is with us bears us up in our weakness and sets our feet on new paths again and again. The community Jesus envisioned is learning to embody values that are different from the structures of power and oppression that are part and parcel of the problem of lust. So the goal of this sermon is to imagine a community that understands itself as "God's good creation," as Hauerwas says. That community is an alternative to the one that limits intimacy by celebrating lust and gratification as a means to finding it.

SERMON

I don't think he meant to say it, but it is what he said. Speaking to a room full of uncharacteristically attentive teens about a subject that is never far from their minds, the dynamic speaker drove his point home holding aloft copy after copy of *Cosmo* and other magazines. Long lean legs and perky breasts emerged from the pages while the preacher pronounced, "This is Satan."

Painfully aware as I am that preachers and teachers often misspeak, I still recoiled at the implication that it is the women who are Satan's emissaries. My twenty-eight-year-old daughter, who is a middle school teacher in the public schools here in the metroplex, was a sponsor for the event. She expressed her anxiety about the subliminal message the youth group would hear. It seems that bottom line is, the girls have to control this thing, and the beauty of their bodies is a problem. Girls are seductresses, toppling society.

I recall the terrible story of Rabbi Jose whose beautiful daughter was the object of a neighbor's attention. Upon learning that the neighbor had bored a hole in the fence so he could catch a glimpse of her, the rabbi turned on his daughter and said, "You are a trouble to mankind, return to dust so that no man may sin because of you."

Our text today, Matthew 5:27–30, has a different perspective. You are familiar with this difficult passage.

> You have heard that it was said, "Do not commit adultery." But I tell you that anyone who looks at a woman lustfully has already committed adultery with her in his heart. If your right eye causes you to sin, gouge it out and throw it away. It is better for you to lose one part of your body than for your whole body to be thrown into hell. And if your right hand causes you to sin, cut it off and throw it away. It is better for you to lose one part of your body than for your whole body to go into hell. (NIV)

It is hard to overlook that Jesus addressed his words to men. Here women are not characterized as Satan. And men are not imagined as being unable to control themselves. While the violent language of cutting off hands and gouging out eyes says this is serious business, isn't it possible that Jesus offered this extreme solution in response to the ludicrous claim some might offer that says, "I just can't help myself, she looks so fine"?

But we find ourselves troubled trying to define terms. What is lust? I recall sermons and bulletin articles from my youth that said something like, "It's not the first look that gets you or maybe even the second; it's that third look that convicts." Somehow this sounds as simplistic as the sermons preached about "mixed bathing." And those were preached mostly to church-goers who lived further away from the beach than my Florida relatives.

This aphorism about looking that third time is an effort to distinguish between the good part of our sexuality that draws men and women to each other in a unique and wonderful way, and the disordered sexual attraction that sees persons as simply physical objects to be used for one's own pleasure. Such a reductionist view of bodies ignores the whole person who has been created for relationships within a community. This disorderly looking is lust. Lustful looking is looking with an intention to act. And it can occur regardless of what people are wearing or not wearing.

Jesus addressed his words to men because they held the social, religious, and political power of their communities. Literature from that time period reveals statements such as, "Though the woman is subject to the commandments, she is disqualified from giving evidence," and, "Better is the wickedness of a man than a woman who does good." In a world like this women can too easily be objectified, abused, and then blamed for the violence.

To his followers, Jesus said, "That is not the way it is to be among you." Among Jesus followers, a higher standard rules how men are to regard women. They are neither husband's property, so that if taken by another man, the offense is really against the husband; nor are they objects, ornaments only for the pleasure of the eye and the flesh. The world may have changed a good bit since that time, but unfortunately we still find ourselves under the leaky canopy of a worldview that blames women for lust and rape and that suggests in some places that women taking public roles in church assemblies might be "distracting" to men.

We are not created men and women only for sexual purposes. We are created men and women—each as expressions of the image of God. Neither one is to be objectified, and each one should be concerned about their own and the other's moral responsibility to God and the community. Each one is responsible to protect the dignity and well-being of the other. And each one has much more to offer than sexual gratification. Reducing others to objects for our pleasure fails to see others as whole people, and the Sermon on the Mount envisions a community moving in a different direction. The axiom, "Isn't life more important than food and the body more than clothes?" can be restated, "Isn't the body about more than sex?"

But perhaps something else is going on in Jesus' bold words. The setting for our text is Matthew's Sermon on the Mount. Matthew includes a number of statements that reveal quite a bit of tension between Jesus and the religious leaders. In fact, today's text is one of six statements in the Sermon that begin with, "You have heard that it was said." The people were used to hearing what the religious leaders said about the law. Jesus told those listening that their righteousness should exceed that of the teachers of the law. Earlier in the gospel, Matthew tells us that John insisted that the religious leaders' lives did not demonstrate righteousness, and at the end of the Sermon Matthew adds that the hearers were amazed because Jesus spoke with an authority that was missing in their teachers of the law.

So perhaps those religious leaders who took pride in their piety and in the fact that they had never actually had another woman in their bed were shocked to learn that Jesus said they were actually no better than the ordinary folk, since he said lusting after a woman is adultery of the heart. Jesus had a way of leveling the playing field. In the world Jesus imagined, legalism isn't enough. Disobedience starts in the heart, and Jesus calls out the heart for examination.

The Sermon on the Mount envisions a world of loving and not hating, of mercy and justice and not oppression, and of real, not pretentious, devotion to God. In this world a person's sexual attractions are not allowed to go unchecked, and blaming another for one's own misconduct is not permitted. What a world Jesus imagines!

Jesus addresses his words to men because of the way power was structured in that society, but since our culture permits more choice and freedom to women than could have been imagined in that day, in this day the words speak to both men and women.

A few months ago the *Dallas Morning News* reported a story of a female teacher having sex with a high school student. Sadly, this is not the first time we've heard of such things. In recent weeks we've been barraged with reports too familiar: sex scandals in Washington. The relationship between lust, sex, and power are undeniable, reminding us again of a definition of terms. Lust is not sexual attraction; it is a disordered understanding of one's self and others. Lust forgets personhood and focuses only on self-gratification. Since lust is a powerful emotion focused on one's own desires and not on the well-being of the other, it has no place in the kingdom of God. We are not a community in which people are available to us for the taking—such a community is tragic indeed and only breeds distrust, jealousy, and heartache that even the most calloused could not survive unscathed.

Jesus calls for sexual restraint of the eyes and of the heart so that the whole body can escape the kind of hell in which people are only objects to be used but not honored, to be taken without commitment, or to be experiments in a quest for fulfillment. When sexual desire is unchecked, people are diminished; and the possibilities for true intimacy and community are limited. In an early episode of the popular TV show *Lost,* the sexy bad guy Sawyer's deep need for community and forgiveness for a past that haunts him was unfulfilled by his sexual objectification of Kate, one of the characters who might offer a redemptive relationship to him. His lusty innuendos drove her away in the early episodes, an unfortunate loss for a man with no friends in the first place. In the church we can extend and receive true community by resisting the order of this world that says we should try to fix our needs for intimacy by lust and casual sex instead of through the hard work of disciplined affection for each that is based on honoring God and each other.

This is a hard teaching for the world we live in. We are tested at every turn. Young people and adults face the constant barrage of messages that say sex is the main thing. Healthy enjoyment of sexuality is threatened by our own insatiability and tendencies toward excess. With so many images and voices bidding for our souls, we may find ourselves anxious, exhausted, and downright incredulous that Jesus would even suggest such a strict view of things. Perhaps we too had hoped it is enough to stay in our own beds.

The harsh images of cutting off hands and gouging out eyes and whole bodies cast into hell remind us that lust and adultery lead us away from the wholeness we've been invited to in the kingdom of God. But those images call us to take care of our hearts in which the problems of lust reside. We need new hearts that imagine and embody kingdom living.

In God's kingdom people relate to each other as whole beings, not just as temporary fixes for untamed desires. In God's kingdom, sex is only a part of the joy of our lives. It has it's own place within the bounds of marriage—and we are not incapable of controlling our desires for sex. In God's kingdom where sex and sexual desire are not the defining metaphor of life, men and women participate together in God's good order, creating a community of mutual respect and partnership in the work of the kingdom.

As Christians, we probably have to accept our limited influence on the sexual behaviors of people outside the church. But we can cultivate our own hearts so that we can model relationships of love and respect in our marriages and our friendships. We can demonstrate that God does not require that we completely stifle our sexuality, but that we live joyfully together, celebrating the fullness of both genders as we work and serve together.

If we dare to live in the world imagined in the Sermon on the Mount, we will do so in the fellowship of the One who originally preached the words. We have not been called to discipleship by one who pushes back and says, "I hope you make it." No, we are called by the one whose name is Immanuel, God with us. Our eyes and hands and hearts are given over to him. We are not dominated by our desires. We can enter into life with our whole bodies and souls.

On the Road with Jesus

Marriage, Divorce, and Trouble in the Sermon on the Mount
Matthew 5:31-32

DAVID FLEER

Compositional Comments

The following sermon was preached before the Westside Church of Christ in Windsor, Ontario, October 2006. I am grateful to several colleagues for their careful reading and insightful suggestions toward improvement, especially Bob Reid, Allen Burris, Jeff Christian, Chase Pratt, Craig Bowman, John Siburt, and Mae Fleer.

I have decided to retain some of the oralisms present in the original in an effort to reflect the rich insights in Dennis Dewey's provocative chapter. This sermon, like other sermons I have preached since experiencing Dewey's stunning performance of the Sermon on the Mount, has been deeply impacted by "learning the text by heart."

In preparation for this sermon, I was especially haunted by Richard Hughes' thesis that the world Jesus imagines is far different from the gospel according to America. The sermon's orienting paragraph and especially its depiction of an empire that *expects* anger to accelerate into violence and *trains* citizens to love the people who love them and hate their enemies are inspired by Hughes' sharp distinctions.

In looking over the sermon's manuscript, one reader said that he wished for something more substantively expositional and clarifying about Jesus' call to a moral center. As with the original manuscript, so with the following sermon, I have decided not to be so direct and, instead, retain a voice that invites the congregation to continue the conversation on a matter of great importance.

A comment on the sermon's contrast between Jesus and Moses is in order. Our pragmatic American vantage makes the word of God in Deuteronomy *appear* more appealing and palatable than Jesus' gospel. Deuteronomy, of course, intends to *protect* the community's marginalized. In contrast, America's privatized reading of scripture tends to focus on personal protection without regard for others who are hurt. Jesus assumes the more difficult way, which was and still is in Torah. I thank Craig Bowman for his clear insight.

Finally, I am unaware of the source for the image of staying on the road with Jesus, but considering that I read an early draft of John Siburt's exceptional sermon before crafting my own, I may owe the image to John. May God grant me courage to live out more of his—and other preachers' in this volume—substantive oratory.

SERMON

Recently, I've been trying to catch up on my reading. So many Christian best sellers to choose from: *Gospel According to the Simpsons, Gospel According to Harry Potter, Gospel According to the Beatles,* and the most recent of these insightful volumes, *Gospel According to America.* A strong current is pulling the church into the mainstream of popular culture.

That makes this morning's text especially difficult. It's from *The Gospel According to Matthew,* and "The Sermon on the Mount." In fact, this text is so difficult I'm tempted to read it as quickly as possible so I can get on with the explanations. It's one of those texts that doesn't travel well alone, doesn't dress up nicely as refrigerator art, not a top ten favorite in any church poll. No one is composing a contemporary Christian song from this passage: "You have heard it said, 'Whoever divorces his wife, let him give her a certificate of dismissal.' But, I say to you that everyone who divorces his wife, except for the cause of unchastity, makes her commit adultery and whoever marries a divorced woman, commits adultery" (NASB).

This gives us reason to ask the obvious question,..."What?"

The Old Testament said, "Divorce? Yes we understand. There are those matters of indecency. Fine."

But Jesus says, "Not so fast," and then he seems to complicate matters and makes you wonder, why didn't he just leave well enough alone? Of the two passages, the one Jesus quotes (Deuteronomy) and the one he creates (The Sermon on the Mount)...we prefer Deuteronomy. *The Gospel According to Moses* looks more palatable than *The Gospel According to Jesus.* To make matters worse, this is a hard passage in a very tough part of town. In the same range of difficulty as "if someone slaps you on the right cheek, turn the other also," or, "If someone demands your outer garment, volunteer your undergarment as well." It's in the same block as, "Love your enemies and pray for those who persecute you." This summer a preacher down in Texas began a sermon from a neighboring text:

> Dear God, we pray this morning that you will be with Al-Qaeda and terrorists around the world who seek to destroy fellow human beings. We pray that you be with the Lord's Resistance Army in Uganda who kidnaps children and brainwashes them into machines of war. We pray that you be with those who do violence in the Philippines, in the Congo, and for racists in Texas who don't think they are racists…Teach us today to be people of love, compassion, and nonviolence as you teach our enemies…to walk in the ways of Jesus in whose name we pray. Amen.[1]

"Be with Al-Qaeda"? This is a rough stretch of road that gets us looking for an exit.

And our text is no easier, "Everyone who divorces his wife, except for the cause of unchastity, makes her commit adultery." You're probably already familiar with several fine off ramps from this difficult road.

Let's try this exit: "Times have changed."

Great Uncle Harold retired after fifty years with the same company. Gave him a gold watch. Not too many today retiring from the same company after fifty years. And we expect the same of marriages as we did last century?

"Friends and houses,
jobs and spouses…
they come and they go."

The fact is, times have changed. Used to be the only divorced family in our entire neighborhood was Debbie Schaeffer's folks. And her Dad was bartender at the Three Monkey's Tavern. What did that tell you?

Used to be, a preacher quoted scripture, "God hates divorce," and even the unchurched Gentiles would say, "Amen."

Used to be, society supported the church.

Used to be, divorce was an unthinkable option.

But, times have *changed!* Society no longer has our back, and churches have drifted into culture's mainstream. Now the banker is divorced; our favorite clerk at Krogers is divorced. Did you hear about the couple who owned the BBQ in Abilene? Divorced. Now there are two BBQs in Abilene. Why, I know preachers who are divorced and friends whose children or parents are divorced. Some of us are divorced.

Preachers don't much quote anymore, "God hates divorce." Now they quote, "Judge not, lest you be judged."

Times have changed. Bishop Spong has created a liturgical ceremony to bless the ending of a marriage. Now, when former partners find themselves "on radically different life paths" and discover "no more potential for life in their relationship," they can go their blessed way.[2] The off ramp reads, "Times have changed."

Early in my first ministry the exit I was tempted to take was marked, "Let bygones be bygones" when one Sunday William came forward and stood before the congregation. He said, with only a little prodding, that if he'd offended anyone, he was sorry and that he'd like to be considered a member in good standing.... He wanted to start out fresh and his fiancée, Rebecca, was studying to become a Christian. But the congregation's elders, who knew William, hesitated. They wondered if there might need to be fruit demonstrating repentance. After all, his affairs and divorce had left his first wife devastated and the congregation reeling. But I stood firm and said, "Do we believe in grace or not? If God can forgive him, then why can't we?" He married Rebecca, and they had a child and then divorced for what seemed good cause. And he married again, and this one lasted a while longer—another child, last I heard. That's life; look around.

The off ramp I helped construct read, "You've heard that it was said, 'Whoever marries a divorced woman commits adultery,' but I say to you, let bygones be bygones, it doesn't matter, time to move on."

Some congregations are tempted to take the exit that demands you just close your eyes and hit the brakes. As in the surprising case of Linda, the pillar of spirituality among the young marrieds. Planning, hosting, and teaching "Ladies' Bible Class" were her specialties. A real beacon. When suddenly and without warning comes the most unexpected news. Linda has left her husband—and their two daughters—and "shacked up" with a local chef. Two weeks after the story breaks, Linda shows up at church. She's out in the parking lot.

"What does she want?" I ask the deacon.

"Wants to talk," he says.

"Only if she's here to repent."

"She's not here to apologize," he says. "She claims a lot happened behind closed doors."

"We cave in on this," I say, "Pretty soon every marriage will crumble."

Hold on tight, slam on the brakes, and hope for as little fallout as possible. It's called "Our Standards," the very kind of attitude Jesus is fighting against in the Sermon on the Mount.

This passage on marriage and divorce is full of exits that want to lure us away.

From the simple, "That *can't mean* what it says…,"

To the theoretical, "It's *symbolic* of what should be but isn't. An *ideal* we cannot reach…,"

To the historic personal, "What about battered wives who *didn't* leave an abusive relationship because they were told it was 'the Lord's will'?"

And thus the young actor in this week's news, "My need for newness and passion and adventure is much greater than my need for any idea of security."

But, what if we stay on the road? Avoid these off ramps? Walk with Jesus, at least for a while, see where he is headed?

What we find, down the road, is that other religious folk seem as troubled over this matter as we are and try to push Jesus into an exit lane. Down the road,[3] we overhear this revealing conversation:

RELIGIOUS LEADERS TO JESUS: "Is it lawful to divorce for any reason at all? Would you please clarify for us your opinion on the text you earlier quoted, Deuteronomy? May a man divorce his wife 'for any matter of indecency.' Yes or no?"

JESUS: "Let's not talk about exceptions. Let's talk about intentions. Let's talk about beginnings, about Genesis. What God has joined together let no man…"

RELIGIOUS LEADERS: "You're not answering the question. Yes or no: May a *man* divorce his wife 'for any matter of indecency'?"

When the smoke finally clears, Jesus is standing next to a wife, saying, "You're not getting rid of her so quickly. You'll not uproot her, cast her away without resources, abandoned, tainted, all because your 'dish was spoiled'[4] or 'she didn't age as expected.'"

In this conversation Jesus isn't dodging bullets, digressing, or taking an off ramp. Jesus is reprogramming our way of thinking to change our way of living.

Jesus isn't parading down the road with a book of codes under one arm and drawing lines in the sand with the other. He's walking with people in need, the hopeless and helpless, women and men on the margins.

Jesus is standing with a wife about to be exchanged. He says, "Not so fast, mister."

Stay with Jesus on the road—in this tough section of town—and listen to the *context* of his words. Jesus says, "No lust," "no anger," "pray for your enemies."

The world Jesus imagines is far different from the gospel according to America—in the empire where we live we *expect* anger to accelerate into violence, lust to explode into adultery. In this world we are *trained* to love the people who love us and to hate our enemies.

But in the world Jesus imagines, we pray for our enemies, address our anger, and—when it comes to marriage and divorce—elevate our concern for human beings, secure the welfare of the marginalized, and don't assume "two consenting adults." There is a whole community to consider: sisters and brothers in Christ, children and other innocents.

These are not ideals beyond reach, an interim ethic, all about the hereafter. This is *reprogramming* for the community who call themselves the Church of Christ. So, imagine a wedding ceremony. Rehearsals and rentals...all past. What you see is the young couple at the altar, your daughter in her beautiful white gown or your son in his handsome black tuxedo.

He says, "I promise before God, our family, and friends, that I will love, honor, and cherish you in sickness and in health as long we both shall live..."

What do you think? Why, you promise, "We will do everything in our power, we will work and give and sacrifice so that this may come true."

Now the bride says, "I promise to be faithful and true to you and to our marriage vows now and forever."

What do you think? Why, you promise, "We will give our life that this be true."

Imagine now that the audience is the church and the couple is every couple who marries for all the seasons of life—Spring and Summer and Fall and Winter. With all the different demands, hardships, dreams, and possibilities each season brings? The same person? Yes! In this community of mentors, supporters, sacrificers, givers, and fellow travelers. Yes! By the grace of God.

And what of divorce? Like Jesus, we are sensitive to the pain and recognize the fallout of this exceptional and tragic experience. And, just as Jesus, we embrace, forgive, and accept every broken person.

We'll not take these easy exits: "Times have changed," "bygones," or, "our standards." We will not ignore anyone. We will not deny anyone. No, we will stay on the road with Jesus, among the people he loves that we might learn to live in the world he imagines.

13

People of Integrity
Matthew 5:33–37

DAVE BLAND

Compositional Comments

Warren Carter emphasizes Jesus' instructions to the disciples to imagine a different way of life than that practiced by the empire of the day and the empire of our day. We envision different social and political structures, and we live into the world Jesus imagines for the disciples. To begin living into this world does not necessarily mean that we have to begin with attacking the major power structures of the day. Like a mustard seed, we can begin with the smallest and most common activities of daily life; we can begin with words. In Matthew 5:33–37 Jesus describes how his disciples must use words and how those words reflect their true character. Jesus' disciples use words to serve others and treat others with respect. They use words to support and deepen their relationships, not to protect their own interests.

One of the most accessible resources we have to oppress others, whether we are in positions of power or not, are our words. We can use words to exploit others. However, as Charles Campbell observes, words are tools the church uses as an alternative to violence.[1] We are to practice good stewardship of our words. We do not use them lightly or deceptively. We see the power words have to heal and transform lives, to mend and serve others. When responsibly used, words are a way of practicing justice; and justice is what separates God's empire from the political empire of the day.

In chapter 6, Dennis Dewey offers provocative insight into how one faithfully performs Matthew's Sermon on the Mount. Though he provides practical suggestions for faithful text-performance, at the core the performance has to do with the whole person. He observes, "We are not actors mouthing someone else's words but Word-bearers acting out our lives through and in the Word." We do not just mouth the words of the Sermon; we embody the text in our own hearts. As Dewey says a little later in his chapter, we do not pay lip service to the text but life service. In a real sense that is the essence of Jesus' teaching about oath making. When Jesus speaks of how we use our words, he gets below the surface to the kind of people we are. Our words reflect our innermost being, our character. The purpose of this sermon is to capture the breadth and depth of Jesus' teaching. When Jesus says, "Let your 'yes' be 'yes' and 'no' 'no,'" he calls us to be people of integrity in all avenues of life. A version of this sermon was preached in June of 2006 at the Church of Christ at White Station in Memphis, Tennessee. Though one can still find room for improvement in the sermon, Carisse Berryhill and Bob Reid were especially helpful in sharpening its focus and clarifying its message.

SERMON

When we see a rule, we think exception. When we make a commitment, we think escape clause. When we see law, we think loophole. After all, isn't that why the IRS has written a tax code, as a challenge to us to find the loopholes? In the same vein, human nature tends to reduce religion and religious responsibility to a set of rules, a list of laws. Approaching religion in this manner is a subtle but effective way of segregating our life; religious responsibility is put in one category and personal life in another. That way we can more easily control our life as well as have the best of both worlds. Or so we think.

It doesn't appear to be that much different from the tendencies of the religious leaders of Jesus' day. They took seriously the law regarding the making of an oath. The law said, "You shall not make a false oath, but you must carry out the vows you have made to the Lord." "Yes," they said, "We must honor the commandment." But they thought loophole and contemplated, "What is a false oath?" "We can set up a system that will make sure we do not cross the line and break the law." Thus they developed a scheme of oath taking that technically allowed them to keep the law while at the same time serving their own purposes (Mt. 23:16–22). They strategized, "Only oaths that include the divine name are binding." "If you make a promise that does not include the Lord's name, then you have leeway to fudge a little on keeping it." Jesus, observing their true intentions, replies, "However hard you try, you cannot exclude God from your oaths. If you vow by heaven, it is God's throne; if by earth, it is his footstool; if Jerusalem, it is his city. Even if it is by the hairs on your head, they, too, belong to God." In other words, nothing the religious leaders say exempts them from being in the presence of God; all of life belongs to God. In reality they used oaths to practice a duplicitous life. So Jesus cuts right to the chase, "Don't make an oath at all. Just say 'yes' or 'no,' that will suffice."

We, too, want to take Jesus' words seriously. However, in our desire to keep them we fall into the same quagmire the religious leaders fell. We end up interpreting Jesus' words narrowly, applying them only to a small segment of life. Our reasoning goes like this, "Jesus said, no oaths at all; just 'yes' or 'no' is sufficient. Therefore, we must be on guard about violating this command in settings where oaths are required." We surmise, "Whenever someone asks us to swear to God, we will refuse. When we're in a courtroom or under some kind of legal obligation, we will not in good conscience make an oath. We will just say 'yes' or 'no' and thus satisfy the requirements."

Without realizing it, and often in good conscience, we've approached Jesus' instruction in the same way the religious leaders approached the law, narrowly and rigidly. We approach it looking for the escape clause. We apply Jesus' teaching to a particular dimension of life, believing that when we are in these contexts, we refrain from oath making and thus fulfill its requirements.

If, however, we follow this line of reasoning legalistically, it would mean Christians could not complete business transactions. Doctors could not take the Hippocratic Oath in vowing to preserve life. Couples could not make marriage vows. One could not swear before a Notary Public.

Yet Jesus himself testified under oath during his trial.[2] Paul invoked oaths on numerous occasions.[3] Jesus' words are not confined to formal occasions or legal systems. They have greater breadth and depth. His teachings on speech and oath making have to do not with a particular aspect of life but with our whole lives, not with lip service but with life service.[4]

Jesus calls his followers to embody truth telling as a lifestyle, to refuse the pervasive practice of engaging in imaginative ways of avoiding *telling* the truth while maintaining an *appearance* of truth. Jesus' concern is broader and deeper than simply the judicial or court settings of life. He says, "Don't try to find creative ways to avoid telling your neighbor the truth. Through your speech, respect others in the same way you want them to respect you."

Jesus looks behind the law on oath taking to reveal its intention. He does not approach it legalistically but through the context of the most fundamental law, the law of love as described in Leviticus, "You shall love your neighbor as yourself" (Lev. 19:18b).[5] That is, truth telling becomes a way of fleshing out how *love* fulfills the law.[6] It's not just about legal practices and public vows and official documents. Jesus brings fresh perspective to the Old Testament law on oaths by including its full implications: God's people are people of integrity.

A Christian's speech and life are marked by integrity. Our "yes's" and "no's" are clear; we do not mix them. We do not try to make it appear we are telling the truth when we aren't. We do not try to appear to live one style of life when we are actually living another.

I like the currently popular commercials on television advertising the city of Las Vegas. The one I find most amusing is a lawn care man after completing a job going to the door of the customer to collect payment, "That'll be $75." The customer, shocked at the price, replies, "$75! Last time it was $30." "Yes," says the man, "But you know, I was in Las Vegas this past week, and I had a good time, and I noticed that you were there and you were really enjoying yourself too!" The customer, embarrassed, stammers, "$75? Okay that'll be fine...Good job on the lawn!" The caption then flashes on the screen, "What happens here, stays here."

Jesus' teaching to say just yes or no calls us to be who we say we are. We do not claim to be someone we are not, pretending our lives are in sync with God on Sunday, and the rest of the week live inconsistent with that proclamation. Our Christianity is not a glossy coat covering over hidden compartments of our lives. Jesus says, "Don't try to conceal the truth about who you are. Don't disguise your 'yes' as something it is not. Don't deceive others with your words. Be people of character so that others can trust what you say and who you are."

Jesus' words touch every aspect of existence. We do not quarantine Jesus from lifestyles or habits or relationships or pleasures that serve our own agenda. "Let your yes be yes and no no" means we are people who practice honesty in every facet of daily living; it is our DNA. We are people of integrity. We are who we say we are.

Mark Snyder has developed an instrument identifying the degree to which an individual is able to "self-monitor." Self-monitoring, he says, "refers to a person's ability to adjust his or her behavior to external situational factors."[7] Those who are high in self-monitoring demonstrate the ability to easily adapt in their relationships with others. They display more flexibility to their environment than do low self-monitors. They adjust their leadership style to fit the situation. In contrast, low self-monitors are less concerned with the way others perceive them and are less likely to adjust their character to fit the demands of different contexts.

Snyder argues that managerial and CEO type positions demand high self-monitoring to be effective.

While it is true that an essential quality of leadership requires leaders to adapt to changing situations and adjust speech to fit the occasion, the rigors of such demands can potentially cause leaders to lose perspective on who they really are and the authenticity of their lives as disciples. Jesus calls disciples to demonstrate consistent character that reflects inner attitudes and values, character that, while able to adapt to its surroundings, displays authenticity in word and deed. We are who we say we are.

Michael Faraday, a chemist and physicist during the nineteenth century, established a worldwide reputation. His book, *Fundamental Researches in Electricity,* is now a classic in science.[8] Since his death, twenty-three major biographies have been written about his life. Faraday was a member of a Church of Christ in London. In 1840 he was appointed an elder in that church. Three years after being appointed, he was dismissed. It seems that he had been chosen by Queen Victoria to have lunch with her at Windsor Palace. In complying with her request, Faraday missed a Sunday worship service. The congregation did not accept his reason for the absence and declared that he was no longer fit to serve as an elder!

Few churches today would dismiss an elder, or any other church leader for that matter, for one absence from a Sunday service. But what was most impressive about Faraday's dismissal was his subsequent behavior. He continued to worship and work in the church as faithfully as ever, and seventeen years later was reinstated as an elder. There is no indication that Faraday was striving to regain the office or that his ego was involved in these years of service. He was not using the church for any sort of self-enhancement. He worked and served because of a strong sense of responsibility and commitment. His life was consistent with his beliefs. He was a man of character.

When Jesus says, "Let your 'yes' be 'yes' and 'no' 'no,'" he describes a life characterized by integrity. His admonition addresses not just legal settings, not just truth telling, but the issue of character as it touches every corner of life. We strive to become who we say we are. We live into the world imagined in the Sermon on the Mount.

14

Imagine

Matthew 5:38–42

CHARLES CAMPBELL

Compositional Comments

When I preach, I try to focus as concretely as possible on both the text and the context. This sermon was no exception; the challenges I faced revolved around these two poles. In preaching from the familiar text of Matthew 5:38–42, I wrestled with two specific challenges: (1) engaging the congregation with a new, and potentially quite foreign, interpretation of the text; and (2) speaking a word to the specific context in which I was preaching.

My interpretation of the text presented two distinct challenges. First, I wanted to depict Jesus as a jester. I sought to capture the jesterlike way in which Jesus in the Sermon on the Mount humorously and even satirically subverts the presuppositions and rationalities that hold us captive. My attempt to capture this dimension of Jesus' words began with my reading of the text. As Dennis Dewey recommends in his essay in this volume, I tried to read the text in the spirit of the jester or fool–though this approach obviously cannot be captured on the printed page in this volume.[1] Through such an oral presentation of the text I hoped to prepare the way for the sermon and to provide consistency between my reading and interpretation of the text.

The second interpretive challenge involved interpreting Jesus' words, not as a counsel of passive nonresistance, but as a counsel of *active nonviolent resistance* to evil. This shift also began with my reading of the text;

following Walter Wink and Warren Carter, I translated the traditional, "Do not resist an evildoer," as, "Do not *violently* resist an evildoer" (5:39). More importantly, because I knew this interpretation would be new and possibly even questionable to many in the congregation, I spent a significant amount of time developing this interpretation through a detailed presentation of the three examples Jesus provides. This move required me to avoid a significant danger: I could not allow my necessarily detailed treatment of the text to become tedious, more like an exegetical presentation than a sermon. Consequently, I tried to present Jesus' examples in a lively, engaging, jesterlike way. This effort required some significant body language (particularly in relation to "turning the other cheek"), as well as humor and satire. My presentation seemed to work—there was significant laughter during this section of the sermon—though, again, these aspects of the sermon are difficult, if not impossible, to capture in written form.

In addition to these two interpretive challenges, I also wrestled with the contextual challenge. I was preaching in a eucharistic chapel service at Columbia Theological Seminary, which was attended by students entering Greek school and visiting Doctor of Ministry students (some of whom were taking a course on Matthew!). In addition, I was aware of the larger world context, in which the Iraq War continued to rage and in which Israel had been fighting with Hamas in the Palestinian territories and had just recently entered into war with Hezbollah in Lebanon.

In the sermon I sought to hold these various contexts together. I addressed the violent response to enemies that is embodied in war, including the "war on terror" and the fighting in the Middle East. In addition, to address the seminary context, I broadened the focus to that of imagination and explored the seminary as a place where an alternative imagination—like that of the Sermon on the Mount—can be formed. This word seemed to be an appropriate one, particularly for students just entering seminary. Finally, I sought to bring together my interpretation of the text and the eucharistic table by suggesting that the table is both a place where we embody a "foolish" alternative to the violence of the world and a place where an alternative imagination is nurtured through our weekly participation in the meal. In the bulletin, as well as in the eucharistic liturgy, I referred to the table as the "Feast of Fools." And the music during the eucharistic celebration was a lively, even playful, jazz piece that gave the table itself an odd, off-balance feel. In these ways, I hoped the liturgy would not only help bring together text and context, but would also help people actively participate in the gospel we shared that morning. This sermon was preached on July 14, 2006.

SERMON

Many people today read the Sermon on the Mount as a set of rules for the Christian life. I know I have read it that way in the past. I hear people talk about the Sermon in these terms. And maybe some of you read the Sermon that way as well. And, of course, that reading is not completely wrong. The Sermon does provide directives and practices for the life of the Christian community.

At the deepest level, however, the Sermon is not primarily a set of rules or directives. At the deepest level the Sermon on the Mount is an act of imagination—and a rather wild and crazy act of imagination at that. In the Sermon Jesus reimagines the world and invites the church to live into this new, alternative reality.

And the world Jesus imagines is a crazy, upside-down world—sort of like the world of carnival, in which everything is turned on its head. Those on the bottom are on the top. Those on the top are on the bottom. All of the old, rigid rules are suspended. Everything is out of whack. It is a world that runs counter to the presuppositions, rationalities, and myths of Jesus' day—and our own:

"Blessed are the poor in spirit…"

"Blessed are those who mourn…"

"Blessed are the meek…"

"Blessed are you when people revile you and persecute you…"

And that's only the beginning of the Sermon!

In the Sermon Jesus tries to dislocate and disorient us, to shock us out of our commonsense, taken-for-granted presuppositions so we might see the world differently—and possibly begin to live in it differently.

We might even think of Jesus here as a kind of jester. Yes, you heard me correctly—a jester. We often read the Sermon so seriously (indeed, we often read scripture as a whole so seriously, especially here at seminary) that we miss its startling craziness. Thinking of Jesus as a jester may help us get at this.

The jester is a figure who has a fundamentally different perspective on the world. He or she (and there *were* women jesters) is one who sees the world in odd or unusual ways, often from the place of an outsider. And through often comical antics, the jester seeks to startle and dislocate people, so they might be set free from the commonsense presuppositions that hold them captive.[2]

As someone has written, the jester "melt[s] the solidity of the world."[3] The jester melts away all those things that are supposedly "written in stone." He or she subverts the myths, rationalities, and presuppositions that everyone takes for granted, but that often are the ways of death and not life. And Jesus does that a lot in the Sermon on the Mount.

Nowhere does Jesus play the jester more clearly than in the words he speaks to us today. "You have heard it said, 'An eye for an eye and a tooth for a tooth'" (5:33, author's trans.). Here Jesus tackles the "law of retaliation." It's in Exodus. It's in Leviticus. It's in Deuteronomy. It's important. Interestingly, the law was actually meant to limit violence–to check the kind of uncontrolled vengeance that was common in the day. It limited retaliation to retaliation "in kind": "No *more* than an eye for an eye. No *more* than a tooth for a tooth." It was a piece of progressive legislation. But still the deep presupposition remains: the way to respond to the enemy–the way to respond to one who has harmed you–is through violent retaliation.

That presupposition is not just in the law–in Exodus, Leviticus, and Deuteronomy. It's in the very air we breathe–even today. It drives our world–from the war on terrorism (both the acts of the terrorists and the United States' responses to them) to the conflict in the Middle East (as we have seen all too clearly over the past two weeks) to the death penalty and at times even to our interpersonal relationships. As a result, the cycle of violence seems unending. We can hardly even imagine alternatives.

"You have heard it said, 'An eye for an eye and a tooth for a tooth.'"

"But I say to you…"–and here Jesus begins to melt the solidity of the world–"But I say to you, "Do not violently resist an evildoer."

Then Jesus invites us to imagine alternatives. He puts on the cap and bells, and he plays the fool. Humor becomes the vehicle to set us free. Jesus challenges the powers of domination and violence through burlesque and lampooning. He imagines antics worthy of any jester. The audience surely would have been chuckling–or even laughing out loud.

Consider what Jesus says about giving the cloak also.[4] Here's the situation: A poor person who literally owns nothing but the clothes on his back–an outer garment and an undergarment–is being sued for what little he has left. So Jesus counsels, "If anyone wants to sue you and take your outer garment, give your undergarment as well." Which means the person would take off his undergarment and walk out of court stark naked. Curious folks would undoubtedly crowd around and ask, "What's going on?" The entire economic system would be unmasked for what it is–a system that milks the poor for the benefit of the rich. It is the jester's way of "speaking truth to power."

Or consider what Jesus says about turning the other cheek. Notice that he says, "If someone strikes you on the *right* cheek." That's important. Because the striker would always use the right hand, a blow to the right cheek would have to be a backhanded slap. It was an act of humiliation. It was a way of putting someone down, keeping someone in his or her place. Masters did this to slaves; husbands to wives; superiors to inferiors. It was a way of reinforcing the social hierarchies of the day. So Jesus says, "Turn the other cheek"–the *left* cheek. Now, this is not an act of passivity. Instead such a move creates an extraordinary situation. You see, a person can't backhand someone with the *right* hand on the *left* cheek. Just try it. It makes you look ridiculous. The only way someone can strike a person on the *left* cheek with the *right* hand is by striking the person with an open palm or a fist. And striking someone in that way would *make the person an equal!* The social superior, the abuser is stuck. What to do? And for a moment, the social order is interrupted. Possibly a space is created where something new might happen.

Or consider "going the second mile"–my favorite example. A Roman soldier was permitted to force someone to carry his equipment for one mile–*but no further.* The practice had been abused, so a law was enacted to limit the demands a soldier could make: *one mile, no more.* So Jesus says, "If anyone forces you to go one mile, go also the second mile." Can you imagine the scene at the end of that first mile:

The soldier says, "Okay, that's enough. We've gone one mile. You can put down my stuff and return to your business."

But the person carrying the equipment replies, "Oh, I'd be happy to carry the equipment a second mile."

"What?" the soldier replies, "You can't do that. It's against the law."

"But I'd really like to help you out. Please let me carry it another mile."

"Hey, I could get in trouble for that–fined or flogged. What are you up to?"

"I just want to help out. Could I *please* carry the equipment another mile?"

A wrench is thrown into the entire Imperial Machine, and it grinds to a halt, even if just for a minute. Possibly a space is opened up for something new and surprising to happen.

This is what's going on here. Jesus, the jester, lampoons and burlesques various aspects of an oppressive social order. At the same time, Jesus subverts the "law of retaliation" by imagining alternatives to violent resistance. Jesus seeks to set us free from the presuppositions that are killing us–such as the necessity of violent retaliation. He invites us to live in the world in new, imaginative, even foolish ways.

This is what seminary ultimately should be about. It should be about nurturing our imaginations–setting them free in Jesus Christ. Indeed, I think this is what the church desperately needs today: imagination. The church doesn't really need any more committees and task forces. And I don't think we need more seminars on conflict resolution or church development. To be honest, I don't even think we need more "decency and order."[5] What the church really needs is imagination and foolishness shaped by the way of Jesus Christ. What the church really needs are some holy fools, who will help nurture a church that is crazy enough and odd enough to offer a genuine alternative to the violence and domination of the world.

That's one reason coming to this table is so important here at seminary. This table nurtures an alternative imagination. For this table continues the foolish, crazy table manners of Jesus. Jesus' meal practices certainly qualify as the actions of a jester. Jesus was always eating with the wrong people: the unclean, the outsiders, the tax collectors and sinners. He just never seemed to "get it." At the Last Supper he even ate with the one who would betray him and those who would desert him. At Jesus' table, everybody was welcome. It was just one big feast.

Through these crazy meal practices, Jesus was reimagining the whole social order. Meals in that culture reinforced the social hierarchies; they intentionally reinforced the distinctions between insiders and outsiders, honored and shamed, clean and unclean, us and them. That was one of the primary functions of the theater of the table.

But as he ate and drank, Jesus was turning that old world upside down and inviting everyone to feast together in a new creation. That's the crazy vision of this table, much like the vision of the Sermon on the Mount: This is the joyful feast of people of God. People will come from north and south and east and west. All people will come and sit at table together in peace and justice–Shalom.

So come to this feast of fools. Come…and imagine.

15

Perfection

Matthew 5:48

DEAN SMITH

Compositional Comments

The following sermon was delivered in the opening worship for the 2006 Rochester Sermon Seminar before approximately two hundred ministers from thirty states or provinces and more than twenty Christian groups. At the outset of a conference dedicated to the question, *Dare We Live in the World Imagined in the Sermon on the Mount?* this sermon dares to ask whether our desires are even inclined in that direction. It was intended not to convey new information or challenging new interpretations, but simply to be confessional about the challenges we face when we seek to take the Sermon on the Mount seriously. The following text is expanded from the oral presentation, which was abbreviated by time restraints. The additional material is elaborative rather than substantive.

As Warren Carter observes in his earlier chapter, one of the most common approaches to the Sermon on the Mount is the spiritual one—interpreting the Sermon as an ideal to be devoutly revered, but rarely obeyed. This sermon, written from a personal and pastoral perspective, confirms that impression and suggests some reasons for it. It further proposes that the answer to this evasion may be found in the heart of the Sermon itself, the Lord's Prayer, which, when prayed, strips away our pious pretensions and draws us into a reorienting engagement with the living God.

SERMON

I must confess to a healthy amount of skepticism when I approach the Sermon on the Mount. My attitude is best conveyed by something I once heard Dallas Willard express in an interview. He was asked what advice he would give new ministers starting out in a new ministry. He suggested that they begin by preaching a series on the Sermon on the Mount...just to determine how many still believed it.

Sören Kierkegaard once wrote that there are two kinds of Christians: those who want to imitate Jesus and those who only want to admire him. In many ways that represents our approach to the Sermon on the Mount. Most Christians today aren't looking to be like God—to be accepted by God, loved by God, approved by God, but not to imitate God. Many Christians I know regard Jesus' teachings in the Sermon on the Mount as an impossible and unrealistic ideal that one can certainly admire, but never actually follow. In fact, many regard its lofty expectations as little more than a vehicle to appreciate God's "amazing" grace by demonstrating just how far we "fall short" of God's righteousness—just another form of admiration without imitation (and a rather legalistic view of grace).

Thus when Jesus calls would-be disciples to "be perfect, therefore, as your heavenly Father is perfect" (5:48, NIV), I wonder if any of us take that seriously anymore. For most of us the phrase, "Nobody's perfect," is not only our favorite description of what it means to be human, it is our favorite excuse for ignoring Jesus' radical call. But discipleship is all about imitation. Jesus says as much in the conclusion to this Sermon when he addresses the foolishness and self-deception of simply hearing his words (perhaps even admiring them) with no serious intention of actually living them out in everyday life. Matthew continues this warning throughout his gospel, culminating in an entire chapter devoted to chastising the hypocrisy of some religious leaders who want to appear righteous without actually becoming so.

But can we handle the honesty of Jesus that unmasks our arrogant attempts at self-justification? The Sermon on the Mount has a strange way of either making us better people or better liars. Either we are compelled by Jesus' vision of living under the reign of God and are transformed by that encounter, or we attempt to follow Jesus' teachings as a perfect system of ethics and behavior apart from this relationship. The latter almost invariably results in perfection*ism* and utopian*ism*, the very human effort to do God's will independent of the serious engagement of a relationship with God. We end up giving lip service to a system of rules rather than submitting ourselves to a challenging, and often unpredictable, relationship with the living God.

Now, I know that sounds rather naïve and simplistic—rules versus relationship—especially when you consider examples of some who have seriously applied the ethics of this Sermon apart from a belief in Jesus as the Son of God. I'm thinking particularly of Gandhi, who was deeply affected by the ethics of nonviolent resistance conveyed in the Sermon on the Mount. In fact, his uncompromising application of those principles reminds me of Jesus' words that only those who do God's will have any chance of entering the kingdom of heaven (Mt. 7:21). That, coupled with our general failure as Christians to faithfully live out his teachings in this Sermon, makes my conclusion seem even more naïve and perhaps even patronizing.

Yet for one who has been haunted by this Sermon all his life, I have found my attempts to honestly live it out to be a dismal failure apart from a genuine desire to imitate God. They have resulted in the very hypocrisy and self-deception Jesus warned about. I realized this several years ago while doing some background research on the Pharisees in an attempt to gain a better understanding of their motivation and approach beyond the rather one-dimensional portrait offered in the gospels. I kept wondering why the gospels, and Matthew in particular, were so brutal in their critique of this group. Surely they had *some* redeeming qualities. After all, they represented a reformation movement within Judaism that attempted to focus on a serious engagement with the Law of Moses, believing that if they could systematically follow it God would bless them and restore their fortunes as a nation.

As I dug deeper, I began to see that they had *many* redeeming qualities, especially as you compared them to the other religious sects of that day. In fact, the more I examined the profile of a Pharisee, the more uncomfortable I became until one day I came to the conclusion that, in more ways than I care to admit, *I am a Pharisee.* I am inordinately concerned with the perception others have of me, much more concerned with being perceived as righteous than actually being righteous. I devote more of my time interpreting the word of God in a way that makes me, and others, feel more comfortable and acceptable than seeking the truth that unmasks my own, and others', self-deception. I have spent far too much of my time educating people in the distinctive practices of a particular religious tradition so they might become like me rather than become like Jesus. In short, I have admired the teachings of Jesus more than I have made any serious attempt to embody them.

One turning point for me came in a most unexpected way—through a reexamination of the prayer Jesus taught his disciples to pray. Deceptively simple and direct, it has a way of stripping away all attempts at self-justification and manipulations of the truth and opening our hearts to really hear the truth of Jesus' teaching. As I was reading the history of interpreting the Lord's Prayer, I noticed that many of the saints had a practice of reciting it three times a day, much like the practice of Jews reciting the Shema. So I adopted the practice, at first because it was so foreign to me. Now, I recite the prayer before every meal for two reasons. First, because I rarely eat alone, so the prayer prepares me for conversations in which I am most tempted to forget who I am. Second, so I won't forget (since I rarely miss a meal). At first it seemed rather mechanical, but then I began to experience changes in my attitude and behavior that were not present before—apologies offered, gossip withheld, criticisms resisted, and a whole lot more courage and compassion. This simple practice awakened in me a desire I had not experienced in a long time—a deep desire to imitate the character of God.

You see, my weakness isn't a failure to understand Jesus' teachings or a lack of conviction that they are true and right. I think I understand most of Jesus' teachings quite clearly. Rather, my weakness is rooted in a deeply ingrained skepticism about whether they are relevant in the "real world" and, specifically, whether I am willing to live up to their expectations. I think I share this weakness with a lot of other Christians (and preachers). The widening chasm between the humble, self-sacrificing lifestyle portrayed in Jesus' teachings and the one practiced by many Christians in America reveals the self-deception Jesus warned of at the end of his Sermon.

I was reminded of that just recently when my wife and I were out running errands. I asked her to maneuver our vehicle through traffic to a particular store and wait for me as I ducked in to get something I needed. It wasn't easy, but finally she managed to get me there. I ran in and began looking for the particular item, but I couldn't locate it so I asked a clerk to help me find it. He didn't speak English very well, and I grew increasingly frustrated as I tried to describe to him what I was looking for. Finally I became so irritated that I simply threw up my hands and walked out. As I returned to the car, Carolyn noticed I was empty-handed and asked if they were out of the item I was seeking. "No," I angrily replied, "*Abu* couldn't understand what I was looking for!" Pretty ugly, don't you think? Especially when you consider the patriotic rhetoric in our country right now that fans our emotions and clouds our judgment. My excited utterance betrayed an attitude of heart that was far from the heart and character of the heavenly Father. Fortunately, I am married to a woman who never lets me get away with things like that. (And after thirty-four years, she shows no signs of changing.) "That's pretty racist, don't you think?" But rather than being defensive I found myself feeling deeply embarrassed and contrite. Even she was surprised.

That incident reminded me of two things. First, of just how far I have to go to become like God. (I believe much of our problem as preachers is simply acknowledging that chasm.) Second is the virtual impossibility of such imitation apart from a community of fellow disciples who are committed to "speaking the truth in love." In such a community the possibility exists that someone might question our facile reading of the gospel to justify a comfortable status quo. That someone might actually stand up and ask, "What would Jesus do?" to address an ethical dilemma greater than whether we should return a ten dollar bill we found in the parking lot. In such a community painful truths could be spoken because deep in our souls we know all too well what Jesus would say and do.

However, the problem for most churches, indeed most preachers, is not only a failure to live in the world imagined by the Sermon on the Mount, but to even imagine or desire such a life. In the words of the immortal Pogo, we have met the enemy and it is us—which is a helpful insight these days, especially when we consider that the particular way that Jesus teaches us to be like the Father is to love our enemies and pray for those who threaten us (Mt. 5:44). Given our present distress, this seems like the most radical and powerful "preemptive response" one could ever imagine. Perhaps if we followed that simple command in our churches, we might begin to imagine such a radically transformed world.

In the end it may be the concluding words of Dietrich Bonhoeffer's famous prayer poem "Who am I?", which struggle with the chasm between knowing the truth and doing it, that provide a ray of hope for us. "Whoever I am, Thou knowest, O God, I am thine."[1] Given our propensity for obscuring the demands of Jesus' teaching, words like these might appear to be just another example of that, except for how extensively and passionately Bonhoeffer lived out the ethics of this Sermon. Indeed, the brutal honesty and humility of his prayer could only have come from one so intimately connected to the person and teachings of Jesus. Reading of his execution, we witness a powerful imitation of Jesus' own death and are reminded that it is only when we are willing to follow Jesus anywhere he leads us that we can follow him at all. Surely then, if our desire to be perfect is not the calculating strategy of a religious professional, but the simple, unpretentious desire of a child to be like the Father, we may discover the courage and honesty to live in this world imagined by the Sermon on the Mount and may truly become the "children of God" (Mt. 5:9).

"Our Father in heaven, may your name be honored in our lives. May your kingdom be realized, your will be on done on earth as it is in heaven. Give us what we need this day and forgive us of our sins as we forgive those who sin against us. Do not lead us to despair, but deliver us from the evil that is around us and within. For it is your reign and your power and your glory, that we so earnestly desire. In the name of Jesus we pray. Amen."

16

May I Have Your Attention Please

Matthew 6:1-18

JERRY TAYLOR

Compositional Comments

The following sermon was preached at the 2006 Sermon Seminar at Rochester College to an audience of scholars and preachers. Four panelists evaluated the sermon by measuring it against the visiting scholars' analysis of the first-century imperialistic world of evangelist Matthew. The panel also evaluated the sermon's effectiveness in speaking authoritatively to those living in the twenty-first–century world of empire.

The sermon interacts with Warren Carter's excellent historical analysis of the first–century world of empire and his current statistics on the plight of children living in poverty. He provides statistics from the Children's Defense Fund declaring that 37 million people, including 13 million children, are living in poverty in America, the richest nation on earth.

The sermon immediately gives attention to the children, the most vulnerable in an imperialistic society. Starting with children gives natural expression to my voice. As an African American child, I lived in extreme poverty during the 60s and 70s in racially oppressive southwest Tennessee.

As a result of growing up on the underside of oppression, I gained a unique perspective that enables me to see and speak about the painful realities of living without power and visibility at the bottom of the social

138

heap. On the back of the American dollar bill is a pyramid with an eye at the top. Is this the all-seeing eye of justice, or is it blind to the needs of the poor who are being crushed at the bottom of the global pyramid?

Matthew's Sermon on the Mount declares the good news of the "Unseen Seer" as seeing the ones that Caesar overlooks. Authentic communal acts of worship connect the powerless and the overlooked to the "Unseen Seer." Caesar's empire, as all empires, is only a temporary replica, emulating Pharaoh's empire that will also one day lay fallen in ruins under the collapsed structures of history.

SERMON

Last week I had the special privilege of sharing with two couples in the joyful celebration of the birth of their firstborn child. These infants enter the world with the cry of, "Give me your attention please!" Their instinctive cry is a protest against aloneness in a strange and mysterious world wherein they feel so vulnerable. As these precious little ones grow into adulthood, they will learn to use more sophisticated means such as conversation and behavior to attract the attention of others. They will learn that many adult conversations and interactions are fierce competitions of tug of war, wherein people pull hard against each other in the persistent pursuit to possess each other's undivided attention. These little ones will continue to grow in their awareness that being seen or noticed can make one feel significant and special. Being seen or noticed makes one feel that one actually does exist.

One of the most painful feelings is the feeling of being invisible. Being born into the invisible 97 percent poverty underclass in the Roman Empire was a painful experience for many of Matthew's audience. In modern times being born into the wrapping of a skin color that causes one to automatically be consigned to an invisible underclass in today's empire is a painful experience. Being born on the other side of a national border and fleeing to a country for economic refuge where your cheap labor is more valued and visible than your humanity is a painful experience.

Inattention to the humanity of others is a passive act of hatred that subtly denies the significance of their existence. Another word for authentic human attention is *love*. To affirm the existence of others by attending to their needs and making them feel visible is an act of love. Love has been found so vital for babies that a total absence of it will either kill them or reduce them to imbecility or madness.

A disease known as Marasmus is common among infants who are war victims or who are poorly cared for in orphanages. Marasmus is a medical term for starvation or a gradual wasting away of the body, generally associated with severe malnutrition or inadequate absorption of food. Marasmus worsens when infants are not picked up, held, cuddled, caressed, kissed, hugged, squeezed, and generally loved. A child with Marasmus doesn't develop socially, psychologically, or physically, and often wastes away and dies. This disease is not exclusively caused by food or material deprivation, but is also caused by emotional trauma and the deprivation of love.

As Warren Carter points out, according to the Children's Defense Fund there are 13 million children in the wealthiest nation on earth who are living in the overlooked grips of poverty, many of whom are also starving for love and authentic human attention.

In Romans 16:16 Paul shows the importance of recognizing each other's existence by saluting and greeting one another with the physical touch of a holy kiss. Much of our culture today is cold and disconnected. People walk past each other without speaking or making any eye contact. We live among each other as zombies, with our imagination and cognition short–circuited by consumerism and greed.

Children growing up in cold and unaffirming social environments often suffer from a twisted and distorted need for attention. The distorted need for attention creates within them a Grand Canyon–sized starvation for attention. People with a distorted need for attention become emotional vagabonds scrounging through the garbage cans of life searching for the leftover scraps of human praise. They are emotionally homeless searching for cognitive shelter in the eyes of other people.

Television and the movie industry have become sophisticated homeless shelters that Hollywood uses to house celebrities in the eyes of the watching masses of fans. Some celebrities feel significant only when they are seen in the public's eye and given ovations. When they become invisible to the public's eye during a career low, they feel like they are dead and have nothing to live for. It is as if they no longer exist. When their careers rebound, it is said that they have made a comeback. The question is, Where have they come back from? Such actors have come back from obscurity. They have reappeared on the public scene onscreen. The public can once again go to the movies to "see" them and "watch" them on television.

In the first century when Matthew lived, actors in the theater were known as hypocrites. They were stage actors acting out the parts of a character in a play. It was a custom for Greek and Roman actors to speak in large masks painted to represent the character they were portraying. They used mechanical devices for augmenting the force of the voice. They were not being themselves in the public's eye, only impersonating others.

In life, the hypocrite is a person who masks his or her real self while he or she plays a part to capture the undivided attention of his or her audience. Matthew's gospel addresses religious people who are using pious acts of worship as a form of pretentious playacting. In the name of God they are seeking public notoriety. In the name of God they are seeking to make a name for themselves. Their publicly professed love for God and the poor is nothing more than an actor's costume designed to cover the hidden lust for human praise. This unhealthy religious atmosphere prompted Jesus to say to his disciples, "Be careful not to do your 'acts of righteousness' before men, to be seen by them. If you do, you will have no reward from your Father in heaven" (6:1, NIV).

Jesus knew that a self-centered attempt to impress others with our self-righteousness would contaminate all three areas of piety—giving to the poor, prayer, and fasting. When we seek to win the hearts of others by impressing them with how good we are, we end up tainting our good deeds with the poison chemical of self-promotion. Jesus says, "So when you give to the needy, do not announce it with trumpets, as the hypocrites do in the synagogues on the streets, to be honored by men. I tell you the truth; they have received their reward in full."

When we are good to those who are less powerful and less wealthy only for the purpose of winning their hearts to our political or social causes, we are simply engaging in a covert form of manipulation. Disciples of Jesus understand that for rich nations to throw economic crumbs at countries sleeping at their gates only for the purpose of giving the fake appearance of national generosity is simply another form of victimizing the poor. Disciples of Jesus know that it is national hypocrisy when our domestic policies and politics only give the false impression that we genuinely care about the poor, the elderly, the children, and the alien in our society while at the same time we pass laws that favor the wealthiest segment of our nation.

In the first century among the elite, relief action for the poor was seen more in terms of its benefit in enhancing the giver's image and reputation. The elite were more concerned about their image than about addressing the desperate needs of the poor from whom they were extracting their great wealth.

Jesus says, "But when you give to the needy, do not let your left hand know what your right hand is doing, so that your giving may be in secret. Then your Father, who sees what is done in secret, will reward you." Jesus instructs his disciples to protect the integrity of their giving. Giving loses its integrity when we seek to use it as a tool to draw attention to our own goodness.

The praise seeker always uses giving as a weapon to rob God of the praise and attention that's due God. It is only when our giving springs forth from God's being that we cease seeking to steal God's glory for ourselves. Our giving must be prayerfully planted in the soil of God's being for it to produce the fruits of genuine goodness.

According to Matthew's Sermon on the Mount, Jesus' instruction on prayer is centrally located between his instructions on giving and fasting. One should immediately pin down the conclusion that our acts of giving and fasting are to be inspired by our prayerful communion with God. Our prayerful relationship with God bleaches the clothing of our religious acts of the stains of hypocrisy and grandstanding. Prayer internally cleanses our hearts so that our worship will be carried out without the dirt and grime of narcissistic egotism. In prayer God teaches us how to become comfortable within the invisible realm of spirit. In prayer God gives us the keys that can unlock the doors of our imprisonment to the physical attachments of this world. As God sets us free from physical attachments, God also sets us free from the drug addiction to human praise.

Jesus says, "And when you pray, do not be like the hypocrites, for they love to pray standing in the synagogues and on the street corners to be seen by men. I tell you the truth; they have received their reward in full. But when you pray, go into your room, close the door and pray to your Father, *who is unseen.* Then your Father, who sees what is done in secret, will reward you."

When we go into our prayer room and close the door, we realize that we are encountering the Unseen Seer. Here the spiritual eyes of God are found to be of greater worth than the faultfinding eyes of human beings. What God sees within us is far better than what people are able to see about us. In prayer we discover that we truly are the apple of God's eye and that God is the chief overseer of our souls. It is here that we learn that we are more than our physical bodies. Because prayer empowers us to know that we are more than what meets the human eye, we don't have to spend our energy trying to look good in the eyes of others.

In connection with Jesus' instructions on prayer, he says, "When you fast, do not look somber as the hypocrites do, for they disfigure their faces to show men they are fasting. I tell you the truth; they have received their reward in full." He says, "But when you fast, put on oil on your head and wash your face so that it will not be obvious to men that you are fasting, but only to your Father, who is unseen; and your Father, who sees what is done in secret, will reward you."

Spiritual power is not based on the approval rating we receive for the performance of our pious acts of religion. We become spiritually impotent when we allow our righteousness to walk around on the broken crutches of religious showmanship. Jesus' instructions on prayer remind us that genuine spiritual power grows out of our prayerful meditation upon the Presence of God, the Unseen Seer. The spiritual power that comes as a result of prayer is a power that the Simon the Sorcerers of the global economy cannot buy. Spiritual power that comes from prayer is not a commodity that can be traded on the New York stock exchange.

On the other hand, religious people who worship their religious acts of worship and their religious symbolisms are easily hijacked by the Simon the Sorcerers of this world. The Simon the Sorcerers of the world use religion and its symbols as a means to financial gain. Religious people who are dependent on the external forms of religion are easily misled into supporting political agendas that have a form of godliness but deny the very power thereof.

We experience more spiritual power in the invisible Presence of God than we ever will in our sole dependence on the external form of religion. In the prayer room we come to understand the sovereignty of God. There we stop believing that despotic tyrants and political empires have the divine right to control our minds and our destinies. In the prayer room we lose our fascination with imperial pomp and pageantry designed to seduce undiscerning subjects into a state of soul surrender and worship of empire.

In the prayer room we receive our inoculation against the shock and awe of great military might. In this sacred space we learn no longer to fear despotic regimes that threaten to use physical force against us when we dare challenge their right to extract cheap labor from our brothers and sisters at home and abroad to feed the greed of an exploitative global economy. In the prayer room outrage is transformed into courage that inspires us to look beyond the fake smiles and false handshakes of false prophets and lying politicians to behold God's vision of a world that embraces the humanity of every human being.

In the prayer room we find the strength to revolt against the categories of race that the empire confines us to. In the prayer room we learn that God is not sectionalized, racialized, and privatized. God is not the God of the South, or the God of the North. God is not the God of whites only or the God of blacks only. God is not a God that wears a tag that says, "Made in America." This is why when we pray we say, "Our Father." God is our shared spiritual resource. I might be blacker than a million midnights, and you might be as white as the driven snow, but when we pray as Christ's disciples, and not disciples of empire, we say, "Our Father."

God's name is hallowed. No human on earth bears a name as sacred as God's name, including the Roman emperor. Courage found in the prayer room empowered many Christians to face death at the hands of Domitian. He executed many Christians for "atheism," because they refused to worship the gods of Rome. Nero referred to himself as "Nero, Lord of all the earth" and accepted divine accolades from his subjects. Faithful Christians in the Roman Empire were accused of being unpatriotic because they refused to participate in the worship of the Roman state.

In prayer Jesus' disciples know that it is God and not the economy that provides us with our daily bread. We will not worship the idol god of the economy despite the fact that it has upgraded the golden calf in the wilderness into a bull market on Wall Street. In prayer Jesus' disciples know that God has the only power to deliver us from evil, not any president or any political party. In prayer Jesus' disciples know that the kingdom, power, and the glory belong to God, not to any nation. We cry forth that Jesus is Lord.

- In the face of threat and intimidation, we say Jesus is Lord.
- In the face of lynchings and church bombings, we say Jesus is Lord.
- In the face of water hoses and police dogs, we say Jesus is Lord.
- In the face of assassinations, we say Jesus is Lord.
- In the face of economic slavery and sexism, we say Jesus is Lord.
- In the face of the World Bank and the military-industrial complex, we say Jesus is Lord.
- In the face of false accusations and severe persecutions, we say Jesus is Lord.
- In the face of domestic terrorists that have infiltrated our own government, we say Jesus is Lord.

We do not fear him who can destroy the body; we fear the one who can destroy both body and soul. Because we know this we do not fear what man can do to us.

- What is man that we should seek to impress him? Man is only a dressed-up piece of earth walking about as potential dust for some well-kept cemetery on some lonesome hillside.
- What is man that we should seek to impress him? Man is only a flicker of light that flashes for a moment and is soon blown out into the darkness of eternity.
- What is man that we should seek to impress him? Man is nothing but a breath (a bad breath at that). He is swiftly inhaled into this earthly existence and is soon exhaled into an invisible region from which no traveler has returned.

- What is man that we should seek his honor? For he has been created and set at the pinnacle of creation, yet he chooses to live as an enemy to creation, making himself to be pitied as an endangered species within creation, facing the threat of self-annihilation.
- What is man that we should seek his honor? For he has been given the lofty place just beneath the angels, yet he chooses to live on a level beneath the demonic.
- Our reward comes from being seen by the Unseen Seer. Only God's Spirit can touch and caress our human spirit. It is God's silent voice that speaks so loudly that it drives out all fear from the inner regions of our being.
- In spite of all the external arrangements of war taking place in the world today, we as God's children remain secure in our secret place of prayer within the sacred temple of our being.
- We are encouraged by the Unseen Seer who is with us even to the end of the age. Faith is the substance of things hoped for and the evidence of things not seen. That which is seen is temporal, that which is invisible is eternal.
- Why should I feel discouraged, and long for heaven and home, when I've got Jesus as my portion? He is a constant friend. His eye is on the sparrow, and I know he watches me. I sing because I am happy. I sing because I am free. His eye is on the sparrow. I know he watches me.

17

New Rules for the Game of Life

Matthew 6:19–34

CHRIS ALTROCK

Compositional Comments

Charles Campbell urges us to see the Sermon on the Mount as a vision for an alternative world, a vision that, in contrast to the contemporary culture, may seem like folly.[1] Thus, in this sermon I invite the listener to consider a particularly "crazy" slice of that vision—using possessions for neighbor rather than self. Jesus turns the ancient and contemporary view of wealth on its head, showing that we tend to value what is ultimately worthless and we tend to overlook what is truly priceless. As Warren Carter reveals, the Sermon on the Mount was originally preached in a context of social inequality and to a culture in which the elite "stored up treasure" for themselves. It therefore has challenging implications for the consumeristic society in which we currently live.[2] This sermon strives to name the financial "powers" at work against us and against God in modern life. It invites listeners to take up residence in a different world, the world of generosity, hospitality, and simplicity imagined by the Sermon on the Mount.

This sermon was preached at the Highland Street Church of Christ in July 2006 as our congregation began its new fiscal year and was part of a larger effort to call congregants to examine not only their weekly giving, but their entire approach to possessions. Ours is an upper-middle–class congregation that meets in one of America's poorest cities—Memphis, Tennessee.

SERMON

I recently played the game of LIFE with my daughter Jordan. To begin, you pick a career. I was a physician pulling in $60,000 each time I crossed a Pay-Day. Jordan was an accountant pulling in $50,000 each time she crossed Pay-Day. As we moved our miniature cars around the board, we frequently landed on spaces marked "LIFE." Here, we picked up LIFE tiles that awarded us in ways such as, "Win dance contest $10,000." Eventually, Jordan and I reached the game's final space. On the last page of LIFE's rule booklet there is printed in very large letters "How To Win." Here's what it says: *The player with the highest total value wins!"* Predictably, the goal of LIFE is to get the most money. As the creators sought to simulate what life is like, they chose to focus on money. You don't win by demonstrating loyalty to friends. You don't win by giving away dollars to charity. You win by collecting the most money. That's the rule.

I put the game and the booklet away; but ever since, it seems to pop up everywhere I am. When I drive by the University of Memphis, I see students' backpacks with LIFE's booklet sticking out–three-fourths of them say that "becoming wealthy" is an important goal.[3] When I see teenage girls at the mall, many of them have the rules of LIFE jutting out of their purses–over 90 percent of them say that shopping is their favorite activity.[4] And as I drive through for burgers and dig around in my glove box for change, LIFE's booklet falls out–people like me spend fifty times more on fast food than on helping the poor.[5] It seems that many of us live as if there were some merit to the rules of LIFE.

But we are not alone. Two thousand years ago some lived by a philosophy similar to: *The player with the highest total value wins!* Listen to Jesus' description of his own peers. [*The text of Mt. 6:19–34 was read out loud at this point.*] As Jesus searches for a way to summarize this ancient culture's take on money, he puts it this way: they were "storing up" for themselves "treasures on earth." Literally, Jesus says they were "treasuring treasure on earth" for themselves; that is, for selfish purposes.[6] In addition, Jesus notes that they were "worrying" about possessions. At least five times Jesus describes his peers as "worrying" about wealth. They were ambitious about food and fashion.[7] Finally, Jesus describes his ancient world as *"running after all these things."* The elite, who controlled most of the wealth, were running to keep that wealth. The nonelite were running to gain that wealth.[8] Like us, the lives of both were governed by things financial.

But Jesus invites us to take a closer look at these rules of LIFE. First, he reveals the transient nature of our material obsession: "Do not store up for yourselves treasures on earth, where moth and rust destroy, and where thieves break in and steal" (6:19, NIV). A life focused on gaining more is focused on things transient. With no climate-controlled storage or modern savings-and-loan, most in Jesus' day kept their fine clothes at home and their savings in a strongbox in the home or buried beneath it. Thus, the clothing could be destroyed by insects, the buried treasure could be corroded by rust, and the strongbox could be stolen by thieves.[9] It was all terribly transient.

It still is. For example, my friend Kevin was so excited when he had finally saved enough to buy a car. It was used, but it was new to him. Not many in our small high school had their own car—now Kevin did. We who had to bum rides from friends or parents envied him. But one day Kevin sped down Cox Canyon, skidded around a curve, off the road, and totaled the car. In an instant, his prized possession became a hunk of junk. Just like that, Jesus says, all those possessions we ambitiously run after can disappear.

But Jesus invites us to consider not just the transient nature of possessions. He urges us to understand their darkly powerful nature. In Jesus' world, something sinister lies behind money. Possessions have the power to impact our hearts: "For where your treasure is, there your heart will be also" (6:21). The heart is Jesus' way of talking about that place where we establish commitments and make decisions.[10] Just as we have a physical organ called the "heart" that governs the rest of our physical activity, so we have a spiritual "heart" that governs the commitments and decisions we make. Those of us who treasure treasure will find that same treasure corrupting our hearts—impacting the commitments and decisions we make. Similarly, Jesus reveals that treasuring treasure results in a dark life: "The eye is the lamp of the body. If your eyes are good, your whole body will be full of light. But if your eyes are bad, your whole body will be full of darkness. If then the light within you is darkness, how great is that darkness!" (6:22–23, NIV). The "eye" is Jesus' way of talking about our focus. Just as we have a physical organ called an "eye" that governs the rest of our body's activity, so we also have a spiritual "eye" that governs the quality of life. What you focus on will either fill your life with light or darkness. It's not just money. It is a power that corrupts the heart and fills life with blackness.

But Jesus' most alarming statement about money is found in these words: "No one can serve two masters. Either [you] will hate the one and love the other, or [you] will be devoted to the one and despise the other. You cannot serve both God and Money" (6:24, NIV). In calling money a "master" or "lord," and in contrasting serving God with serving money, Jesus almost elevates money to a supernatural entity with supernatural power.

C. S. Lewis illustrates this in his book *The Voyage of the Dawn Treader*. Eustace is the well-educated and well-to-do cousin of the Pevensies, who fantasizes about riches and power. During an adventure on an island in Narnia, Eustace stumbles upon a dragon. He watches the dragon leave its cave, limp to the edge of a pool, and die. Curious, Eustace explores the dragon's cave. It is filled with coins, jewelry, and precious stones. As he imagines all he might do with his secret treasure, he falls asleep. When he awakes, he feels awkward; not himself. He lopes out of the cave to the pool of water nearby. When he stares at its surface, he sees a dragon reflected back: "In an instant he realized the truth. The dragon face in the pool was his own reflection. There was no doubt of it. It moved as he moved: it opened and shut its mouth as he opened and shut his. He had turned into a dragon while he was asleep. Sleeping on a dragon's hoard with greedy, dragonish thoughts in his heart, he had become a dragon himself."[11] What Lewis wrote as fiction, Jesus says is nonfiction.

All of us who are governed by the rules of LIFE will wake up one day amazed at the dark ways in which those rules have transformed us. For example, a friend of mine who races cars as a hobby was talking to me about his finances. His church had asked him to consider contributing significantly to some new church initiatives. He said that request became a clarifying moment, because it forced him to look at what he was actually doing with his money. He said, "I had no idea how much I was spending on my hobby. When I sat down and actually looked at how much I was spending on that hobby, I was shocked. I saw just how much money I could be using for others if I weren't spending it on cars." The transformation from human to dragon happens without us even noticing it.

Thankfully, Jesus offers a different perspective on life. "Is not life," he says, "more important than food, and the body more important than clothes?" (6:25, NIV). Of course, he says, there's more to life than what so many of us have been living. Jesus invites us into a new life and a new way of approaching treasure: "But store up for yourselves treasures in heaven, where moth and rust do not destroy, and where thieves do not break in and steal" (6:20, NIV). Jesus' world features an approach to finances that overcomes their transient nature. Jesus will echo these words later in Matthew 19:21 when he says, "If you want to be perfect, go, sell your possessions and give to the poor, and you will have treasure in heaven." In Jesus' world, when we use money for others, especially the poor, we make eternal investments—no insect, rust, thief, or slippery road can touch them. How encouraging to consider that every penny, stock, vehicle, square foot of your home, or hour on the company clock can become an eternal investment. Jesus invites us to live in a world where, when we use possessions for others, those finances take on an enduring quality.

Jesus invites us into a world where the dark power of money can be transformed into a positive force: "If your eyes are healthy, your whole body will be full of light." Jesus' word "healthy" can mean "generous." It is a life-focus that looks generously toward others.[12] In Jesus' world, life is about seeing what possessions can do for others; it's about focusing on the use of earthly possessions in heavenly ways, righteous ways. When money is invested in the needs of people, those of us who are dragons are transformed into angels. In the dark world of greed, we become sources of light.

For the past few months some members at Highland have experienced this light. Rick is a young boy who's been staying with his mother and father in our congregation's "Matthew House"–a free home for cancer patients at Saint Jude. Some Highland members prepared the home for Rick's arrival. Others provided Rick transportation to and from Saint Jude. Still others prepared meals and took the family out for meals. Some worked to get Rick into school. In our consumeristic culture, those selfless acts have been a beacon of light. They've been a death blow to the dragon of greed. They've been an assault against the powers that tell us that financial success is the goal of life. Each hour given up to clean Rick's house, each gallon of gas burned to drive him to the hospital, each grocery or restaurant bill incurred to feed the family, and each dollar potentially given to aid his schooling has become an eternal investment. Even more, they've allowed many to experience the light of Jesus' way of life. They've helped introduce us all to a whole new way of enjoying this game of life.

In Dostoevsky's *The Idiot,* Prince Myshkin is thrust into a culture obsessed with wealth. But the Prince has no greed or envy. He refuses to treasure treasure for himself. In contrast to the surrounding culture, his financial behavior is so abnormal that people don't know what to think of him. Eventually they conclude that he is an idiot.[13] The story raises the question of who is the real idiot–the one who focuses on what is transient and darkly powerful or the one who focuses on what is eternal and a positive force of light. May our faith in a heavenly Father who provides "all these things" lead us to be generous and open-handed–even if the world thinks us fools.

18

You Be the Judge?

Matthew 7:1–6

LUCY LIND HOGAN

Compositional Comments

During his lecture at the Rochester Sermon Seminar, Stanley Hauerwas issued a challenge. We, the church, he argued—we who follow Jesus Christ—should be so happy and filled with joy that everyone who sees us will want the life we are living. They will want to follow Christ. As spiritual writer Evelyn Underhill observed, we need to be "contagious Christians."[1] Unfortunately, we seem to spend less time "infecting" and more time "vaccinating" people *against* Christ with our poisonous, pious, judgmental attitudes.

I begin the sermon by reminding us of the setting and the moment when Jesus went, as the saying goes, "from preaching to meddling." I tried to keep before me the understanding stressed by all the essayists in this volume that the Sermon on the Mount is a message to the church, to a group of people, and should not be privatized. It is the challenge to the church as a whole. By participating in a "community of forgiveness," according to Hauerwas, we learn to name our sins and know ourselves as those who have been forgiven.

As I try to show through examples, judging seems to be part of our very being. Therefore the challenge not to judge seems almost impossible. But I was helped by Warren Carter's reminder that the Sermon on the Mount is not a text that lays before us an impossible and unfulfillable ideal. Rather, it is a vision, given by God, of a new way to live. It is, according to Charles Campbell, not a burden, but an adventure. And it is, according to Hauerwas, a call to live entirely dependent on God and one another. Therefore, we are called upon, not to judge and exclude, but to give our lives willingly and extravagantly to the other, as Jesus gave his life for us. It was this that I hoped to show through the use of the example in *Babette's Feast*, with its strong christological and eucharistic themes.

SERMON

Jesus had been making quite a name for himself teaching the good news of the kingdom of God and, perhaps more spectacularly, curing every disease and every sickness. No wonder great crowds had begun to follow him wherever he went. They watched, they listened, they reflected on what it meant to follow this man Jesus and to live into the reign of God. We join that crowd, listening, reflecting, and wrestling with what it means to live into the life set forward by the preacher Jesus in this Sermon. Dare we, and if we do, how can we live in a world so wonderful, so abundant, so perfect?

What sort of day was it when Jesus went up the mountain? Was it a gentle spring day? Was there a soft breeze blowing the newly growing grass and budding wild flowers promising new life? Was it the kind of day when people would look for any excuse to get away from the work that needed to be done? Was there a joyous festive atmosphere? People were being healed, after all. Paralytics were walking. The blind could see, and the deaf could hear. What more marvelous things might this teacher do? So they followed him, out away from the town and up on the mountain. Again he began to teach.

Like all good speakers, he began by capturing the good will of his listeners. Who doesn't like to hear the good news that we are going to be comforted and inherit the earth? We like being assured that we will receive mercy and not only see God, but be called children of God. I would imagine the nods of agreement and pleasure moved through the crowd like waves. Yes, this was the exciting teacher who they had been following, proclaiming the great good news. Weren't the miracles signs that this was all true?

When did the nodding stop? Did it stop when he praised those times when they would be reviled and persecuted? Did their expressions change and did they begin to exchange disgruntled looks with those nearby when he told them that they might be thrown out and trampled underfoot if they were like useless salt? What kind of good news was that? And then, when he began telling them not to be angry or insulting, that those actions were as bad as murder—well, he went over the top at that point. Did some in the crowd begin to leave?

Matthew's Sermon on the Mount seems to present us with an impossible portrait. How are we, as the church, the descendants of those disciples, the followers of this preacher seated on the side of that mountain, ever going to be able to live the life pictured in this Sermon? How can we be perfect as our heavenly God is perfect? Might we be tempted to join those annoyed spectators and walk out? I think we find it impossibly difficult when this mountain preacher demands that we not judge others. Not judge others at all, ever; how can that be? How can we do that? Should we do that? Aren't there people who deserve to be judged? Do we not live in a world of sinners?

Who is in, who is out? Who is good or bad? Who is first, last, up, down, best, worst? Who should be the highest or the lowest? Who is the insider, and who is the outsider?

Watch young children at play, and you will discover that, very early in life, we begin to judge others. Children love to make up teams or groups. They make selections deciding who will be a part of the group and who will be excluded. The criteria for inclusion or exclusion will be as varied as there are children—everything from gender, to hair color, to athletic ability. The inability to throw or hit a ball means that you will usually be judged as not preferred "team" material.

It hurts to be the one who is banished from the team as a child. Judging others can be damaging, but it can also be an important and crucial skill. Often we encounter people whom we need to avoid, people who will lead us down the wrong path and into things in which we should not be involved. Judgments, therefore, are complex and essential decisions.

Of course, it is not just children who judge one another. We live in a challenging time of sharp divisions in and between churches, in and between political parties, communities, and nations. All you have to do is turn on the news programs filled with "talking heads" and you will see one after another making and pronouncing judgment. Their debates are characterized, not by civility and politeness, but by rancor and rudeness. What are we to make of Jesus' command that we, as individuals or communities, are not to pass judgment on one another?

Over and over Jesus demands of us the extraordinary, the impossible, the perfect. A rich young man hears the demand to follow not only the letter of law, but also to give away everything that he has. Jesus demands that his dear friend Martha, on the death of her brother, realize that Lazarus will live again. Jesus demands that the disciples drop everything, not even taking time to bury a dead parent, and follow him. To Jesus this was all possible, but to us? How are we who are mortal, finite, and imperfect able to do the perfect? Perhaps a clue lies in the riddle of camels and needles.

When that rich young man asks Jesus what he needs to do to have eternal life, Jesus' answer is clear, extravagant, and uncompromising. The young man needs to sell his "possessions, and give the money to the poor" (Mt. 19:21a), and then follow Jesus. As the young man walks away disconsolately, Jesus observes that it is easier for a camel to pass through a needle's eye than it is for persons of wealth to give away all that they have. Is the focus of this riddle money? Somewhat. Is it about divine tricks of magic? Hardly. Is Jesus really speaking about a small gate in the city's wall? We mustn't be so literally minded. No, the disciples do not understand that Jesus in asking the ultimate, the impossible; he wanted us to understand that it is not up to the human. It is never anything that we can do on our own. We are called to recognize that camels can fit through the eye of a needle, the wealthy can give all that they have, only when we rely on God and place our trust in the one who created and loves us. Only when we place our trust in God will we be able to live into that extraordinary perfection, "For mortals it is impossible, but for God all things are possible" (Mt. 19:26b).

Truly, for God and with God, all things are possible. What joyous good news. When we, as both individuals and as church, live into that truth, we begin to realize how foolish it is for us to think that we can do it on our own. We need to divest ourselves of our reliance on our wealth, our investments, and our judgments alone. Our judgments always will be limited, biased, prejudiced, and incomplete. We should hold before us God's rebuke of Samuel, "The LORD does not see as mortals see; they look on the outward appearance, but the LORD looks on the heart" (1 Sam. 16:7b).

We, who follow the preacher, seeking to be poor in spirit, meek, merciful, pure in heart, and peacemakers are challenged to develop "God vision." Jesus asks us to look on the heart of the other and be suspicious of our human tendency to look on the outward appearance. Because we participate in a community of forgiveness, Jesus' command is extraordinary, impossible, and uncompromising—"Do not judge." We are able to live into that command only through our reliance on our forgiving God.

God, who makes these demands, helps us to do the impossible. God also recognizes the complexity of our lives. God knows we will face moments in our lives, in community, and relationship with others when we will need to make judgments. We are therefore given instructions on how to act.

We are called upon to see as God sees, with "God vision." Unfortunately, our vision is hindered by the logs in our eyes. We grow so used to thinking of ourselves as superior to others that when we see the imperfections in the other—the *karphos* or twig that is in their eye, we fail to notice the *dokos* or log that is in our own eye. A *dokos* is the beam that supports the roof of a building. Jesus wants us to laugh at the ridiculous image. There is no way that we could have a *dokos* in our eye; it would crush us. That is the whole point. We do walk around with a *dokos* in our eyes, and it crushes us.

To see with "God vision" is to live into the love and respect with which God accepts us. We love our neighbors as ourselves. It does not mean that we cannot challenge people and call them to accountability before the gospel. It just means that we leave the judging up to God.

What will this look like? *Babette's Feast* gives us a glimpse. The film tells the story of a woman who does an extraordinary, unexpected, and extravagant thing, filling a community with love and grace. A fugitive from the civil war that rages in Paris, Babette arrives on the doorstep of two elderly sisters in an isolated village in Norway. They preside over a small and very contentious pious sect founded by their late father. For many years after, Babette works as their maid and cook. As an outsider, she watches and listens quietly as the group gathers not only for prayers and Bible study, but for quarreling and squabbling. Scrupulously passing judgment on each other had become their way of life, and year after year they fight, take sides, and divide over the slightest of insults and infractions.

One summer day, Babette receives a letter informing her that she has won an enormous sum of money in the French lottery. The sisters are shocked when she asks their permission to spend her winnings on them by preparing a feast for the celebration of their late father's birthday. A somber and fearful group gathers around the sister's now lavishly set dining room table, having vowed to one another that they will eat this luxurious and sinful meal but not enjoy it. They invite wealthy village aristocrat, General Loewenhielm, to join them. This man of the world serves as the narrator of the glorious meal. He explains sumptuous dish after sumptuous dish lovingly prepared by Babette, who is giving them all that she possesses. What none of the guests know is that before Babette left Paris she had been the chef of a famous restaurant where the General frequently dined. The key, however, is that Babette never appears in the dining room, so the General cannot tell the sisters and their guests the true identity of their host.

Gradually, the grace of the food, the wine, and most importantly, the artistry of the woman preparing the dishes, begins to fill the room with the glorious radiance of a heavenly light. Joy and celebration replace discord and friction. Finally, the General proclaims the good news of the gift that has been given them all, "Grace, my friends, demands nothing from us but that we shall await it with confidence and acknowledge it in gratitude. Grace…makes no conditions and singles out none of us in particular; grace takes us all to its bosom and proclaims general amnesty…For mercy and truth have met together, and righteousness and bliss have kissed one another!"[2]

Tears fill their eyes, and forgiveness fills their hearts. Hateful words are forgotten, and the invitation to the table transforms them into a community of love. From that day they began to live into the mercy made possible by that grace and amnesty. And, as they tumble forth from that place, a sort of "upper room," their words of love mingle with the snow that dances in the air. "Bless you," they all call after one another.

We all have been invited by our great preacher, Jesus the Christ, to gather at the table. With overflowing, abundant grace he gathers us to his bosom and proclaims the amnesty of forgiveness and mercy. He commands us in turn to greet our brothers and sisters with that same forgiveness and mercy. Our judgments are replaced with blessings and the humble acknowledgment of our oneness in Christ.

19

God Responds to All Who Seek Him

Matthew 7:7–12

RUBEL SHELLY

Compositional Comments

Dare we live in the world imagined for us in Matthew's Sermon on the Mount? Surely we *desire* it, but we *cannot do so* without the transforming power of the Holy Spirit. Our problems are not the strictly historical, exegetical, hermeneutical, or even "application" issues scholars raise about the Sermon. They are far more existential.

For example, in chapter 3 in this volume, Stanley Hauerwas cites the work of Dietrich Bonhoeffer with this Sermon. One can hardly appreciate what the latter writes without knowing that he was dealing with kingdom life (i.e., what Hauerwas calls "our participation in a community of forgiveness") in the historical context of Hitler and the Nazis. Bonhoeffer was trying to figure out how to live nonresistance to evil in Germany during World War II. For him, great struggles of conscience notwithstanding, it meant not only leading a confessing church over against the anti-Jewish state church but trying to assassinate *Der Fuhrer.*

For me to preach Matthew 7:7–12–as you will see directly–takes me to my own autobiographical and existential province. I have seen religious authority function in ways very different from Jesus' teaching and example. It was used judgmentally and abusively–an observation that entails the awful paradox that Hauerwas named of judging those who judge. So I simply confess the struggle. I hope my "judgment" is indeed simply embracing the verdict God has already made, while being essentially confessional rather than censuring of others.

Recent New Testament scholarship has helped us appreciate the positive aspects of Judaism in the time of Christ. Not every Pharisee, for example, was a hypocrite. We should have known better from having met Nicodemus in the Fourth Gospel and from Paul's recounting of his pre-Damascus Road life as a "Pharisee of Pharisees." Yet the fact remains that our modern problem of the abuse of religious authority has some first-century roots.

Some Pharisees and scribes had made Yahweh into an impossible-to-please Sovereign for Israel and an unappealing-to-us Mystery for pagans. That is part of what I understand Peter to imply when he said the religion he had grown up with was "a yoke that neither our ancestors nor we have been able to bear" (Acts 15:10b). Into that deficient matrix came the Son of God who challenged people to think of God in a new way. The Sermon on the Mount offered them the vision of an alternative community that would model authority in love and reveal truth through gentle fruit rather than overwhelming force. It proposes a community that is countercultural through its confession of its need of forgiveness rather than through its image as a forensic society of "religious fussbudgets."

SERMON

When religion is reduced to an angry God giving orders to cringing subjects through prune-faced messengers, we have abandoned the God of Abraham for the gods of paganism. When our worship of that deity is wringing reluctant concessions from him through rule-keeping and ritual, we have given up the God who spared Nineveh for the one whose lightning bolts are thrown as spears from Olympus. When devotion to Yahweh is about "thee" versus "you" in prayer, *a cappella* music as a test of fellowship, or having a deacon volunteer to keep African Americans (and that was not the term of reference he used!) out of Sunday assemblies, mercy and justice, humility and joy are being shortchanged. When religion becomes institutional and has human clergy hands on the levers of its power to admit and exclude, it is God who soon gets excluded.

My experience of church includes the stone soup and snake sandwiches of legalism, sectarianism, racism, and the like. It was all the more confusing to try to sort out because my experience of church also included gentle, godly people who were caught in the trappings of those institutionalized evils. While my devout parents shaped my heart for compassion, much of my formal instruction in religion shaped my mind and teaching to be that of a religious fussbudget.

Fussbudgets worry endlessly about doctrinal minutiae without realizing they are turning good news into bad. They think the event of baptism, for example, can substitute for the process of conversion. They offer what they believe are sincere professions without realizing that they entail performances that are lacking. To the degree these begin to dawn on a religious fussbudget, he or she becomes a spiritual neurotic. Even to say such a thing—not as indictment but merely as confession—is to enter the paradox of judgment. But even the person who points out the paradox is himself making a judgment!

Jesus had his most caustic exchanges with the religious fussbudgets of his day. He accused them of being more interested in the letter than the spirit of the law. He said they knew how to enforce legal minutiae without ever getting the point that Torah was meant to protect and bless people, not torment them. In a word, he said they had the wrong image of Yahweh. He scandalized them by daring to call God "Abba" and teaching his disciples to pray "Our Father" as well.

In the Sermon on the Mount, Jesus said he had come not to abolish but to fulfill the Law and the Prophets. The Law and the Prophets had pointed for centuries to someone who would come in Yahweh's good time—greater than Moses, writing the very words of God on human hearts rather than stone tablets, and putting a new spirit within humans that would enable them to live out the decrees of God. This is not some simplistic prediction-to-achievement motif. This is not prooftexting from scripture. It is something quite different. It is the divine longing for the whole human race to be "accomplished" and "fulfilled" in Christ Jesus.

Jesus went above and beyond anything law could either do or create and then invited us into a brand new quality of righteousness—one some of us miss still on account of our legalistic preoccupation with the minutiae of law. That way of reading scripture leaves us angry and judgmental, playing God rather than surrendering to God. Christ came to bring something radically different.

Jesus forbids seeing scripture as an end in itself or using it as a sledgehammer for passing judgment on unbelievers. It is neither true doctrine nor right morality that makes us disciples. It is Jesus Christ alone, the mediator and Son of God himself who confers that status by his grace. Yet grace does not become antinomian license to abolish the Law and the Prophets; we know how to treat one another if and only if we pay attention to what the Law and the Prophets say. We must, following Christ, "fulfill" them!

Unbelievers can't hear those teachings, for their hearts are not yet prepared for them by the indwelling Spirit. So they can only hear much of our preaching as judgments—judgments that make them resist not only us but the Jesus in whose name we make our pronouncements. So it is wasted time. It is as smart as giving sacred things for dogs to chew on or pearls for pigs to trample in the mud. Your "prospects" will only trample or otherwise stifle your message, turn on you, and maybe even tear you to pieces. But "people" loved and affirmed by our own confession of sinfulness may give a very different hearing to the gospel.

There really is a better way to explain God to unbelievers! We don't have to come across as self-righteous prudes. We dare not act as their judges. We don't have to alienate the people God wants us to influence and win. We can instead be light and salt, living epistles known and read by all, people who—in imitation of the Lord Jesus Christ—incarnate the message of divine grace.

Matthew's Sermon on the Mount underscores Jesus' teaching about the "interdependent" nature of loving God and loving our neighbors. What I called being a "religious fussbudget" or using one's ecclesial role to bully and abuse altogether misrepresents God. It defies the God who in drawing near to us has also drawn near to our neighbors—and made them the more precious to us.

The misuse of Jesus' words about asking and receiving as a generalized promise about prayer has been stock in trade for the "health-and-wealth gospel" crowd. They have used his words here so as to flatly contradict what James warned against—the offering of brazenly selfish prayers.[1] But what is the context here? The larger context is whole-life discipleship under the kingdom rule of God, and the immediate issue is pointless preaching to the non-disciples around us. What, then, do we need so urgently that we should not only "ask" but "seek" and "knock" to obtain? Delivered from the need to judge one another in the community of faith, we want God to teach us to live within this family so as to bear witness effectively to unbelievers around us. So we pray for it.

No more than I would give stones and snakes to one of my hungry children would God fail to give "good gifts" of righteousness and joy, love and peace, or gentleness and self-control to Jesus' disciples who ask for them. So we ask with absolute confidence. "For everyone who asks receives, and everyone who searches finds, and for everyone who knocks, the door will be opened" (Mt. 7:8). We go to the throne of heavenly grace in boldness. And we are this confident of getting exactly what we desire: "He who did not spare his own Son, but gave him up for us all—how will he not also, along with him, graciously give us all things?" (Rom. 8:32, NIV).

For the second time in the Sermon, Jesus speaks here of the Law and the Prophets. Earlier he declared that he had come to "fulfill" them—to show us in his person and behaviors what the Law and the Prophets had anticipated. Now he reaches the crescendo of his Sermon by proclaiming that the golden rule "sums up" the Law and the Prophets.

Against the reduction of religion to rules, regulations, and–particu-larly–*regulators* with a captious, judgmental, and grim spirit, Jesus tells us that it is people who matter to God. Heaven's rules are to bless and empower people, not to crush their spirits. "The Sabbath was made for man, not man for the Sabbath," he declares. "So the Son of Man is Lord even of the Sabbath" (Mk. 2:27–28, NIV). This is a new way of looking at scripture, at commandments generally, and at Sabbath in particular. More than that, it is a whole new way of looking at *people!* But it is the perfect fulfillment of what the Law and the Prophets had envisioned.

Righteousness is all about people, not religious formality: relation-ships, not rules; caring, not judging. So this is the summary principle by which people with an authentic relationship with God relate to their fellow human beings: *treat them the way God has treated you.* What could be simpler? What could be more demanding?

This climactic text is ultimately less about prayer than about faith over unbelief. *How do you see God?* Far from a critical judge, God is a loving Parent who is eager and quick to give the best gifts to children. *How do you understand discipleship?* Far from demanding the impossible of you, God promises to treat you with grace and kindness and love so that you–by the power of the Holy Spirit–will be transformed into the very likeness of his One Perfect Son. *How do you see yourself?* Rather than aloof and critical of others, you can act out of your sense of security to treat your unbelieving neighbors with the very same grace and kindness and love you have received.

Friends of mine appeared in a foreign court in August 2000 to adopt a little girl named Olona. With about two years of background to the proceeding, they stood with her as a judge read from a document that said things such as, "Inasmuch as Olona Morgan is orphaned and unwanted by any family in this country," and, "Inasmuch as no citizen of this country wishes to have Olona Morgan." At the end of that awful recitation which transferred a little girl from state custody to Rick and Patty White, they dropped to their knees, embraced her, and promised, "You will never hear the word 'unwanted' spoken of you again." That little girl is thriving in her new home now and–at her own initiative and request–has now changed her name from Olona Morgan to Hope White!

You and I are not unwanted orphans in a hostile universe. Dearly loved, sought after, and claimed, we are God's children. We have been given Christ's name as our own. We are secure because of him. On the authority of Jesus, we rest in the confidence that we are more precious than we dared dream and that God will never turn us away so long as we are seeking him.

20

The Rain Came Down

Matthew 7:24–27

JEFF CHRISTIAN

Compositional Comments

"The rain came down…" ended a series I preached with a number of other preachers across the United States, a series I also preached as a part of my doctoral project at Abilene Christian University, where I focused upon the role preaching plays in the formation of a person's character. As a part of the Rochester Sermon Seminar, David Fleer and I invited preachers to join together in an online conversation about the Sermon on the Mount, our sermon preparation, and our actual sermons written in community. (That conversation is located at http://sermonseminar. blogspot.com.) We discovered that preachers are solitary creatures who need more encouragement to make themselves vulnerable to one another, not for their own benefit, but for the benefit of the church that needs fresh speech that calls listeners into communion with God whose empire is greater than all the empty promises of contemporary culture.

Speaking of empire, Warren Carter's material in this volume is the most helpful in the formation of this sermon, as well as the whole series. His work on empire helped give the series focus within an either/or dichotomy. We still live in the Roman Empire as recipients of the Sermon on the Mount; Jesus enables "disciples to envision life shaped by God's reign/empire."[1] Jesus' preaching (and our own as we preach from Matthew) concerns itself foremost with showing disciples how to live differently from the expectations and teachings of the empire. As Stanley Hauerwas notes in his essay, followers of Christ and his Sermon know how to survive good and bad fortune because their lives are more dependent upon God than on the happenings of this world. Compare this with our current setting in the United States where both Christianity and politics are hijacked on a daily basis by whichever side is trying to make a point, and one can see why invitations to mercy and peace and prayer are just as needed today as they were in Jesus' day. As I preached this sermon in an affluent and well-educated upper-middle–class church in East Texas, I could not help but feel some irony in comparison with those poor in spirit mourners of Jesus' original audience. The overlap, however, came within those listeners at the Glenwood Church of Christ in Tyler, Texas, who were ready to give up on the promises of the empire in exchange for the solid, everlasting promises of the reign of God. As I preached through the Sermon on the Mount, I dared listeners to inhabit this imagined world where Christians have reputations for being merciful and pure-in-heart peacemakers. Just imagine a world where Christians take whatever life brings them with the confidence that God's empire is more than our hopes, too often grounded in shifting sand.

Dare we imagine?

SERMON

Some see it as a blessing; some see it as a curse. People in Seattle see it one way; people in Kansas see it another. New Orleans. Phoenix. Not all the same.

Rain.

Far be it from Jesus to preach in ways that leave no responsibility on the listener. "The rain came down" on wise and foolish persons on the same day. Everyone experienced the cruelty of a world drenched with hurricanes, tsunamis, and Saturday thunderstorms. But in typical Jesus fashion, he caps his Sermon with a question in the form of a parable: When the rain comes down, will you remember what I said?

I have noticed something living in Texas all my life: people tend to talk to God more when we need rain. We Texans see rain as a blessing. But for some reason, Jesus pictures rain in Matthew 7 as a type of curse, a method of destruction. It makes you wonder about what Jesus said back in Matthew 5:45 in the midst of loving our enemies: If God sends rain on the righteous and unrighteous, is that a gift, or is it Jesus' way of saying that bad things happen whether you follow God or not? This is a difficult question, to say the least, considering how entrenched American Christianity has become in a theology in which God has become a genie in a bottle. We pray for rain, and God pops out of the bottle and says, "Your wish is my command." Nothing could be farther from the landscape of the last paragraph in the Sermon on the Mount.

The key word in Matthew 7:24–27 that brings the whole Sermon together is one of the most beautiful and meaningful words in the New Testament: "therefore" (NIV). Hopefully the listeners heard a thing or two in a Sermon filled with many things. When Jesus sounds the "therefore," the listeners should remember the teachings and put them into practice. Yet, this is no exercise in neo-legalism. Jesus' "therefore" is an invitation to live in a new world populated by those who love God and love their enemies. The new kingdom is now sopping wet with those who live rejoicing in persecution. The new kingdom is drenched in righteousness, filled with those who say "yes" to God's desire to name us "salt of the earth" and "light of the world." The new kingdom is filled to the brim with listeners who not only listen to the words of Jesus, who not only do the things Jesus teaches, but who dare to live in this world as a way of life. Jesus does not invite listeners to merely do more pious things; Jesus invites listeners to "be" the kingdom of heaven.

By the way, you are now one of those listeners.

When the rain comes down, will you remember to rejoice and be glad because of your heavenly reward?

When the rain comes down, will you remember to seek forgiveness from those who have things against you?

When the rain comes down, will you remember to give to the needy, pray for God's unfolding kingdom, even the most difficult ethic of them all—"not judge"?

But the Sermon leaves you unsettled if you listen closely. Where, by the way, is God in all of this? Is God merely the teacher in this passage hoping to leave us with enough teaching that we may decide everything for ourselves—from drought to flood and everything in between?

Where is God by the time Jesus wraps up the Sermon on the Mount, offers the invitation, and says, "Let's stand and sing"?

Perhaps you know the scenario: two next-door-neighbors are praying. Both are righteous followers of God. One prays for rain; the other prays for sunshine. Whatever is God to do? The neighbor's prayer God chooses to honor will leave the other disheartened, let down, questioning God.

Doesn't God care? I prayed for sunshine. It was supposed to be an outdoor wedding! Doesn't God have any idea how much her dress cost me?

But what if God honors the wishes of the other neighbor?

The crops are thirsty. Government farm subsidies only pay for my losses; they don't feed my family. God, Don't you care?

God is in a Catch-22.

Shall we back up for a moment? Some versions of Western Christianity treat God like a contestant on *American Idol.* We praise God when he does well and critique him when he does something outside our expectations. No way can God win among people who only go to him for their desires. What if we truly learned to pray the prayer we learned earlier in the Sermon, that God's will be done on earth in the same way that God's will is done in heaven? What might that world look like? Maybe one of the points of the Sermon on the Mount has to do with living a godly life no matter what happens. Rain. Sunshine. London. The Gobi Desert.

Rejoice. Live as salt and light. Love. Settle your differences. Keep your promises. Give to the needy. Pray. Fast. Serve God, and trust him. Judge not. Ask, seek, and knock. Bear good fruit.

Then back to the ultimatum-laced closing lines of the Sermon: Will you put these words of Jesus into practice and choose a life of wisdom? Or will you forget the Sermon once you walk out the back door? Will you enter through the narrow gate where you have to wait in line for hours? Or will you meander through the wide gate and spend your life in general admission? Will you come to Jesus with ears to hear, or ears stopped up?

Here's the choice, O faithful sermon listeners: Will you put the words of Jesus into practice? It will not be easy. You will have setbacks. But Jesus has welcomed a new world filled with the ways of God, a kingdom like no other. Dare we join together and live in this new world?

Be careful not to say "yes" too soon. Because if you say "yes" today, it will mean walking across the brittle grass in your front yard as you sing, "All to Jesus I Surrender." If you say "yes" today, you will have to show mercy to your frustrated waitress at lunch who not only has to refill your drink, but has a sick husband, a daughter with an unwanted pregnancy, and a boss whose flirting is getting out of hand. If you say "yes" today, you will have to join fellow Christians around the world who turn the other cheek as they refuse to fight evil with evil, who instead cultivate peace as a way of life. If you say "yes" today and commit to live in the world of the Sermon on the Mount, you will join God in his Catch-22 and look silly to those on the outside who will overhear you praying for your enemies while the streams of violence and hatred continue to rise, not just overseas, but right here in this nation that has become a house divided against itself. The racism so common here in East Texas—and everywhere else it seems—is to be purged from our hearts and minds as those who exchange assumptions built upon the shifting sands for promises to the poor in spirit built upon the rock of all rocks. If you say "yes" today, you will commit to cast aside all arrogance built upon the status anxiety of the upwardly mobile and trade it in for the humility Jesus both teaches and models for those who would dare to hunger and thirst for righteousness above the noise of every commercial that tells you to hunger and thirst for goods and services that will only waste away.

Spend today hungering and thirsting for righteousness. Show mercy to everyone. Cultivate purity when you sit in front of the television or computer. Be a peacemaker in your home.

But where is God in all of this? When you put this Sermon into practice, God is there among your good deeds as people praise the God of your shining light; God is there watching you who keep God's commands, calling you "great" in the kingdom of heaven; God is there every time you love your enemies and pray for those who reject you; God is there rewarding what is done in secret, listening as you pray, storing your treasures in heaven; God is there to feed and clothe you when food and clothes no longer saturate your worried mind; God is there standing at the door waiting to open it as soon as you knock.

Therefore, every man, woman, and child who hears these words of Jesus that we call the Sermon on the Mount and puts them into practice is like a wise builder who knows that every good house begins with good groundwork. The rain comes down. Streams rise. Winds blow. No matter. For in the world imagined in the Sermon on the Mount, we live in a kingdom of rock-solid promises, a kingdom that never falls.

Notes

Introduction: Preaching the Sermon on the Mount

[1]*Detroit Free Press,* July 21, 2006, 10A.

[2]From *Writers' Almanac* broadcast in July 2006; transcript online at http://writersalmanac.publicradio.org/programs/2006/07/17/.

[3]Warren Carter forcefully argues for this assumption in this volume's first two chapters.

[4]Warren Carter, *Matthew and Empire: Initial Explorations* (Harrisburg, Pa.: Trinity Press, 2001), 50–53.

[5]Gillian Flaccus, "Antiwar sermon could cost church its tax-exempt status: IRS wants documents, but rector says court fight is likely," *Detroit Free Press,* September 21, 2006, 7A.

Chapter 1: Power and Identities

[1]My special thanks to David Fleer and Dave Bland for editing this volume, Fleer's leadership of the Rochester Sermon Seminar, and to Craig and Patti Bowman for their hospitality throughout the Seminar.

[2]Ulrich Luz, *Matthew 1–7, A Commentary* (Minneapolis: Augsburg, 1989) 218–23 passim; Hans Dieter Betz, *The Sermon on the Mount: A Commentary on the Sermon on the Mount, including the Sermon on the Plain. Matthew 5:3–7:27 and Luke 6:20-49* (Minneapolis: Augsburg Fortress Press, 1995) 5–50. For more recent interpretations, Daniel Patte, *Discipleship According to the Sermon on the Mount: Four Legitimate Readings. Four Plausible Views of Discipleship and Their Relative Values* (Valley Forge, Pa.: Trinity Press International, 1996); Harvey K. McArthur, *Understanding the Sermon on the Mount* (London: Epworth, 1961); Joachim Jeremias, *The Sermon on the Mount,* trans. Norman Perrin (Philadelphia: Fortress Press, 1963).

[3]Warren Carter, *What Are They Saying about Matthew's Sermon on the Mount?* (New York: Paulist Press, 1994).

[4]This was the 2006 Rochester Sermon Seminar's title. The editors welcomed Carter's gentle critique and after conversation, Chalice Press settled on the current title.

[5]Much Matthean scholarship has emphasized the role of chapters 5–7 in its late first-century Jewish context, and especially in Matthew's dispute with a synagogue community. I am omitting any discussion of this context because of time and space. For discussion, see Warren Carter, *Matthew: Storyteller, Interpreter, Evangelist,* rev. ed. (Peabody, Mass.: Hendrickson: 2005), 66–91.

[6]For elaboration of much of this material, see Warren Carter, *Matthew and the Margins: A Sociopolitical and Religious Reading* (Maryknoll, N.Y.: Orbis Books, 2000), 53–130.

[7]The construction is a genitive absolute.

[8]On 1:1, see Warren Carter, "Matthean Christology in Roman Imperial Key: Matthew 1.1," in *The Gospel of Matthew in Its Roman Imperial Context,* ed. John Riches and David Sim (New York: T&T Clark International, 2005) 143–65.

[9]For a good summary of diverse first-century messianic expectations, see M. de Jonge, "Messiah," *Anchor Bible Dictionary,* ed. David Noel Freedman (New York: Doubleday, 1992): 4:777–88.

[10]On 1:21, see Warren Carter, "'To Save His People from Their Sins' (Matthew 1:21): Rome's Empire and Matthew's Salvation as Sovereignty," in *Matthew and Empire: Initial Explorations* (Harrisburg, Pa.: Trinity Press International, 2001), 75–107.

167

[11]See Warren Carter, "Matthew's People," in *Christian Origins: A People's History of Christianity*, ed. Richard A. Horsley (Minneapolis: Fortress Press, 2005), 1:138–61.

[12]Exodus 19:3, 20; 24:9, 13, 15, 18; 34:4; Deuteronomy 9:9; 10:3; compare Exodus 24:12; 32:30; 34:2; Deuteronomy 10:1.

[13]Isaiah 2:3; 30:29; Micah 4:2; Psalm 24:3; Zechariah 8:3; 1 Maccabees 5:54; compare Isaiah 40:9; Jeremiah 31:6; Obadiah 21; Haggai 1:8; 1 Maccabees 7:33.

[14]Author's translation.

[15]Matthew 5:3, 10, 19, 20; 6:10, 33; 7:21.

[16]On preaching and imagination, see Walter Brueggemann, *Finally Comes the Poet: Daring Speech for Proclamation* (Minneapolis: Fortress Press, 1989); Brueggemann, "Preaching as ReImagination," *Theology Today* 52 (1995): 313–29; Brueggemann, *The Prophetic Imagination*, 2d ed. (Minneapolis: Fortress Press, 2001); Mary Hilkert, *Naming Grace: Preaching and Sacramental Imagination* (New York: Continuum, 1997).

[17]See Carter, *Matthew and the Margins*, 1–49; Carter, *Matthew and Empire*, 9–53. On models of empires, see Dennis C. Duling, "Empire: Theories, Methods, Models" in *Gospel of Matthew in Its Roman Imperial Context*, ed. Riches and Sim, 49–74. For wider discussion, see Warren Carter, *The New Testament and the Roman Empire: An Essential Guide* (Nashville: Abingdon Press, 2006).

[18]Several factors point to the 80s C.E. as a likely date. (1) Matthew inserts a reference to the destruction of Jerusalem into the parable in 22:7, indicating a post-70 C.E. date. (2) All but 50 verses of Mark's gospel appear in Matthew, suggesting Matthew used Mark's gospel as a source. Mark was written around 70 C.E. For discussion, Carter, *Matthew: Storyteller*, 13–29, 47–65. (3) Texts written by around 100, including the *Didache* (see *Did.* 8.1–3) and letters from Ignatius (to Smyrna, see 1:1; to Polycarp, see 2:2 and Matthew 10:16b; to the Philippians, see 3:1 and Matthew 15:13; to the Ephesians, see 19:1–3 and Matthew 1–2), seem to know the gospel and cite material in the form that it appears in Matthew. See Meier, {Author: Need first name of "Meier".} "Matthew and Ignatius: A Response to William R. Schoedel," in *Social History of the Matthean Community: Cross-Disciplinary Approaches*, ed. David Balch (Minneapolis: Fortress Press, 1991), 178–86. There is no certainty about Antioch as the place of writing. Several factors justify it as at least a reasonable guess: (1) the association with Antioch and Syria of the *Didache* and Ignatius of Antioch; (2) the addition of Syria to 4:24; and (3) the prominent role of Peter in the gospel and in Antioch (Gal. 1–2). For further discussion, see Carter, *Matthew and the Margins*, 15–17.

[19]Josephus, *JW* 3.8, 29. Josephus places three legions in Antioch in 40 C.E. (*JW* 2.186). The governor Cestius took troops from Antioch in 66 C.E. to quell the revolt but was driven back to Syria (*JW* 2.499–555). Tacitus asserts four legions in Syria but does not identify where they are stationed (*Ann* 4.5).

[20]Josephus, *JW* 5.520.

[21]Josephus indicates a long tradition of Syrian conflicts with Jews, *JW* 1.88; 2.266; 461–65, 477-78; 5.550–51).

[22]Jews were blamed for a disastrous fire that destroyed a number of public buildings, which led to violence against some Antioch Jews (Josephus, *JW* 7.47, 54–62).

[23]Josephus, *JW* 7.96, 100–111.

[24]Josephus, *JW* 7.218; Dio Cassius, 65.7.2; for discussion, see Warren Carter, "Paying the Tax to Rome as Subversive Praxis: Matthew 17:24–27," in *Matthew and Empire*, 130–44.

[25]Virgil, *Aeneid*, 1.277–79; Suetonius, *Vespasian*, 5.7; Tacitus, *Hist.*, 1.86; Dio Cassius, 64.8.2; 64.9.1; 65.1.2–4. See Carter, *Matthew and Empire*, 20–34.

[26]Carter, *Matthew and Empire*, 44–45, for discussion and illustrations.

[27]Daniel J. Harrington, *The Gospel of Matthew*, Sacra Pagina 1. (Collegeville, Minn.: Liturgical Press, 1991), 10–19.

[28]Anthony J. Saldarini, "The Gospel of Matthew and Jewish-Christian Conflict," in *Social History*, ed. Balch, 38–61; also Anthony J. Saldarini, *Matthew's Christian-Jewish Community* (Chicago: University of Chicago, 1994).

[29]Matthew 2:15, 19, 20.

[30]Carter, "Evoking Isaiah: Why Summon Isaiah in Matthew 1:23?" in *Matthew and Empire*, 93–107.

[31]Warren Carter, "Are There Imperial Texts in the Class: Intertextual Eagles and Matthean Eschatology as 'Lights Out' Time for Imperial Rome," *Journal of Biblical Literature* 122, no. 3 (Fall 2003): 467–87.

[32]Carter, *Mathew and the Margins*, 130–37.

[33]For an excellent discussion of the poor, see C.R. Whittaker, "The Poor," in *The Romans*, ed. A. Giardina (Chicago: The University of Chicago Press, 1993), 272–99.

[34]I have heard this story used in several sermons, though I have not remembered the preacher, place, or date. The reader might recall its use in the movie *Fried Green Tomatoes*, with slight cosmetic differences.

[35]For the roles and power of governors as representatives of the Roman Empire, and the scenes between Pilate and Jesus in the four canonical gospels, see Warren Carter, *Pontius Pilate: Portraits of a Roman Governor* (Collegeville: Liturgical, 2003).

[36]Further examples follow in Matthew 5:13–16, and 5:21–48. Carter, *Matthew and the Margins*, 143–57.

Chapter 2: Embodying God's Empire in Communal Practices

[1]Children's Defense Fund, *The State of America's Children, 2005* (Washington, D.C.: Children's Defense Fund, 2005), chapter 1:1, 18.

[2]Ibid., 5.

[3]Ibid., 3.

[4]Ibid., 1.

[5]Ibid., 4.

[6]Ibid., 5.

[7]Chuck Collins and Felice Yeskel, *Economic Apartheid in America* (New York: New Press, 2000), 39. Quoted in Jack Nelson-Pallmeyer, *Saving Christianity from Empire* (New York: Continuum International, 2005), 163.

[8]CDF, *The State*, chapter 2:4–5.

[9]Bill Moyers, "The Fight of Our Lives," AlterNet, posted on June 16, 2004; quoted in Nelson-Pallmeyer, *Saving Christianity*, 163.

[10]CDF, *The State*, chapter 2:1.

[11]Ibid., 1.

[12]James R. Nieman and Thomas G. Rogers, *Preaching to Every Pew: Cross-cultural Strategies* (Minneapolis: Fortress Press, 2001); Joseph R. Jeter Jr. and Ronald J. Allen, *One Gospel, Many Ears: Preaching for Different Listeners in the Congregation* (St. Louis: Chalice Press, 2002).

[13]Leonora Tubbs Tisdale, *Preaching as Local Theology and Folk Art* (Minneapolis: Fortress Press, 1997), 56–90.

[14]Author's translation.

[15]Dwight D. Eisenhower, "Farewell Address to the Nation," January 17, 1961; quoted in Nelson-Pallmeyer, *Saving Christianity*, 162.

[16]The phrase, of course, derives from Ronald J. Sider, *Rich Christians in an Age of Hunger* (Dallas: Word, 1990).

[17]For discussion, see Warren Carter, *Matthew and the Margins: A Sociopolitical and Religious Reading* (Maryknoll, N.Y.: Orbis Books, 2000), 305–8, 326–28.

[18]In recent decades there has been much rethinking of some standard claims about first-century Judaism. For a very helpful discussion, see George W.E. Nickelsburg, *Ancient Judaism and Christian Origins: Diversity, Continuity, and Transformation* (Minneapolis: Fortress Press, 2003).

[19]Carter, *Matthew and the Margins*, 159–60; Arthur Robinson Hands, *Charities and Social Aid in Greece and Rome* (Ithaca, N.Y.: Cornell University Press, 1968), 26, 77, passim.

[20]Edward P. Sanders, *Paul and Palestinian Judaism* (Philadelphia: Fortress Press, 1977); Nickelsburg, *Ancient Judaism and Christian Origins.*

[21]Bruce Malina, "Wealth and Property in the New Testament and Its World," *Interpretation* 41 (1987): 354–67.

[22]Ulrich Luz, *Matthew 1–7, A Commentary* (Minneapolis: Augsburg, 1989), 211–13 with diagram.

[23]The Massah incident in which Israel doubts God's faithfulness appears in Exodus 17:1–7 and Deuteronomy 6–8. The same noun for "temptation/testing" appears in Exodus 17:7; Deuteronomy 6:16; 7:19. See Carter, *Matthew and the Margins,* 168.

[24]*Acts of Augustus,* 34.

Chapter 3: The Way of the Church

[1]This sermon is one of the "exhibits" in my *Unleashing the Scripture: Freeing the Bible from Captivity to America* (Nashville: Abingdon Press, 1993), 64.

[2]Dietrich Bonhoeffer, *Discipleship* (Minneapolis: Fortress Press, 2001), 169–70.

[3]Augustine, *Confessions,* translated with an introduction by R.S. Pine-Coffin (Baltimore: Penguin Books, 1961), 7, 12.

[4]Ibid., 7, 18.

[5]Bonhoeffer, *Discipleship,* 172.

[6]Ibid., 173.

[7]John Howard Yoder, *The Christian Witness to the State* (Newton, Kans.: Faith and Life Press, 1964), 9.

[8]Ibid., 9.

[9]Ibid., 31–32.

[10]John Milbank, *Being Reconciled: Ontology and Pardon* (London, New York: Routledge, 2003), 156. Earlier in *Being Reconciled,* Milbank put this understanding of gift in a more theoretical mode. He argues, "To offer charity, whether as original gift or restorative forgiveness, is only possible if one is *already* receiving the infinite divine charity, since charity is not an empty disposition (as it later became), but the ontological bond between God and creatures, whereby creatures only are as the receiving of the divine gift and the unqualified return of this gift in the very act of receiving…Hence giving, since it is not enacted in order to achieve purity of motive but to establish reciprocity, is already a receiving according to a reception transcendentally prior to any purely possessive calculation of what one might, perhaps, receive by giving. And, likewise, to forgive is to re-establish reciprocity only possible as the attainment of a mysterious harmony through its participation in the divine infinite harmony. As the human forgiver is himself a sinner, he must re-receive this harmony in order to be able to forgive. His forgiving of the other, therefore, shows that he is divinely forgiven, or rather his forgiving of the other is the very instance of himself being divinely forgiven," 57.

[11]Milbank observes, "Parents who entirely sacrifice themselves for their children thereby betray them, since they fail to present them with any *telos* and example of a lived, enjoyed (and sexual) adult life." *Being Reconciled,* 159–60.

[12]Thus Kant says in the first paragraph of his essay, "What is Enlightenment": "Enlightenment is man's release from his self-incurred tutelage. Tutelage is man's inability to make use of his understanding without direction from another. Self-incurred is this tutelage when its cause lies not in lack of reason but in lack of resolution and courage to use it without direction from another. *Sapere aude!* 'Have courage to use our own reason!'–that is the motto of the enlightenment." "What Is Enlightenment" is an appendix to Kant's *Foundations of the Metaphysics of Morals,* 85.

[13]For Kant's reflections on the atonement, see his *Religion Within the Limits of Reason Alone,* trans. Theodore Greene and Hoyt Hudson (New York: Harper and Brothers, 1960), 106–7.

[14]Rowan Williams, *Ponder These Things: Praying with Icons of the Virgin* (Norwich: Canterbury Press, 2002), 35.

[15]Bonhoeffer, *Discipleship*, 176.

[16]Bonhoeffer says in *Ethics* (New York: Simon & Schuster, 1995) that Jesus' sayings in the Sermon on the Mount interpret his existence.

Chapter 4: Dare We Live in the World Imagined in the Sermon on the Mount?

[1]Garry Wills, *What Jesus Meant* (New York: Viking, 2006), 40.

[2]Bill Wylie-Kellermann, "Foreword to the 2004 Edition," in William Stringfellow, *An Ethic for Christians and Other Aliens in a Strange Land* (Eugene, Oreg.: Wipf and Stock, 2004), 3.

[3]Stringfellow, *Ethic*, 14–15.

[4]Ibid., 152–53.

[5]Timothy Weber, *Living in the Shadow of the Second Coming: American Premillennialism, 1875–1982* (Chicago: University of Chicago Press, 1987).

[6]George W. Bush, "Address to the Nation," September 7, 2003.

[7]George W. Bush, "State of the Union Address," 2003.

[8]Ron Suskind, "Without a Doubt," *The Washington Post*, October 17, 2004.

[9]Author's paraphrase.

[10]Charles Marsh, "Wayward Christian Soldiers," *The New York Times*, January 20, 2006.

[11]Jim Lobe, "Conservative Christians Biggest Backers of Iraq War," *Common Dreams News Center* (www.commondreams.org), October 10, 2002.

[12]Marsh, "Wayward Christian Soldiers."

[13]Charles Reed, "Pax Americana and Christian Values," *Zion's Herald* 180 (March-April 2006): 4.

[14]Jim Wallis, *God's Politics: Why the Right Gets It Wrong and the Left Doesn't Get It* (San Francisco: HarperSanFrancisco, 2005), 212.

[15]Ibid.

[16]David Lipscomb, *Civil Government* (Nashville, 1889), 28 (cf. 83–84, iv) and 97.

[17]David Lipscomb, "Babylon," *Gospel Advocate* 23 (2 June 1881): 340.

[18]Lipscomb, *Civil Government*, 25, 27–28 (cf. pp. 83–84), 96.

[19]Ibid.

[20]David Lipscomb, "Religion and Politics," *Gospel Advocate* 32 (26 March 1890): 199.

[21]David Lipscomb, "New Publications," *Gospel Advocate* 8 (1 January 1866): 11–12; *Gospel Advocate* 8 (27 February 1866): 141; and *idem*, "Tolbert Fanning's Teaching and Influence," in *Franklin College and Its Influences*, 59–60.

[21]David Lipscomb, "The Cholera," *Gospel Advocate* 15 (26 June 1873): 619.

[23]Michael Sattler, "Schleitheim Confession of Faith," 1527, in Walter Klaassen, *Anabaptism in Outline: Classics of the Radical Reformation* (Scottdale, Pa.: Herald Press, 1981), 269.

[24]Jacob Hutter, "Letter to the Vice Regent," 1535, in Klaassen, *Anabaptism in Outline*, 275.

[25]Balthasar Hubmaier, "Conversation on Zwingli's Book on Baptism," 1526–27, in Klaassen, *Anabaptism in Outline*, 233.

[26]"God's Green Soldiers," *Newsweek* (February 13, 2006): 49.

[27]Michael Janofsky, "When Cleaner Air Is a Biblical Obligation," *The New York Times*, November 7, 2005.

[28]Cornel West, *Democracy Matters: Winning the Fight Against Imperialism* (New York: Penguin Press, 2004), 150.

[29]Stringfellow, *Ethic*, 46.

[30]William Stringfellow, *Instead of Death*, reprint (Eugene, Oreg.: Wipf and Stock, 1976, 2004), 100–101.

Chapter 5: The Folly of the Sermon on the Mount

[1]Matthew 21:1–11 and par.

[2]The image of "street theater" is taken from Ched Myers, *Binding the Strong Man: A Political Reading of Mark's Story of Jesus* (Maryknoll, N.Y.: Orbis Books, 1998), 294.

[3]Martin Hengel, *Crucifixion: In the Ancient World and the Folly of the Message of the Cross,* trans. John Bowden (Philadelphia: Fortress Press, 1977), 1.

[4]On the tradition of holy fools, see, for example, John Saward, *Perfect Fools: Folly for Christ's Sake in Catholic and Orthodox Spirituality* (Oxford: Oxford Univ. Press, 1980).

[5]On the Sermon on the Mount as vision, see Charles L. Campbell, *The Word before the Powers: An Ethic of Preaching* (Louisville: Westminster John Knox Press, 2002), 94–95; also Warren Carter's treatment of the Sermon in *Matthew and the Margins: A Sociopolitical and Religious Reading* (Maryknoll, New York: Orbis Books, 2000), 128–95. See also Carter's first essay in this volume, in which he highlights the visionary character of the Sermon on the Mount.

[6]As Walter Wink has persuasively argued, the actions in 5:38–42 ("turning the other cheek," "giving the cloak also," and "going the second mile") are not acts of passivity, but acts of nonviolent resistance. See, for example, Walter Wink, *The Powers that Be: Theology for a New Millenium* (New York: Doubleday, 1998), 98–111. See also the discussion of these verses later in this essay and in my sermon elsewhere in this volume.

[7]Beatrice K. Otto, *Fools Are Everywhere: The Court Jester Around the World* (Chicago: Univ. of Chicago Press, 2001), 13, 27, 38.

[8]Carter, *Matthew and the Margins,* 160.

[9]As Carter notes in his second essay in this volume, honor was a particularly important value in Roman culture and was especially associated with acts of beneficence, such as the act of giving alms, which indebted the recipients to the person performing the beneficent act and actually maintained the economic status quo.

[10]My interpretation of this text follows Wink, *Powers that Be,* 103–6.

[11]Walter Wink, "Neither Passivity nor Violence: Jesus' Third Way," *Forum* 7 (March–June, 1991): 12.

[12]Ibid.

[13]My discussion of the "myth of redemptive violence," including some of my examples, is taken from the work of Walter Wink. See, for example, Wink, *Powers that Be,* 42–62.

[14]In the Enuma Elish, the Babylonian creation myth, the god Marduk brings order out of chaos by killing his mother, Tiamat, and then fashioning the world from her dead corpse. See James B. Pritchard, *Ancient Near Eastern Texts Relating to the Old Testament,* 3rd ed. (Princeton: Princeton Univ. Press, 1969), 60–72.

[15]Walter Wink, *Engaging the Powers: Discernment and Resistance in a World of Domination* (Minneapolis: Fortress Press, 1992), 17.

[16]In Chapter 5 of the Book of Revelation, it is not the Lion King who is able to open the scroll and provide the meaning to history, but rather the Slaughtered Lamb King. Can we even imagine an animated film entitled "The Slaughtered Lamb King" being a blockbuster in theaters today?

[17]I am focusing on some of Jesus' direct challenges to this myth. Other parts of the Sermon indirectly challenge the myth. For example, Jesus' admonition not to be anxious about the possessions of this world (6:19–34) indirectly challenges the myth of redemptive violence. As Rene Girard has argued, acquisitive, mimetic rivalry and desire lie at the heart of society's violence—and such rivalry and desire are precisely what Jesus challenges in this section of the sermon. See Rene Girard, *The Girard Reader,* ed. James G. Williams (New York: Crossroads Publishing Company, 1996), 9–65. In Matthew 6:19–34, Jesus replaces such desire with trust in God and pursuit of life in God's new order.

[18]Carter, *Matthew and the Margins,* 133. On "the meek," see also Carter's first essay in this volume.

[19]Carter, *Matthew and the Margins*, 135-36.

[20]See Exodus 21:24; Leviticus 24:20; Deuteronomy 19:21.

[21]The Greek word is *antistenai.* See Wink, *Powers that Be*, 99-101; Carter, *Matthew and the Margins*, 150-51.

[22]For a description of these other two actions, see my sermon later in this volume.

[23]This statement is an adaptation of Cardinal Suhard's famous affirmation: "To be a witness does not consist in engaging in propaganda, nor even in stirring people up, but in being a living mystery. It means to live in such a way that one's life would not make sense if God did not exist." I do not know the original source of this widely quoted saying, but it is available on many Web sites, including http://www.cambridgestudycenter.com/quotesMindCulture.html.

Chapter 6: Great in the Empire of Heaven

[1]I use the term *telling* intentionally and have made many a teaching moment of requesting that church secretaries not label what I do as "reading." I also sometimes use the term "text telling," a form popular with my storyteller colleagues in the UK to distinguish between a performance of the actual text and a loose paraphrase or a first-person monologue.

[2]Although we think of *text* as denoting ink on paper, the word originally referred to the spoken word. The root of the word is also the root of *textile*, and the familiar expressions "weaving a tale" and "spinning a yarn."

[3]The Network of Biblical Storytellers, 1000 West 42nd Street, Indianapolis, IN 46208-3301; www.nobs.org.

[4]Thomas Boomershine, a Second Testament scholar, is the cofounder of NOBS and the author of *Story Journey: An Invitation to the Gospel as Storytelling* (Nashville: Abingdon Press, 1980).

[5]Boomershine's term.

[6]My coinage of the verb "to remembrance" intends deliberately to echo the familiar words of eucharistic liturgy. The internalizing and telling of the text is more than a memory exercise; it is virtually sacramental.

[7]Dennis Dewey, "The Mnemonics of the Heart: Marinating in the Stories of Scripture," presented at the Conference for Orality and Literacy III: Memory, The Center for the Study of Cultures, Rice University, October 2003.

[8]Daniel Goleman, *Emotional Intelligence: Why It Can Matter More Than IQ* (New York: Bantam Books), 1995, 8f.

[9]Thomas Aquinas, *Summa Theologica* II-II, 49, translation at http://www.niagara.net/hyoomik/phi205/memory.htm (accessed October 12, 2006).

[10]Jonathan Cott, *On the Sea of Memory* (New York: Random House, 2005), 36.

[11]From http://www.aish.com/spirituality/48ways/Way_3_Say_It_Out_Loud.asp (accessed July 8, 2006).

[12]Walter Ong, *Orality and Literacy* (New York: Routledge, 1982), 186.

[13]Richard Lischer, "Martin Luther King, Jr.: 'Performing' the Scriptures" in *Anglican Theological Review* 87, no. 2 (Spring 1995): 161.

[14]Gilbert Bartholomew, "Feed my Lambs: John 21:15-19 as Oral Gospel," *Semeia* 39 (1987): 72f.

[15]David Rhoads, "Performance Criticism: An Emerging Methodology in Second Testament Studies—Part I," *Biblical Theology Bulletin* (forthcoming).

[16]Whitney Shiner, *Proclaiming the Gospel: First-Century Performance of Mark* (New York: Trinity Press International, 2003), 27.

[17]See Warren Carter's essays in the first two chapters in this volume.

[18]Lawrence L. Welbourne, *Paul, the Fool of Christ: A Study of 1 Corinthians 1–4 in the Comic-Philosophic Tradition* (London: T & T Clark International, 2005), 11. See also the insights of Charles Campbell on the foolishness in the Sermon and in Paul in chapter 5 of this volume. Welbourne cites evidence to the effect that church tradition

has perpetuated a major mistranslation as regards Paul's occupation as "tentmaker," that *skenopoios* should instead be understood (as it is in every extra-biblical context of the time) as "prop maker," Paul's familiarity with the theater making obvious the extended conceit about foolishness in 1 Corinthians.

    [19]In this I follow the lead of the late Donald Juel, who gave eloquent testimony to his "conversion" as a scholar to a radically new understanding of Mark's gospel as performed text ("The Strange Silence of the Bible," *Interpretation* 51, [1997]), after which conversion Juel *encouraged* his students to speak the words of the stories in different, even outlandish ways—to have the centurion at the cross say in a mocking/ironic tone, for example, "Ha! Truly *this* was a Son of God!"

    [20]See Charles Campbell's essay in chapter 5 of this volume for further elaboration.

    [21]Shiner, *Proclaiming the Gospel,* 27.

    [22]Ibid., 171.

    [23]Richard A Horsley and Jonathan A. Draper, *Whoever Hears You Hears Me: Prophets, Performance and Tradition in Q* (Harrisburg: Trinity Press International, 1999), 16.

    [24]"The Confession of 1967," in *The Book of Confessions,* Presbyterian Church (USA) (Louisville: The Office of the General Assembly, 1999), 259f.

    [25]Walter Fisher, "*Homo Narrans:* Story-Telling in Mass Culture and Everyday Life," *Journal of Communications* 35 (1985).

    [26]Cott, *On the Sea of Memory,* 86.

Chapter 7: The Suprising Blessing of the Beatitudes

    [1]Charles L. Campbell, *The Word Before the Powers: An Ethic of Preaching* (Louisville/ London: Westminster John Knox Press, 2002).

    [2]Note Campbell's discussion of the beatitudes in the latter part of his essay (pp. 66–68). While Campbell focuses on the beatitudes as depicting an alternative to the myth of redemptive violence, he rightly notes that they sketch general qualities of an alternative world.

    [3]To use Warren Carter's words (from the end of chapter 1 of this book), the sermon is intended to help the congregation imagine "a different identity for themselves and for this world. Envisioning sermons help people imagine and live into being practices and habits that do not exercise or exploit power over others but are empowering for all. Envisioning sermons help the people of God imagine and live into being a way of life that is not a religious variation of our dominant cultural values but a way of life that enacts God's good and just transforming and redemptive purposes for all people. Envisioning sermons represent God's saving presence, the reign or empire of God. Envisioning sermons help folks develop strategies, formulate plans, and commit to concrete enactments of God's just and good and life-giving purposes for all of creation."

    [4]For exegetical expansion on the interpretation that follows, see Ronald J. Allen, "Fourth Sunday after the Epiphany, Year A," in *The Lectionary Commentary: Theological Exegesis for Sunday's Texts. Third Readings: The Gospels,* ed. Roger Van Harn (Grand Rapids: Eerdmans, 2001), 26–30.

    [5]See chapter 1 in this volume by Warren Carter for further details of Roman oppression.

    [6]For more detailed exegesis of the beatitudes, see Warren Carter's comments. While my discussion moves in the same stream as Carter's, I differ on some details.

    [7]Note Carter's expansive treatment of the phrase "poor in spirit" in his first essay.

    [8]Note the similarity between this comment and Warren Carter's remarks on praying the prayer that Jesus taught in Matthew 6: "To pray for God's empire to come is to commit to live out God's reign now. To pray for God's will to be done is to commit to live it now" (found in chapter 2 of this book, under Carter's seventh "aspect").

[9]Joseph M. Smith, *Three Years in the Fish's Belly or The Years the Locusts Ate* (Indianapolis: Privately Published, 2004), 13.
[10]Ibid., 16–17.

Chapter 8: Salt and Light, Salsa And Tortillas

[1]It is, of course, a matter of debate about what "American culture" actually comprises. Thus the "scare quotes."
[2]"Remarks by Sen. Miller to the Republican National Convention," from http://www.washingtonpost.com/wp-dyn/articles/A54300-2004Sep1.html.
[3]Gerhard Lohfink, cited in Richard Gardner, *Matthew,* Believers Church Bible Commentary Series, ed. Elmer A. Martens and Howard H. Charles (Scottdale, Pa.: Herald Press, 1991), 101.
[4]See Matthew 4:17.
[5]The phrase "if the salt μωρανθη," literally means if the salt becomes *insipid* or *foolish.*

Chapter 10: The Power of Anger in an Imperialist America

[1]Charles L. Campbell, *The Word Before the Powers: An Ethic of Preaching* (Louisville/London: Westminster John Knox Press, 2002), 177.
[2]Ibid.
[3]Cited on http://en.wikipedia.org/wiki/Cop_Killer_(song).
[4]Curtiss DeYoung, *Reconciliation: Our Greatest Challenge–Our Only Hope,* (Valley Forge, Pa.: Judson Press, 1995:13), 106.
[5]Martin L. King, Jr., *The Autobiography of Martin Luther King, Jr.,* ed. Clayborne Carson (New York: Warner Books, 1998), 328, 331.
[6]James Cone, *Black Theology and Black Power,* 20th anniversary ed. (New York: Harper & Row, 1989), 140, 143.
[7]Matthew 12:43–45; Revelation 12–13.

Chapter 12: On the Road with Jesus

[1]Jeff M. Christian, "Faithful and True" [on-line]; available from http://www.sermonseminar.blogspot.com: Sermons from Matthew 5:43–48; accessed 26 October 2006.
[2]John Shelby Spong, cited in Richard B. Hays, *The Moral Vision of the New Testament: A Contemporary Introduction to New Testament Ethics* (New York: HarperCollins, 1996), 348f.
[3]I am paraphrasing here Matthew 19:3–12, Matthew's companion discussion on marriage, divorce, and remarriage.
[4]For helpful background and as an excellent reading companion, see David Instone-Brewer, *Divorce and Remarriage in the Bible: The Social and Literary Context* (Grand Rapids: Eerdmans, 2002). Especially clarifying is his discussion on the Hillelite/Shammaite debate, 110–17.

Chapter 13: People of Integrity

[1]Charles L. Campbell, *The Word Before the Powers: An Ethic of Preaching* (Louisville/London: Westminster John Knox Press, 2002), 72–73.
[2]As in Matthew 26:63–64.
[3]As in Romans 9:1; 2 Corinthians 1:17–18.
[4]Statement made by Dennis Dewey in chapter 6 of this volume.
[5]David Buttrick, *Speaking Jesus: Homiletic Theology and the Sermon on the Mount* (Louisville: Westminster John Knox Press, 2002), 96.
[6]See Romans 13:8–10.

[7]Mark Snyder, "Self-Monitoring Scale," 1974, http://pubpages.unh.edu/~ckb/SELFMON2.html.

[8]See Herbert T. Pratt, "Brother Faraday," *Restoration Quarterly* 31, no. 4 (1989): 219–29.

Chapter 14: Imagine

[1]See Dennis Dewey's essay.

[2]Beatrice K. Otto, *Fools Are Everywhere: The Court Jester Around the World* (Chicago: Univ. of Chicago Press, 2001), 13, 27, 38.

[3]Enid Welsford, *The Fool: His Social and Literary History* (1935; reprint, Gloucester, Mass.: Peter Smith, 1966), 223.

[4]My interpretation of the text at this point relies on the work of Walter Wink. See Walter Wink, *The Powers that Be: Theology for a New Millennium* (New York: Doubleday, 1998), 98–111.

[5]Doing things "decently and in order" is a mantra among Presbyterians.

Chapter 15: Perfection

[1]Dietrich Bonhoeffer, "Who Am I?" Christianity and Crisis (March 4, 1946), cited online at http://www.religion-online.org/showarticle.asp?title=385.

Chapter 17: New Rules for the Game of Life

[1]See Charles Campbell's essay in this book, "The Folly of the Sermon on the Mount," chapter 5.

[2]This is the subject of Warren Carter's essay, "Embodying God's Empire in Communal Practices: Matthew 6:1–18," chapter 2 in this book.

[3]Higher Education Research Institute, UCLA, reported in *U.S. News & World Report,* March 4, 1991.

[4]Michael Schut, ed. and compiler, *Simpler Living, Compassionate Life* (Denver: Living the Good News, 1999), 10, 24–25, 60–61.

[5]*Outreach* (Jan./Feb. 2004): 18. Study conducted by the Barna Research Group for Compassion International.

[6]Warren Carter, *Matthew and the Margins: A Sociopolitical and Religious Reading* (Maryknoll, N.Y.: Orbis Books, 2000), 172.

[7]John R. W. Stott, *The Message of the Sermon on the Mount,* The Bible Speaks Today (Downers Grove, Ill.: InterVarsity Press, 1978), 169.

[8]Ibid., 18-21.

[9]D. A. Carson, *Jesus' Sermon on the Mount and His Confrontation with the World* (Grand Rapids: Global Christian Publishers, 1991), 230–31.

[10]Carter, *Matthew and the Margins,* 173.

[11]C.S. Lewis, *The Voyage of the Dawn Treader* (New York: Harper, 1952), 91.

[12]Craig S. Keener, *A Commentary on the Gospel of Matthew* (Grand Rapids: Eerdmans, 1999), 232.

[13]As discussed in Richard Foster, *Money, Sex & Power* (New York: Harper & Row, 1985), 4–5.

Chapter 18: You Be the Judge?

[1]Evelyn Underhill, *The House of the Soul; Concerning the Inner Life* (Minneapolis: Seabury Press, 1947), 96.

[2]Isak Dinesen, "Babette's Feast," in *Anecdotes of Destiny and Ehrengard* (New York: Vintage International, 1993), 52.

Chapter 19: God Responds to All Who Seek Him

[1]See James 4:3 and 1 John 5:14.

Chapter 20: The Rain Came Down

[1]See Warren Carter's essay in chapter 1 in this volume.